Getting Off at
ELYSIAN
FIELDS

Getting Off at ELYSIAN FIELDS

OBITUARIES FROM THE *TIMES-PICAYUNE*

John Pope

UNIVERSITY PRESS OF MISSISSIPPI • JACKSON

www.upress.state.ms.us

Designed by Peter D. Halverson

The University Press of Mississippi is a member of the Association of
American University Presses.

First printing 2015
∞
Library of Congress Cataloging-in-Publication Data

Pope, John (Reporter)
Getting off at Elysian Fields : a collection of obituaries from the
Times-picayune / John Pope.
pages cm
ISBN 978-1-4968-0375-7 (cloth : alkaline paper)
ISBN 978-1-4968-5362-2 (paperback)— ISBN 978-1-4968-0376-4 (ebook)
1. Obituaries—Louisiana—New Orleans. 2. Funeral rites and ceremonies—
Louisiana—New Orleans. 3. New Orleans (La.)—Biography.
4. New Orleans (La.)—Social life and customs—Sources.
I. Times-picayune. II. Title.
F379.N553A275 2015
976.3'35—dc23
2015005239

British Library Cataloging-in-Publication Data available

FOR MY WIFE,
DIANA PINCKLEY,
WHO CONTINUES TO INSPIRE ME

BLANCHE DU BOIS: They told me to take a streetcar named Desire, and then transfer to one called Cemeteries and ride six blocks and get off at—Elysian Fields!

— from *A Streetcar Named Desire* by Tennessee Williams, copyright 1947

CONTENTS

THE FUNERALS

Getting Off at
ELYSIAN
FIELDS

INTRODUCTION

Obituaries matter. To the friends and family of someone who has just died, a newspaper obituary, accompanied by a fairly flattering picture, is a sign that that individual played a role in community life.

Newspaper obituaries find their way into scrapbooks and, in at least one case I can cite, the *Congressional Record.*

Despite their importance, writing obituaries has been regarded for too many years as the scutwork of journalism, a chore that a harried assignment editor hands out to rookies to help them learn how to organize information quickly—and to give them something to do on a slow day.

These stories generally run a few paragraphs and include information about the dead person's education, career, family, and funeral arrangements.

Too often, that's it—a life summed up in what I call a résumé obit, which offers no hint of what might have made that individual different from someone whose similarly written obituary appears nearby.

I confess to writing many of these bland obituaries in my early years.

I started to think about breaking out of that mold when I made the acquaintance of Alden Whitman in the pages of the *New York Times.*

Whitman spent most of his professional life writing long, flavorful advance obituaries. In addition to doing thorough research, he sometimes interviewed the subjects, who were thrilled that someone was paying attention. Bette Davis even mixed a pitcher of martinis for herself and a *Times* reporter once she realized he had come to interview her for her obituary.

Whitman's stories were replete with fascinating details. For instance, Elizabeth Arden, the queen of a beauty empire, had her laboratory develop creams for rubbing down her racehorses. And Walter Winchell, the acerbic gossip columnist who delivered his scoops in a rat-a-tat bark to a vast radio audience, celebrated making his first million dollars by arranging a special lunch, which he ate by himself.

Fascinating stuff, I thought. Since New Orleans is overflowing with distinctive characters, I was convinced by the late 1970s that I could do that, too, relying on reportorial nosiness and a history degree that helped me appreciate the importance of context and the way people fit into their environments.

I knew that people would read these stories because New Orleans, where I grew up, is a big small town, where folks make a point of knowing all they can about other people's lives.

Charlie Ferguson, my editor at the *States-Item* (and, later, the *Times-Picayune*), agreed, and he encouraged me to start reporting and writing longer obits.

I wrote many on deadline. On the ones I did in advance, I had the gift of time, although, of course, I never knew how much lead time I had. One obituary was ready for sixteen years; I finished another one six hours before the subject died.

Charlie became a great source, pulling me aside every so often to whisper that I had better get cracking on a certain individual's obit because that person didn't look so good.

Doing long obituaries involves not only imposing some order on a person's history but also limning that individual's personality so readers will wish they had made that person's acquaintance.

The latter task can be tough because it sometimes involves armchair psychoanalysis, but it has often been wonderfully rewarding. When I was researching Walker Percy's obituary—a task that took more than a year—Charlie encouraged me to call other writers to get their opinions on Percy. I was only too happy to use company time and money to chat up authors whom I had idolized, including Eudora Welty, William Styron, and E. L. Doctorow.

This full-bore approach to obituaries paid off early. One of my first big projects was the obituary of Edith Stern, one of New Orleans' great philanthropists. Her relatives liked the story so much that they asked Lindy Boggs, New Orleans' congresswoman at the time, to put it in the *Congressional Record*.

Doing advance obituaries does have its jarring side. I met Mrs. Stern at a party three weeks after I had written her obituary. One Christmas, my wife, Diana Pinckley, and I walked into a party where three people whose obituaries I had written were sitting together on a sofa, laughing it up and having a splendid time. I came close to hyperventilating, but I somehow managed not to let on to anyone but Diana.

I regard these obits as profiles, and that's the line I use—truthfully—to start people talking if I think they might be uneasy about being interviewed for an obituary, be it their own or someone else's.

I employed that approach when, at my publisher's behest, I interviewed his father-in-law, a former king of Carnival, for his obituary. We were having a fine time, and then he asked, "When will this story run?"

"Oh, I don't know," I said—and quickly changed the subject.

One more story. In 1982, when Charlie was convinced that Albert Dent, the greatly respected president of Dillard University, was about to die, he sent me out to interview what seemed like most of the city for this great man's obituary.

One interviewee was Rosa Keller, a member of the city's white aristocracy who became a trustee of that historically black university and a major force in the local civil rights movement. We had a grand conversation.

I wrote the obituary. Mr. Dent didn't die for nearly eighteen months.

So at a party a year later, while Mr. Dent still was alive, Rosa came up to my wife and me, grabbed my arm, and said, laughing, "Well, we haven't needed that obit yet, have we?"

Diana grew silent, and her eyes widened.

After Rosa had moved on, Diana told me that she admired Rosa's grip on her own mortality because she thought Rosa was talking about her own obituary, which Diana knew that I had written. I quickly reassured Diana that Rosa had no idea that her own lengthy obit was ready to run.

After researching and writing these stories for more than thirty years, I have a stable of knowledgeable folks whom I can rely upon for educated commentary for obituaries about most facets of New Orleans life. I've relied on them so much for these stories that when I call them when I'm not doing an obituary, I always put them at ease by saying, "Hi, it's Pope. Nobody died."

In writing obituaries, some subjects, such as politicians, major artists, former Carnival royalty, and civic leaders, are obvious choices. But I also like to write about the people most folks wouldn't know about, like the letter carrier who was a spy in World War II, the woman who collected Judith Leiber handbags, and the waiter who collected money in gay bars for men and women who were hospitalized with AIDS.

I call that category of obits my Linda Loman moments, after the character in *Death of a Salesman* who stands at her husband's grave and says, "Attention must be paid."

I like to think that the obituaries I have written have provided that opportunity.

I'm providing a bit of lagniappe, a term we New Orleanians use to denote something extra at no extra cost. My lagniappe comprises stories of four funerals, and it's not because of the sassy bumper sticker proclaiming: "New Orleans—We Put the Fun in Funeral."

I'm including them to carry out a theme of this book—New Orleans' distinctive character—by showing how we honor our dead.

THE OBITUARIES

Edith Rosenwald Stern

A philanthropist who "invested in humanity"

E dith Rosenwald Stern, a New Orleans philanthropist who was determined to use her wealth wisely to benefit a long list of organizations
involved with the arts and public affairs, died Thursday in her suite at the
Pontchartrain Hotel. She was 85.

"Money is wasted on many people," said Mrs. Stern, who was born into
one affluent family and married into another. "Our families always regarded
wealth as a trust to be invested judiciously in humanity."

These "investments" touched nearly every major charity in New Orleans
and, through the Stern Fund, many others that were headed by people Mrs.
Stern never saw.

In New Orleans, Mrs. Stern founded the Newcomb Nursery School and
the Metairie Park Country Day School; was a member of the boards that
ran Dillard University, the New Orleans Museum of Art, and the New Orleans Philharmonic Symphony Orchestra; and established the Voters Registration League Inc. (later Voters Service Inc.) to weed out illegally registered
people and to encourage others to exercise their right to register and vote.

She and her husband, Edgar B. Stern Sr., the president of the Cotton Exchange, set up the Stern Fund with his money and the fortune she had inherited from her father, Julius Rosenwald, a president of Sears, Roebuck & Co.

More than $10 million was given by the foundation to advance such
diverse enterprises as Ralph Nader's campaign for a federal "sunshine"
law and the Freedom of Information Act, the work of the biologist Barry
Commoner, studies into the side effects of nuclear energy and the Fund for
Investigative Journalism, which helped pay the expenses Seymour Hersh
incurred while researching his Pulitzer Prize-winning story of the My Lai
massacre.

Mrs. Stern also was a mother, grandmother, and great-grandmother who delighted in receiving letters from younger members of her large family. She gave Sears stock to the staff at her massive house, and she helped some of her employees through their financial difficulties. And when she felt pride in a friend's accomplishments, she used to say, "I put on my 'mama' face when I think about what you've done."

She spent most of her life in New Orleans, but she was born in Chicago to parents she adored. She grew up with money, but, she said in a 1974 interview: "We were reared in the tradition of good works, culture and public service. If any of us indulged in personal extravagances, we had a guilt complex."

Her father was a model for the philanthropy she later practiced. Julius Rosenwald, who was Sears' president from 1910 through 1924, once remarked that it was easier to make $1 million honestly than to give $1 million away wisely. He gave away more than $63 million.

He established Chicago's Museum of Science and Industry and contributed to Jewish charities and a wide array of educational, scientific, and community causes and organizations. Through the Julius Rosenwald Fund, he helped finance the building of more than 5,000 schools for African Americans, the establishment of clinics to treat their illnesses, and the development of grants to aid black artists, writers and musicians.

When she was growing up, Edith Rosenwald "went to a progressive-education school in Chicago, one of those schools where you learn nothing," she recalled in a 1974 interview. "Then I went to high school but never graduated."

She also attended a finishing school in Germany, where she studied German and learned the language's guttural sounds because her teacher pressed her hand against her vocal cords as she spoke.

"I developed a *basso profundo* speaking voice," she said. "That was a blessing because Edgar told me later he could never have married a girl with a Chicago voice."

Before she met Edgar Stern, she was married at 18 to a man she later refused to name. The union did not last, and, after a divorce, she went to live in New York City, where she met Stern, a Harvard student who was the son of Maurice Stern, a cotton merchant.

The two became engaged, but Edith Rosenwald's father summoned her back to Chicago, and she obeyed.

She and Stern were eager to be married, but as an Illinois resident once more, she faced a legal problem: State law required a person to wait a year after a divorce decree became final before getting a license for a second marriage.

By the time the couple learned of this hitch, they had already booked passage on a ship to Europe for their honeymoon. So they started looking for a state with more lenient laws, and they found Indiana.

"I had a brainstorm," she said. "Why not get a private railroad car, hitch it to the train going from Illinois to Indiana, get married on the train in Indiana and return home to Chicago for the reception?

"My parents agreed. The family decorated the car with so many flowers it looked like a gangster's funeral. About 30 guests, including family, crowded the car. The rabbi performed the ceremony as soon as we drew into Indiana. Then we got back to Ravinia, our family estate. We had a big reception—champagne, wedding cake, music—then off to New York to sail for Europe the next day."

The date was June 28, 1921. In the 1974 interview, she referred to it as "my finest hour."

The couple moved to New Orleans, and, Mrs. Stern said, "I had three babies (two sons and a daughter) in less than four years, and I thought I was a much-put-upon young woman."

In 1926, when the Sterns' oldest child, Edgar B. Stern Jr., was 2, Mrs. Stern wanted to enroll him in a nursery school like those she had seen in the East.

No such school existed in New Orleans, so she and a group of parents started one: the New Orleans Nursery School, which became the Newcomb Nursery School, a part of Tulane University.

She went through a similar process when her children reached elementary-school age because, she said, she wanted them to attend a progressive coeducational school in a rural atmosphere. The result was Metairie Park Country Day School.

In adult education, Edgar B. Stern was a leader in negotiations that led to the formation of Dillard University in 1930 from two black colleges. He was the first president of Dillard's board of trustees, and Mrs. Stern succeeded him as a board member after his death in 1959.

On the Dillard campus, one building is named after her husband, and another is named after her father.

Mrs. Stern also was active in Democratic Party politics and attended several national party conventions. During the 1945–46 mayoral campaign of deLesseps S. "Chep" Morrison, the reform candidate, Mrs. Stern led a group of women marching on St. Charles Avenue with brooms across their shoulders to dramatize Morrison's intention to sweep out the practices associated with his predecessor.

After Morrison's election, Mrs. Stern was appointed to the Parkway and Park Commission. She also was executive secretary of New Orleans' housing projects and, in 1951, she was named Louisiana's representative to serve on a 48-woman commission—one member per state—to advise the Defense Department on matters relating to women in the armed forces. A decade later, President John F. Kennedy appointed her to the National Cultural Center Advisory Committee on the Arts.

But her principal political activity was the organization of the Voter Registration League Inc., which fought with local and state officials to have the city's rolls purged of voters improperly registered as disabled and illiterate.

Through this crusade, the number of people so registered dropped from nearly 10,000 in 1951 to 4,075 the next year, and the method of registering such people was changed to require voters needing help at the polls to fill out colored cards.

Mrs. Stern also set up a filing system to give complete information on each voter and to ease the task of spotting improperly registered people.

The organization mailed letters to voters urging them to correct or revise their registration forms to keep from being eliminated from the rolls and, to keep elections as honest as possible, worked to retain voting machines throughout the state.

"The vote is something so precious," Mrs. Stern said in a 1958 speech. "It should not be tampered with. The privilege of voting is one of the most priceless things we have in America today."

The organization was nonpartisan and nonprofit, but it had to raise money to meet its annual operating expenses of about $20,000. One fundraising method that candidates found invaluable was the sale—at $5 per precinct—of complete lists of voters for the entire city. These names were printed on gummed labels, ready to be stuck onto campaign literature to be mailed.

The Sterns lived on an estate on Garden Lane, a private path off Metairie Road near the New Orleans Country Club golf course. Among the scores of guests who stayed there were artists, musicians, Eleanor Roosevelt, and Adlai Stevenson.

Early in her career, Marian Anderson sang at Longue Vue for the Sterns' friends. Among the others who performed there were Pablo Casals and Jack Benny.

In 1940, Ellen Biddle Shipman, a landscape architect, laid out the large formal garden that became Longue Vue Gardens, a spot that took its name from the Hudson River estate where the Sterns became engaged. The site has been declared a National Historic Landmark.

In 1968, Mrs. Stern opened Longue Vue Gardens to the public. When she heard that admission fees would be charged to help pay for the site's upkeep, she quipped, "Can't you see me there with my tin cup?"

She donated her house and surrounding land to the New Orleans Museum of Art, and it has been converted into a center of decorative arts. To underwrite the work, Mrs. Stern provided a $5 million endowment.

While her home was the most conspicuous gift to the museum, it wasn't her only donation. Among the art she gave were "Coup ou Fruit," a sculpture by Jean Arp; "Ballatrix C" by Victor Vasarely; and a sketch Wassily Kandinsky made for his painting "Several Circles."

Mrs. Stern was instrumental in helping the museum develop its Arts of the Americas collection, including a trove of Peruvian art. She also paid for the construction of the museum's Stern Auditorium.

She received scores of honors, and *Life* magazine declared her one of the United States' 12 *grandes dames*. In its centennial issue in 1977, the (New Orleans) *States-Item* newspaper named the Sterns the city's outstanding philanthropists during its first century.

— *September 11, 1980*

Alton Ochsner

A renowned surgeon who inveighed against smoking

Dr. Alton Ochsner, an internationally known surgeon and anti-smoking crusader, died Thursday in the suburban hospital he helped found. He was 85.

Although he was acclaimed as a surgeon and a medial innovator, Dr. Ochsner was modest about what he thought a doctor could do.

"Eighty-five percent of your patients will get well no matter what you do," he said, "and a few will die. The doctor can influence the outcome of maybe 10 percent."

During his long career, Dr. Ochsner tried to influence the outcome of as many cases as he could. He performed surgery until April 4, 1968—four days before his 72nd birthday. On that day, he went through 11 operations before laying down his scalpel for the last time.

He performed more than 10,000 operations—including, in 1934, the first lung removal in the South—and his long roster of patients included the actor Gary Cooper, the golfing great Ben Hogan, the former Argentine President Juan Peron and a former president of Panama.

But Dr. Ochsner's reputation reached beyond the operating room. His primary joy was teaching, and he had more than 3,000 students, including Dr. Michael DeBakey, who was a baby sitter for Dr. Ochsner's children and went on to become an internationally famous heart surgeon.

On a broader educational level, Dr. Ochsner was one of the first to warn Americans about the health hazards of cigarette smoking. He began his anti-smoking crusade in 1936.

He also helped found the medical institution that bears his surname. Since its 1942 opening in an Uptown New Orleans building near Touro Infirmary, the facility has expanded into an medical colossus with offices throughout south Louisiana.

Dr. Ochsner was president of several prestigious organizations related to his work, including the American College of Surgeons and the American Cancer Society. In addition to professional activities, he reigned over Mardi Gras as Rex, king of Carnival, in 1948, and was named one of 13 fathers of the year in a nationwide poll.

In the *States-Item*'s centennial issue in 1977, Dr. Ochsner was named the newspaper's Man of the Century in medicine.

He was born Edward William Alton Ochsner on May 4, 1896, in Kinball, S.D., and he received his undergraduate degree from the University of South Dakota. Two years later, he earned his medical degree at Washington University in St. Louis.

Dr. Ochsner, who dropped his first two names, was an intern at the Barnes Hospital in St. Louis and a surgical resident at Chicago's Augustana Hospital under Dr. A. J. Ochsner, a cousin who took an interest in the young doctor's career because his own son did not go into medicine.

Acting on his cousin's suggestion, Dr. Ochsner went to Europe in 1922 as an exchange surgical resident at the universities of Zurich and Frankfurt. While abroad, he wrote—in German—the first of more than 500 medical articles he would publish.

When Dr. Ochsner returned to the United States, he opened a surgical practice in Chicago with Dr. D. A. Orth. But after a year, he said, "I found myself driving 100 miles a day to visit patients. It was a waste of time. I liked what I was doing, but I knew by then that I wanted to teach."

Even though it meant a loss of more than half his annual pay—from $11,000 to $5,000—he accepted an offer to join the University of Wisconsin's surgical faculty. A year later, he succeeded the acclaimed Dr. Rudolph Matas as professor of surgery at Tulane University School of Medicine.

At Tulane, Dr. Ochsner instituted an educational method known as "the bull pen," in which a student had 30 minutes to examine a patient, diagnose his illness and defend that judgment before his peers—and his instructor.

This method of teaching resulted in scores of anecdotes. In a documentary on Dr. Ochsner, one of his former students recalled panicking because his patient spoke nothing but Cajun French. In another case, after hearing a student's diagnosis, Dr. Ochsner shouted, "Why? Why? Why?" and the doctor-to-be fainted.

"I don't know who was more scared, he or I," Dr. Ochsner later said of that incident. He justified this method of instruction by saying that a doctor must learn to perform quickly and under stress.

He gained respect at Tulane, but his life there was not easy. Tulane's medical school was affiliated with Charity Hospital, a state-run facility, and

Dr. Ochsner ran into opposition early on from hospital administrators, who were aligned with Huey P. Long's political machine.

At one point, Long wanted a friend of his put on the Charity staff, but Dr. Ochsner objected because he felt the man was not qualified, said Gertrude Forshag, who became his secretary in December 1929 and held that job for the rest of his life.

Because of this climate, Dr. Ochsner wrote a despairing letter in 1930 to a friend, asking about an opening at another medical school. He explained that he was making the request because the political atmosphere at Charity Hospital made progress impossible,

Dr. Ochsner, who wrote the letter at work, planned to take it home to show his wife. He put it in the pocket of his coat, which he hung up while he made his rounds at Charity.

Someone pilfered the letter and showed it to Long, who was so enraged that he had the young physician stripped of his affiliation with Charity. Until he could be reinstated there, Dr. Ochsner arranged with Tulane administrators to perform his surgery at Touro Infirmary in a 20-bed sector that became known as "the Tulane ward."

That was one of several incidents that led to the formation of the Louisiana State University School of Medicine.

Dr. Ochsner's banishment "was almost a blessing," said Forshag, who explained that he used it for research and reading that he would have been unable to do if he had been continuing his Tulane duties.

During the 1930s, Dr. Ochsner began talking with Tulane colleagues about the possibility of forming a private clinic where they could combine their medical skills.

He and the four department heads who were interested in the idea—Drs. Edgar Burns, Guy Caldwell, Francis LeJeune and Curtis Tyrone—wanted Tulane to operate the facility, but the university's administrators voted against the concept. Nevertheless, they let the doctors proceed on their own.

The idea continued to grow, and the doctors were able to get $500,000—the amount they figured they would need to open the clinic—from Hibernia National Bank by using no more collateral than their signatures after convincing Rudolf S. Hecht, chairman of the bank's board of directors, that it would be good for the city.

But not everyone was so enthusiastic. Many doctors were wedded to the idea that a physician should practice alone, and some doctors even felt that Dr. Ochsner and his partners were traitors to their profession.

On a spring day in 1941, a messenger dropped off a small leather bag at the home of each founder. Each bag contained 30 dimes and this message:

"To help pay for your clinic. From the physicians, surgeons & dentists of New Orleans."

Despite this none-too-subtle analogy to Judas' betrayal of Jesus Christ, plans for the clinic reached the point where the founding doctors had to name their fledgling enterprise. New Orleans Clinic and Southern Clinic were suggested, but while Dr. Ochsner was in Ogden, Utah, on a professional trip, he received this telegram from his colleagues: "The baby has a name: the Ochsner Clinic."

On Jan. 2, 1941, Ochsner Clinic opened in a building in Uptown New Orleans across Prytania Street from Touro Infirmary. At the end of World War II, it took over Camp Plauché, an Army medical facility near the East Bank approach to the Huey P. Long Bridge. Because it was a series of one-story frame buildings connected by walkways, it acquired the nickname "Splinter Village."

It 1954, the medical facility moved to 1516 Jefferson Highway, which still is its headquarters. In addition to Ochsner Foundation Hospital, the complex houses the Ochsner Clinic for outpatient treatment, cancer and research institutes, and a hotel for patients' families and friends. A heliport is used for emergencies, and the hospital houses an Ochsner innovation: a family waiting room near the operating area where a patient's relatives can wait in privacy—and comparative silence—until the doctor tells them the outcome.

At this facility and at other hospitals, Dr. Ochsner continued to perform surgery until he was nearly 72. When he established the clinic, Dr. Ochsner set 70 as the mandatory retirement age, but as a founder, he was able to bend that rule and continue operating for nearly two more years.

"The nurses all admired him for his daring ability to take on cases that no one was doing at the time," said Julie Carnahan, the nursing supervisor of Ochsner Clinic's surgery department.

Carnahan described Dr. Ochsner as a "court of last resort" for some patients and explained why: "He was the man who would do something if it had to be done. In the early days, before antibiotics, if a patient had something that seemed hopeless, like a brain tumor, he'd operate.

"He wasn't trying to be any miracle man, but he wasn't afraid. He felt that if he made the correct diagnosis, he would want to do the thing that got the patient well. He'd tell people, 'If there's a reason for doing it, there's a reason for not putting it off.' That's the way he was."

Among his more dramatic moments in surgery were his use of a blowtorch in radical mastectomies, the first successful separation of conjoined twins in Louisiana, and the removal of the thyroid gland of Tómas Gabriel Duque, a former president of Panama

Dr. Ochsner performed the thyroidectomy in Panama at the request of Secretary of State Cordell Hull, who asked him to operate because Duque had helped the United States by engineering the overthrow of a pro-Nazi government.

Firsthand glimpses of most of Dr. Ochsner's surgical triumphs generally were limited to the people in the operating room with him. But a closed-circuit television hookup let a roomful of doctors—meeting for a national convention in a New Orleans hotel—see how well he could work under pressure.

The operation was a removal of a cancerous lung. It seemed routine and Dr. Ochsner was patiently describing each step to his enthralled audience. But suddenly, blood started gushing from a pulmonary artery because the tumor had penetrated the artery, and Dr. Ochsner's dissection of the cancer had punctured the blood vessel.

The commentary stopped; the surgeon had to act quickly to save the patient's life. He squeezed the artery to halt the flow of blood, holding it with one hand while sutures were put in to close the artery wall. He won that race with death.

Lung cancer was a disease Dr. Ochsner had observed as a medical student. One of his professors summoned his class to see a person with this disease because, the instructor said, "you may never encounter another lung cancer in your entire careers."

But in 1936, Dr. Ochsner saw nine lung-cancer patients in six months. By investigating their medical histories, he learned that each had started smoking during World War I. This discovery, which led to more research into the link between cigarette smoking and health, was the start of his war against cigarettes.

Dr. Ochsner took his battle to the American Cancer Society and persuaded the board of directors to go on record in favor of a resolution, backed by evidence from intense research, that cigarette smoking causes cancer.

Although the fiercely conservative Dr. Ochsner railed against government intervention in many facets of American life, including medicine, and opposed the Medicare program, he believed the federal government should take a stronger role in the war against smoking.

He preached his anti-tobacco gospel to anyone who would listen. While Juan Perón was president of Argentina, Dr. Ochsner was flown to Buenos Aires to examine the dictator's vascular ailment. The doctor recommended surgery and began to prepare for Perón's incognito visit to Ochsner Clinic. But the Argentine strongman was overthrown in the mid-1950s and banished to Spain before he could make the journey.

Dr. Ochsner, who visited his patient twice in exile, told Perón he could avoid the operation by stopping smoking. The deposed despot took his advice.

One man whose life Dr. Ochsner saved on the operating table was Ben Hogan, the professional golfer. In 1949, while Hogan was recovering in a Texas hospital from injuries he had suffered in an automobile accident, he developed blood clots in veins. Anti-coagulants were prescribed to thin his blood, and they touched off massive internal bleeding.

Dr. Ochsner was summoned, and he was rushed to Texas in a B-29 bomber, where he was forced to sit in the only available spot: the bombardier's seat.

To keep the clots from reaching the golfer's heart, Dr. Ochsner tied off the vena cava and gave Hogan medication to thicken his blood and stop the hemorrhaging.

On Hogan's recommendation, Gary Cooper came to Dr. Ochsner to get him to repair a hernia, a task that had daunted doctors in four previous operations. The operation was vital, Cooper explained, because he had to be ready to ride horseback and perform some strenuous stunts in his next picture.

Working at Touro, Dr. Ochsner repaired the hernia and cleared Cooper for the movie. The film was "High Noon"; Cooper won his second Academy Award for his performance.

Until he was in his early 80s, Dr. Ochsner maintained an intense daily routine. After arising at 4 a.m. and performing the Royal Canadian Air Force exercises, including as many as 100 pushups, he worked until midnight. At Ochsner Medical Institutions, he insisted on using stairs until advanced age, coupled with arthritis in one knee, forced him to rely on elevators to get from floor to floor.

After Dr. Ochsner's last operation, colleagues gave him an abstract-looking collage made of gleaming surgical instruments set against a wooden block. The proud physician hung it on a paneled wall in his office.

Among his fellow workers, Dr. Ochsner was remembered as the sort of man who could inspire tremendous loyalty.

"Even when he was a young man, he was so appreciative and very helpful, and he hasn't changed too much since he's gotten older," Carnahan said. "He was the kindest man I've ever known."

After he stopped his operating work, Dr. Ochsner continued to make his rounds, to treat patients—as many as four per day—and to keep up a schedule of speaking engagements. Among his favorite topics was the danger of communism in the Western Hemisphere.

In addition to writing more than 500 articles for medical journals, he wrote six books and 24 sections of books.

Dr. Ochsner received honorary degrees from 10 universities and he was given orders of merit by Ecuador, Panama, Guatemala, and Venezuela. These and other decorations and citations filled the walls in his and Forshag's offices, and others were displayed in stacks atop filing cabinets ringing his secretary's desk.

In an interview with the *Journal of the American Medical Association*, Dr. Ochsner said he had been blessed through his long life with "Presbyterian luck": "If you do the right thing, no matter what happens, it will turn out for the best."

"I believe in luck," he said. "The harder I work, the luckier I get."

— September 25, 1981

Albert Walter Dent

He had his own strategy for advancing civil rights

A lbert Walter Dent, a leader in education and health who was Dillard University's president for 28 years, died Sunday at his New Orleans home after a long illness. He was 82.

For four decades, Mr. Dent worked hard to improve the lives of black people, but he never joined a lunch-counter sit-in or picketed a department store. Except for the March on Washington in 1963, he never participated in a demonstration.

In a 1974 interview, he explained why.

"While there must be someone sitting in at a lunch counter, there has to be another person sitting somewhere else at the same time, talking with the people in power and deciding how best to work out the problem," he said. "That was the role I chose, and for me, it proved the most effective way of helping."

With these words, Mr. Dent summed up the philosophy behind his long service in New Orleans as the superintendent of Flint-Goodridge Hospital, a hospital built for black patients; business manager and president of Dillard, a historically black university; and the member of dozens of boards.

For many years, Mr. Dent was a steadfast participant in community activities, even though he was often the only black member of certain groups and even though, in the days before integration, he had to attend some functions in hotels by using their freight elevators.

"He would take these positions, knowing he was a token, but he took them knowing he was opening doors," said Rosa Freeman Keller, a longtime Dillard trustee.

For that reason, there was no plan to give Mr. Dent a key to the city when he retired in 1969, City Councilman John Petre said.

"He needs no key," Petre said. "He already has opened so many doors for so many people for so many years."

"Some of the most effective leadership in New Orleans, among both whites and Negroes, is not vocal," Mr. Dent said in a 1974 interview. "The more positive their thinking and actions are, the less vocal and conspicuous they are. After all, isn't it a much more dramatic and effective thing to quietly change a man's way of thinking than to go out and loudly make a speech or participate in some publicity-oriented event?"

Consequently, until segregation was outlawed in public places, he never created a scene by trying to go where he would not have been welcome, and he and his wife, Jessie, did not attend events where they would have been forced to sit in a section set aside for black people.

"I never knew of a motion picture, a concert or any other type of entertainment that was worth being segregated to attend," he said in the 1974 interview. "I also knew that I really had nothing to gain from social events of that kind. I didn't want to embarrass the other members or myself by attending and perhaps creating an awkward situation.

"Besides, I knew that one day things would change. It took 15 or 20 years, but the change finally did come."

This self-imposed restriction gave Mr. Dent an excellent reason to make Dillard's Gentilly campus an important center. In the opinion of his peers, he succeeded.

Besides raising money, erecting most of the buildings on campus, and recruiting top-rank faculty members, Mr. Dent brought to campus—and his home—such speakers as Ralph Bunche, the United Nations diplomat and Nobel Peace Prize recipient; Haile Selassie, the emperor of Ethiopia; and Eleanor Roosevelt. Mr. Dent counted several Rockefellers among his friends, and he spent weekends at their country retreats.

"For more than a decade—perhaps two decades—he was the most influential black leader in New Orleans," said Daniel Thompson, a social scholar who used to be Dillard's vice president for academic affairs. "For years, he and Mrs. Dent set the standard for social acceptability in the black elite."

By being influential in the lives of others, Mr. Dent was doing what had been done for him as he grew up in Atlanta.

He was born there on Sept. 25, 1904. His father, a day laborer, died when his son was an infant; consequently, his widow had to take a series of jobs—chiefly as a domestic—to support her son and an older daughter.

In Atlanta then, public education for black children stopped at the seventh grade. To fill that need, Morehouse College was also an upper elementary school, junior high school, and high school.

He enrolled and held a series of jobs until he graduated in 1926. During his senior year, he worked for Atlanta Life Insurance Co. He was hired as an auditor and went to Houston a year later to open up a branch.

He returned to Atlanta in 1928 because Morehouse hired him to be a fundraiser and, then, alumni secretary.

In 1932, a year after Mr. Dent married Ernestine Jessie Covington, he was hired to be superintendent of Flint-Goodridge Hospital, which was considered the nation's foremost hospital for African Americans. Before he took that job, Mr. Dent never had been inside a hospital, even as a patient.

[Dillard owned the hospital until 1983. The hospital closed two years later.]

He quickly gained a reputation as an innovator, starting in the obstetrics department. When Mr. Dent took over, 20 percent of all black babies in New Orleans were born at home with the assistance of midwives, many of whom did not have up-to-date training.

To reduce that number, Mr. Dent reduced the hospital's maternity fee to $10, set up a series of pre- and post-natal clinics for 10 cents per visit, gave refresher courses, and taught pregnant women how to grow vegetable gardens, not only to provide healthful food but also to give women some exercise.

His strategy worked. By the mid-1940s, the at-home birth rate for black babies had plunged to 4 percent.

Mr. Dent also set up programs to fight sexually transmitted diseases and tuberculosis, and he brought hospitalization insurance to black New Orleanians for $3.65 per year. That figure, based on the average cost per patient per day, was called the penny-a-day plan. The program eventually was merged into the Blue Cross system.

While he was Flint-Goodridge's director, Dillard hired Mr. Dent to be its business manager in 1935, meaning he was holding two full-time jobs. Six years later, he was picked to be Dillard's president.

In that job, Mr. Dent was successful at raising and managing money. Even though he believed in integration, he also believed in black colleges because, he said, they serve a purpose.

"A student from a low-income family who has had little or no opportunity at home for reading and for an awareness of community affairs and little or no parental guidance has no hope of competing equally with students from higher-income brackets who have had all the advantages," he said in the 1974 interview. "There should be some compensation somewhere along the way for the inequities of the past.

"You cannot expect anyone to win a race or even have a chance of tying it when they're 10 yards back at the beginning."

To ensure that more students would have such opportunities, he and four other educators founded the United Negro College Fund in 1944. From 1965 to 1970, he was its chairman.

He ran Dillard in the same no-nonsense fashion he had run Flint-Goodridge, said Geraldine Amos, who worked with him at both institutions.

That included going ahead with a faculty meeting on Sept. 9, 1965, even though Hurricane Betsy was bearing down on the city.

"Some people were absent because the weather looked terrible," Amos said. "He said: 'There are a number of people absent. I'll check with them in the morning.'"

But after the storm hit, Mr. Dent's attitude changed from being concerned about absence from a meeting to being concerned about the losses that Dillard employees had sustained, Amos said. He got a list of things that had been lost and contacted foundations and agencies for help.

During the civil rights period, Mr. Dent worked quietly to make change happen, using the connections he had built up.

One day, when Dillard students were planning a march on a nearby shopping center, Amos said that Mr. Dent addressed them—not to talk them out of marching but to remind them to behave.

"He said, 'Be representative of Dillard,' and that says a lot,'" she said. "The police were out there. They had no reason to touch anyone because everything went according to his directions."

Because of Mr. Dent's approach to civil rights, Thompson said, "there was a time when he was so trusted by the white power structure that some blacks worried about him, but he never betrayed them."

While he was lobbying for change, one man asked Mr. Dent, "Where does this stop?"

His reply: "It doesn't stop."

— February 13, 1984

Muriel Bultman Francis

Giving generously to the arts was a family trait

Muriel Bultman Francis, a philanthropist who gave generously to nearly every facet of New Orleans' cultural life, died Thursday at Southern Baptist Hospital after a long illness. She was 77.

Mrs. Francis was a director of the New Orleans Philharmonic Symphony Orchestra, the New Orleans Museum of Art, the New Orleans Opera Association, the Contemporary Arts Center, and Dashiki Theater.

Although she gave generously of her time and money and was known for her skill at raising money, Mrs. Francis once said: "I have no appreciable talents at all. I'm that necessary part of the arts, which is an audience."

She inherited her interests in the arts and philanthropy from her father, A. Frederick Bultman Jr. Besides running the House of Bultman Funeral Home, he was president of the opera and gave more than $50,000 to it.

Giving to the arts was natural in her family, Mrs. Francis said. "It was just taken for granted. You did your bit."

For three decades, that included being a public relations agent for several artistic enterprises. For 15 years, she had a New York publicity agency that specialized in classical-music performers. But after her father's death in 1964, Mrs. Francis returned home and stepped into his place at the funeral home and in New Orleans' cultural life.

She lived in the family's Garden District house, right behind the funeral home. During the early years of Tennessee Williams' career, she let the playwright move in. He used the house's plant-filed conservatory as the setting for "Garden District," which was made into the movie *Suddenly, Last Summer*.

Mrs. Francis, who was born in New Orleans in 1908, was a Phi Beta Kappa graduate of the University of Alabama.

After two years of theatrical publicity work in Chicago and St. Louis, she returned to New Orleans in 1936 and did public relations for the symphony and the Arts and Crafts Club. She also worked for the insurance company that used to be part of the funeral home.

In 1941, her brother, A. Frederick "Fritz" Bultman III, an art student, persuaded her to move to New York City, where they shared an apartment.

She started doing public relations for performing artists, specializing in opera singers and classical musicians. She eventually ran her own company.

Her clients included the violinist Yehudi Menuhin and the opera stars Lily Pons, Rise Stevens, Ezio Pinza, Leonard Warren, and Marguerite Piazza, a New Orleans-born soprano.

"She did my first publicity," Piazza said. "She was a good friend, too. Her family had buried my family for years."

Mrs. Francis, who became a fixture on New York's social scene, had a lifelong infatuation with fine clothes. Among the designer originals in her closet were a dress made by Christian Dior himself and a gown Yves Saint Laurent fashioned for her out of silk cloth ordinarily used to make obis, the sashes for Japanese kimonos.

Mrs. Francis was interested in the visual arts, too, and she started accumulating art in 1937, when she paid $2,400 [the equivalent of about $39,000 today] for paintings by Claude Monet and Odilon Redon. When she was in New York, she bought works by Jackson Pollock, Robert Motherwell, and David Smith when they were struggling artists.

With her brother's guidance, she built a collection of 19th- and 20th-century drawings, paintings and sculptures. Among her holdings were drawings by Pablo Picasso, Pierre Renoir, and Edgar Degas, and surrealistic paintings by Rene Magritte.

In buying art, she said, "I don't go looking for anything. It just looks for you. It reaches out and grabs you."

Her collection was displayed at Gallier Hall, which used to be New Orleans' City Hall, and the New Orleans Museum of Art.

Even though Mrs. Francis appeared frail—she was painfully thin and possessed a voice that sometimes was barely audible—she kept busy. She served on a host of community boards and was active with committee work, but she always seemed to turn up at every civic activity, smoking unfiltered Chesterfield cigarettes in theater lobbies as she held court.

When asked why she was so heavily involved, Mrs. Francis replied: "Why not? I can find the time and the energy. I've always felt that when you want something done, you ask a busy person, not a do-nothing person."

— *May 2, 1986*

Robert Gordy

His distinctive style drew from many sources

Robert Gordy, a New Orleans artist celebrated for whimsical paintings with repeated patterns and for arresting abstract studies of human heads, died Wednesday at his home of complications from AIDS. He was 52.

Mr. Gordy, a native of southwest Louisiana who became one of New Orleans' most influential and widely known artists, created a distinctive style by borrowing from a wide variety of sources: cubism, surrealism, impressionism, abstract expressionism, art deco, and even African tribal art.

"He was a hard worker, and he was disciplined," said E. John Bullard, director of the New Orleans Museum of Art, who called Mr. Gordy "one of the best-known New Orleans artists of the last 25 years."

His pictures were widely exhibited, and they were in the permanent collections of such institutions as the New Orleans Museum of Art, the Whitney Museum of American Art, and the Museum of Modern Art.

The early decorative paintings featured repeated images of animals, geometric shapes, and female nudes set against unreal landscapes. In the last years of his life, Mr. Gordy concentrated on painting heads, creating a series of characters that displayed such diverse emotions as frenzy, fatigue, skepticism, resignation, and the stoicism associated with primitive masks.

Once he knew he had acquired immune deficiency syndrome, a terminal disease, Mr. Gordy seemed to spend even more time at his work, putting in as much effort as his depleted strength would allow, said Arthur Roger, the owner of the New Orleans gallery that represents Mr. Gordy.

He was born Oct. 14, 1933, on Jefferson Island, La., where his father was manager of a salt mine, and he went to school in nearby New Iberia.

When he was a freshman in high school, he started painting every day and was encouraged by Weeks Hall, a New Iberian who had studied at the Pennsylvania Academy of Fine Art.

In college, Mr. Gordy became influenced by the abstract expressionists, especially Willem de Kooning, and he spent the summer of 1952 studying with Hans Hofmann, one of the foremost practitioners of this style.

Mr. Gordy received an undergraduate degree from Louisiana State University in 1955, and he earned a master's degree there a year later. Mr. Gordy traveled to Europe, Mexico City, San Francisco, and New York, and he taught in Kansas, Vermont, and New Orleans, where he settled in 1964.

In 1967, when he was the artist in residence at Loyola University, Mr. Gordy was starting to show the flat color and repeated images that became the hallmarks of his pattern paintings.

In creating these pictures, Mr. Gordy acknowledged the influences of several artists, especially Paul Cézanne and Henri Matisse.

He drew on a variety of inspirations. For example, in a lush series called "Tortola Stomp," he painted what he thought tropical life might be like.

"Subjects quite often reveal themselves in accidental ways," he said in a 1978 interview, "and, having chanced upon a subject, I immediately try to integrate it with a style."

Mr. Gordy won two fellowships from the National Endowment for the Arts and the Mayor's Arts Award, and his work was included in exhibitions around the country.

But after a 1981 exhibition of his work at the New Orleans Museum of Art, Mr. Gordy felt he was wasting too much time and talent in planning the details that are an important part of the pattern paintings, Roger said.

He found a new outlet for his talent on a trip to New Mexico, where he was shown how to make pictures called monotypes. He was fascinated with the process, and he stayed with it for the rest of his life.

To make a monotype, he painted an image on Formica and pressed it onto paper. Since the inks cannot be allowed to dry on the plate, a picture has to be finished on the day it is started, Roger said.

Because of the required speed, he said, Mr. Gordy could bring a sense of immediacy to his work that he had not been able to do with the pattern paintings.

"Gordy has made a unique and secure place for himself in contemporary American paintings," wrote Gene Baro, a Brooklyn Museum curator, in the catalog for the 1981 New Orleans exhibition of Mr. Gordy's work. "You can be sure with Gordy, no matter how simple the work seems, there will be more to see and more than meets the eye."

— September 25, 1986

J. Skelly Wright

He desegregated New Orleans' public schools

J. Skelly Wright, a federal judge who changed the course of New Orleans' history in 1956 when he ordered the desegregation of the city's public schools, died Saturday of cancer at his home near Washington. He was 77.

Judge Wright, who never used his first name, James, had retired last October from the U.S. Circuit Court of Appeals for the District of Columbia, where he had served since 1962 after leaving his native New Orleans. President Truman had named him to the federal bench in 1949.

In New Orleans, Judge Wright was best known for his 1956 order that New Orleans' public schools had to be integrated.

"I knew that it was not going to be easy," he said in a 1981 interview.

That was an understatement. The ruling, which was followed by four years of appeals and strong opposition from segregationists in the Legislature, ignited a firestorm of hatred. Judge Wright was hanged in effigy, friends spurned him, and someone shoved him into traffic in the Central Business District.

His unlisted telephone number had to be changed frequently to avoid abusive calls, and a cross was burned on his front lawn one night while he was inside his Uptown home. His wife, who had been at the opera, rushed inside to comfort him and found him asleep.

"If they did that to intimidate me, they wasted their time," Judge Wright said, "because I missed the whole show."

After four years of resistance, four black girls entered William Frantz and McDonogh No. 19 elementary schools Nov. 14, 1960.

Despite that victory, the war was hardly over. Federal marshals were stationed around the clock outside his home until President John F. Kennedy appointed him to the District of Columbia Circuit Court of Appeals in 1961.

This gesture was not only a reward for good service but also a way to get Judge Wright out of the city where he had become a pariah to many whites. Although Judge Wright became widely regarded as a trailblazer in race relations, he later said his credo did not always include equal rights for blacks.

"I was insensitive to the problem most of my life," he said. "I didn't perceive any problem."

But it was there early. When he and his six brothers and sisters were growing up near Napoleon Avenue, they lived across the street from McDonogh No. 6 Elementary School, but they went around the corner to McDonogh No. 7 because it was for white children only. McDonogh No. 6 was for black pupils.

After Mr. Wright finished Warren Easton High School in 1927, his family had no money to send him to college, so he went to work as a messenger for a law firm, where his interest in the law was born.

Loyola University approved his application for financial aid, and he earned undergraduate and law degrees there.

When he finished law school in 1934, there were few jobs in his field during the Depression, so Judge Wright had to teach at Fortier High School until 1936, when his politically powerful uncle, Joseph P. Skelly, had him appointed an assistant U.S. attorney.

During World War II, Judge Wright joined the Coast Guard and was stationed in London, where he met Helen Patton, a U.S. Embassy employee whom he married before returning home.

The war, he said in 1981, was the turning point in his attitudes toward race relations. "I saw segregated armies," he said, "and I didn't like that. Americans would have race riots among themselves: Blacks in one camp were attacking the whites in another. We were going out to fight the same enemy, and here we were, fighting each other."

His thinking on this subject evolved more after the war, he said, when he was at a Christmas party, standing on a Camp Street balcony across from the Lighthouse for the Blind.

As he watched, he said, buses pulled up with people bound for a holiday party there. Partygoers were directed to two doors—one for white blind people and another for black blind people.

Seeing that extreme example of segregation that made no sense—especially not to the blind people—made him question even further the whole idea of separating people by race, Judge Wright said in the 1981 interview.

In 1948, he expressed interest in succeeding Herbert W. Christenberry as U.S. attorney when President Harry S. Truman made Christenberry a federal judge. He became U.S. attorney and was appointed to the federal bench a year later.

In 1954, the U.S. Supreme Court declared segregated public schools unconstitutional. Two years later, Judge Wright did the same thing in New Orleans, and he ran into a series of roadblocks from the Legislature, under the direction of Gov. Jimmie Davis, when he tried to put his order into effect.

Judge Wright struck down more than 100 laws to stop desegregation, sometimes acting within minutes of their passage.

"During those days, he was always available, 24 hours a day," said Sam Rosenberg, the attorney for New Orleans' public schools. "If the Legislature was passing bills to close the public schools . . . or fire the superintendent or fire me, he was always available to sign temporary restraining orders to prevent them from doing it."

"As president of the board, I was faced with obeying Judge Wright's order or seeing the public schools destroyed," Lloyd J. Rittiner said. "I couldn't see that happening, so along with three other board members, we decided to comply. It took time to comply, but the judge gave us time."

Although many New Orleanians ostracized Judge Wright, others hailed him, and Yale University gave him an honorary degree. But the reward he wanted—a seat on the 5th U.S. Circuit Court of Appeals—was out of his reach because Sen. James O. Eastland, D-Miss., a staunch segregationist, was chairman of the Senate Judiciary Committee, which had to approve the appointment.

In late 1961, Kennedy named Judge Wright to the District of Columbia Circuit Court of Appeals. That meant he no longer would rule on civil-rights cases in his—and Eastland's—part of the country.*

— *August 7, 1988*

*Blake Kaplan contributed to this article

Norman N. Newhouse

A news executive who was deliberately low-key

Norman N. Newhouse, the quiet-spoken, New Orleans-based key executive of the family communications empire that owns the Times-Picayune Publishing Corp., died Sunday in New Orleans. He was 82.

Mr. Newhouse had been battling leukemia for years, but the immediate cause of death was a heart attack. He had been given five years to live when doctors diagnosed his leukemia in 1971, but continued his rigorous schedule almost until his death.

An early riser, he was at his desk by 6 a.m., and he flew regularly to three Alabama cities and Cleveland to visit Newhouse newspapers.

In New Orleans, he had an office in the Times-Picayune Publishing Corp.'s building, and he participated in and approved decisions on such major matters as spending millions of dollars on presses.

As one of the family members who ran the business, he talked regularly with other Newhouses to keep up with developments at the family's holdings. But, like the other members of his family, he did not take a role in the newspaper's day-to-day operation, and he didn't have a formal job title.

"We never went in for titles," he said in a 1985 interview. "We are, basically, anonymous people. If I were to walk into a room in New Orleans with the 100 most prominent people in town, there may be two who would know me personally. Most would probably know the name and the connection, but they wouldn't know me personally or recognize me by my face because my public position is non-existent."

This low profile was part of the philosophy he and his brothers, S. I. and Ted, developed in 1939, when they bought the *Syracuse* (N.Y.) *Herald-Journal*.

Before this acquisition, their newspapers had been on Staten Island and Long Island and in Newark, N.J.—close enough to let S. I. Newhouse,

Norman Newhouse's older brother and the head of the family business, visit them every day. Because Syracuse was too far for daily visits, the brothers gave editorial control of the paper to its publisher and editors.

Although it started as a practical matter, local autonomy became a tenet of the Newhouse philosophy. The brothers established the policy with all their holdings because, Mr. Newhouse said, they believed the people who lived in the cities knew what the local problems were and had the best ideas for solving them.

"The basic policy is simple," he said. "If it's good for the town and its people, it's good for us."

It may be a simple policy, but, he said, it hasn't made the family immune to criticism. "If you interfered with or dictated editorial policy, you'd get clobbered, like (newspaper czar William Randolph) Hearst was clobbered," he said. "If you failed to do it, they'd say you don't care about editorial policy. So you're damned if you do, and you're damned if you don't."

But when S. I. Newhouse died in 1979, the *New York Times* praised this philosophy on its editorial page: "S. I. Newhouse demonstrated that editorial autonomy in newspaper chains could be both good business and good journalism. In an era of growing consolidation in newspaper ownership, that lesson is a legacy."

At Norman Newhouse's death, the empire had grown and diversified to contain 27 newspapers in 10 states; three cable-television companies; five publishing houses, including Random House and Alfred A. Knopf; and 11 magazines, including *Parade*, *Vogue*, *Gourmet*, *Vanity Fair*, and the *New Yorker*.

Advance Publications, the umbrella company for the Newhouse holdings, is privately held and, therefore, releases no financial data. But John Morton of Washington, D.C., a newspaper-industry analyst, estimated that in 1984 total revenues were about $2 billion.

Even though the Newhouse holdings had expanded widely, Mr. Newhouse spent his life in newspapers, where the family business began. Before moving to New Orleans in 1967, he was editor of the *Long Island Press* and, before that, the *Staten Island Advance*. As an undergraduate, he worked on the daily paper at New York University.

Norman Newhouse was the sixth of eight children of Rose Fatt and Meyer Newhouse. The family lived in a five-room, cold-water flat in Bayonne, N.J., where young Norman slept on boards laid atop the bathtub.

Meyer Newhouse had a suspender factory until his partner sabotaged it by running off with the company's money. He later had to move to Arizona because his allergies made life in Bayonne impossible except in summers.

To support herself and her children, Rose Newhouse peddled dry goods in the streets from a pack she carried on her back, and all the children worked, virtually from the time they took their first steps. When he was 5, Norman Newhouse started selling the *Bayonne Times*. The price was a penny apiece, and he was allowed to keep half, plus tips.

In a privately printed memoir, S. I. Newhouse said his brother quickly realized he could sell more if he just held one paper and said, pleadingly, "Mister, please buy my last paper."

As soon as he sold it, the fledgling entrepreneur would run off to fetch another from a nearby stack.

In addition to selling papers, his duties included buying ice and picking up coal dropped from railroad cars at a siding.

As a child he worked in the *Bayonne Times*' composing room. When he was 9 he was severely burned when molten lead—used for casting Linotype bars—was accidentally spilled down his left leg.

"The skin was burned right off," he said. "You see, in those days, children wore knickers and black stockings. Well, I was wearing knickers, and the stockings became a form. The lead poured inside and formed around the leg."

Mr. Newhouse went to New York University, where he was issue editor twice a week for the school's daily paper. During summers, he worked in the classified and advertising departments at the *Staten Island Advance*, which S. I. Newhouse bought in 1922.

After getting a degree in history and geology, he went to the *Advance* as a reporter.

Mr. Newhouse covered the waterfront for three months before being transferred to the police beat, where he spent three years. When it was discovered that the paper's political reporter was on the public payroll, he was removed, and Mr. Newhouse was named his successor. He later became city editor and managing editor.

In 1937, Mr. Newhouse was moved to the *Long Island Press*, where he became editor.

While editor, he became involved in a row with Fiorello LaGuardia, New York's outspoken mayor, over a decision to build a hangar at the airport that would later bear the mayor's name. The *Press* criticized this decision in an editorial because city officials had announced they didn't have enough money to build a school—a project that, Mr. Newhouse said, was needed more and would cost much less.

"It was a simple editorial, nothing to get tough about," he said, "but LaGuardia took it personally."

The mayor claimed he was attacked because he had refused a favor to S. I. Newhouse. When the publisher heard that, he called the mayor's bluff, offering $5,000 to anyone who could prove that S. I. Newhouse had been in the mayor's office. There were no takers.

"We never stopped crusading," said David Starr, publisher of the Newhouse newspapers in Springfield, Mass. Starr was hired as a copy boy at the *Long Island Press* in 1940, while he was in college.

"We fought for parks," Starr said, "and we fought to preserve the wetlands. We helped get the subway system extended to Queens. The *Long Island Press* fought to have a college built in Queens—Queens College—and I was a product of that college. We fought to create the State University of New York system, and Norman served on the board of trustees of SUNY at Stony Brook."

During those years, Mr. Newhouse was "a working editor, a shirt-sleeves editor," Starr said. "He read copy, wrote headlines and went down to the composing room."

When the United States entered World War II, Mr. Newhouse decided he should go into the armed forces even though he was 35, which was the age limit for the draft. Mr. Newhouse was determined to be a man in uniform, but poor vision kept him out.

Finally, after speaking to several politicians, he was admitted to the Army Air Corps as a writer and assigned to Mitchell Field on Long Island.

After being transferred to several bases along the East Coast, he was sent to North Africa, where he became executive officer of the Office of Strategic Services, the forerunner of the Central Intelligence Agency. He served with the OSS in North Africa and Italy from 1943 until the end of the war.

During four years of military service—from February 1942 to February 1946—he rose from second lieutenant to lieutenant colonel and was awarded the Legion of Merit and the New York Distinguished Service Medal. The Italian government made him a knight officer of the Order of Saints Maurice and Lazarus.

Among the men who reported to him in Italy was John Gardner, who became secretary of Health, Education and Welfare under President Lyndon B. Johnson and the leader of Common Cause, a reform organization. Gardner was a Marine lieutenant in charge of OSS personnel in Italy, and Mr. Newhouse was the regiment's executive officer.

"I think he was a major at the time," Gardner said. "He was dealing with lieutenant colonels and full colonels, but he had no trouble being clear about what he wanted. He had a gift for running things. . . . He was the heart and soul of running that regiment."

Based on the months they worked together, Gardner said, "I would say he was one of the ablest managers I've ever run into. I'm speaking from the heart when I say I really valued him."

Shortly after resuming his job as editor of the *Long Island Press*, Mr. Newhouse noticed a woman walking across the newsroom. She was Alice Gross, a college student working as a reporter, and Mr. Newhouse, a friend of her father's, introduced himself at once. Within three weeks they were engaged, and within three months they were married after her graduation.

"I saw no reason for waiting," he said in 1985. "I knew what I wanted when I found it."

That, Starr said, showed the way Mr. Newhouse worked.

"He's extremely quick," Starr said. "He takes no time to make his mind up. He doesn't dawdle, and he doesn't worry a problem to death."

Even though the Newhouse empire grew, it never acquired a formal management structure. The Newhouse brothers simply met to discuss plans and problems, and, if a dispute arose, everyone deferred to S. I. Newhouse because he was the eldest.

"We were his younger brothers," Norman Newhouse said. "That was all."

To explain his management strategy, S. I. Newhouse wrote this in his memoir: "This is not something found in an organizational manual, nor is it a formula developed in the Harvard School of Business. It's the outgrowth of that pragmatism we learned in Bayonne from an immigrant lady with a pack on her back—the need to hang together and find the appropriate solution to each problem."

Norman Newhouse was "simply a superb executive," Starr said. "First of all, he's so smart. He has a real feeling for people. He gets the best out of them because he understands them and relates to them."

Flexibility was an important trait.

In 1967, S. I. Newhouse decided a family member had to live in the South to oversee the family's properties in that part of the country.

At a family meeting, Norman Newhouse said, "They looked at me, and I said, 'I'm ready.' And so we came down the following Wednesday."

Besides the New Orleans operation, Mr. Newhouse was responsible for the *Cleveland Plain Dealer*, the *Mississippi Press* in Pascagoula, and the *Birmingham News*, the *Mobile Press*, the *Mobile Register* and the *Huntsville Times* in Alabama.

To keep up with these far-flung properties, he spent much of his time traveling. For years, he flew to Alabama on Mondays, headed to Cleveland on Wednesdays and returned the next day.

On these visits, he talked to department heads, the general manager and publisher to be brought up to date. He received progress reports on every area except editorial policy, which, in keeping with the family philosophy Mr. Newhouse had established, he avoided.

"It was old-fashioned minding the store, paying attention to what's going on," said Ashton Phelps Jr., who was then publisher of the *Times-Picayune.*

At the New Orleans newspaper, "there was no formality" in Mr. Newhouse's day-to-day style, said Phelps, who had worked with Mr. Newhouse since 1970.

"You were talking to someone who understood every facet of the business," he said. "He could empathize with the problems and help you solve them without a lot of written reports and financial projections."

The decision to spend $35 million on presses in 1988 exemplified the way Mr. Newhouse did business, Phelps said.

"There was not a single memo written to justify it or a single projection," Phelps said. "He knew the business and knew what should be done. It's not that he didn't appreciate $35 million or know it was a serious decision. He knew the business better than the people making the recommendation, and he approved it without a lot of formality."

In the Times-Picayune Publishing Corp.'s building, Mr. Newhouse was a familiar figure who wore bow ties and suspenders, greeted everyone and drove Chevrolets with blackwall tires. Three of his sons—Mark, Peter and Jonathan—followed their father into the family business.

During the 1971 Christmas season, Mr. Newhouse was told he had leukemia, and doctors said he had no more than five years to live. His daughter, Robyn, convinced him that vitamins might help, and he soon became a believer in massive doses of them.

"I go to the hospital every two months and run through all sorts of tests," he said in 1985. "They tell me after they're all over that I'm alive. I ask my doctors, 'Don't you give any credit to the vitamins?' and they say, 'No.'"

He continued horseback riding until January 1985, when the girth on his horse's saddle snapped and he was thrown onto concrete on the Mississippi River side of the levee.

After that accident, he exercised by walking and pedaling a motorized stationary bicycle.

He never considered retirement because, he said, nobody in his family ever did.

— *November 7, 1988*

Allen "Black Cat" LaCombe

A promoter famed for his bad-luck bets

Allen "Black Cat" LaCombe, the colorful sports figure and promoter fabled for his string of bad-luck bets, died in his sleep Wednesday at his New Orleans home. He was 71.

Mr. LaCombe, who had had two recent heart attacks, was known for outlandish promotional schemes, colorful turns of phrase and friendships with racetrack types with nicknames like Place 'n' Show Joe, Meyer the Crier, Benny Without a Penny, Alimony Tony, Cream Cheese Louie, and Chew Tobacco Sam. As a result, he possessed the aura that surrounded the flamboyant characters in Damon Runyon's Broadway stories from the 1920s and 1930s.

Mr. LaCombe, who affected a monocle after cataract surgery, came to represent a simpler time when a man with some hustle, some connections, and not much cash could assemble friends in a neighborhood bar, pull together a football game or a prize fight, and promote it as an exciting event.

Although he organized tournaments, fights and—while he was in the Army—camel races around the pyramids, Mr. LaCombe's interests went beyond athletics.

With tongue firmly in cheek, he hitchhiked around Louisiana in a 1959 gubernatorial campaign. Three years later, Mr. LaCombe ran for mayor of New Orleans.

He was asked then if the job would be full-time. "I said I was the only one who could promise that because I was the only candidate drawing unemployment pay," he said in an interview.

To most people, Mr. LaCombe was best known by his nickname, which he received from a *Times-Picayune* sports writer after an ill-fated bet on a boxing match.

Mr. LaCombe was supposed to be a handicapper—he even taught a course on the subject at Tulane University—but many people found his tips more of a jinx than a guarantee of big winnings. Buddy Diliberto, a local sportscaster, recalled that when he bet on a LaCombe choice in a harness race, a wheel on the horse's sulky fell off.

But Mr. LaCombe, who wore mismatched shoes for good luck, said his bad luck extended only to gambling. "Nobody's had more fun than me," he said, "and when I die, I'll know I never missed a thing. God looks after you, and I figure He's on my side."

Mr. LaCombe was born in Echo, a small town in central Louisiana, but the family moved to New Orleans' Irish Channel when he was a baby. He grew up there, picking up the neighborhood's distinctive Brooklynese accent and attending St. Michael's School—sometimes.

He "nearly went to high school" at St. Aloysius because he worked out with the football team, Mr. LaCombe said. "But when Brother Martin, the principal, finds how I never made it out of third grade, he gives me the heave-ho."

He said that he received his "college training" at the Press Lounge, a Poydras Street bar known informally as Raymond's Beach in honor of Lew Raymond, a leading fight promoter. It was patronized largely by the "write and fight" crowd—reporters and boxers. He said he was schooled there by some of the "world's greatest con men in promoting"—Broadway Johnny "the Fox" Cox, Leapin' Lou Messina, and Raymond.

Mr. LaCombe's career as a fight promoter began when he was 13, he said, because "this girl I liked edged [*sic*] me on to do it."

By that time, he had been betting on horse races for three years, even though he was too young to place 25-cent bets himself. At his first race, Mr. LaCombe said, "The horse won and paid $1.40," he said. "I been hooked ever since."

In 1935, he launched his first full-scale promotion, the Thanksgiving Day Turkey Bowl, a football contest between champion sandlot teams in the Irish Channel.

For the first game, there was only one ball, and it sometimes had to be wrested from over-enthusiastic fans. But by the third year, when Skippy's Aces played the Bienville Meat Market Thunderbolts, the Turkey Bowl had moved to City Park Stadium, where it drew 16,000 people.

In 1942, Mr. LaCombe was drafted into the Army. He responded by giving a party for his draft board. He helped stage Army boxing matches in Iran, where the shah sparred with Mr. LaCombe's boxers. Mr. LaCombe also hunted gazelles with King Farouk of Egypt.

After the war, in addition to his ill-starred political forays, Mr. LaCombe moved into special-event promotions. One of his bigger projects was a 1965 benefit at Municipal Auditorium for people who suffered losses from Hurricane Betsy. Loretta Young appeared; so did Eddie Fisher, Mel Torme and Bobby Vinton.

In the 1960s, he was named the Fair Grounds racetrack's public-information spokesman. The job kept him busy and happy—so much so that he never considered quitting, even when he reached the traditional retirement age of 65.

"I got to keep up the contacts, you know?" he said. "When you retire, that's when you die."

Burial followed a lap by the cortege around the Fair Grounds track.*

— *July 20, 1989*

Marjorie Roehl contributed to this article.

Caroline Durieux

Satire was the aim of her art

Caroline Durieux, a Louisiana artist who spent her long career poking fun at the foibles of what she called "la comedie humaine," died Sunday in Baton Rouge of complications from a stroke. She was 93.

Mrs. Durieux was a native New Orleanian who developed her talent in art schools and polished her gifts in Mexico, Cuba, and South America. She was a friend of the great Mexican artist Diego Rivera, who became an admirer of her work.

A 1978 article in the *New Republic* summed up her artistry, saying, "Some satirists go to work with a meat ax and some with a stiletto, but Mrs. Durieux prefers the finest and sharpest needles."

Whether her subjects were South American grandees, New Orleans social climbers, dowagers at Carnival balls, or destitute beggars, Mrs. Durieux sought to capture their personalities in her lithographs.

Her works are satirical, but "they're not all funny because, you see, satire ranges from humor at one end to tragedy at the other," she said in a 1978 interview.

In 1980, Mrs. Durieux was honored by the National Women's Caucus for Art. Her works were featured in many books and exhibitions, most recently at the New Orleans Museum of Art last summer.

Born in 1896 into a prominent New Orleans family, Caroline Wogan Durieux traced her interest in art—especially in satire—to her early life. She started by sketching her teachers, and in 1913 entered Newcomb College, where she studied under Ellsworth Woodward, a demanding teacher whom she credited with making her into an artist.

"If I can draw at all," she said in 1978, "it's because for four years, every day for four hours, we drew. That was the kind of training we got."

Mrs. Durieux also studied at the Pennsylvania Academy of Fine Art in Philadelphia, returning to New Orleans in 1920 to marry Pierre Durieux, an exporter who had been a longtime friend. They moved to Cuba, and, in 1926, to Mexico City, where she turned more and more to satire.

The Durieuxs became acquainted with such celebrated artists as Rivera, David Siquieros and Jose Orozco. Although she and her husband liked their work, Mrs. Durieux did not see their subjects—noble peasants and scenes of ghastly oppression—as subjects for her pictures.

"I didn't come from that background," she said, "but, then, the bourgeoisie is the same all over the world. There were plenty of Mexicans I could caricature."

While in Mexico, Mrs. Durieux kept up her artistic contacts in the United States. Among them was Carl Zigrosser, director of the Weyhe Gallery in New York City, who encouraged her to try lithography, in which an artist creates a picture on a heavy stone and runs off prints on a press.

Pierre Durieux's illness forced the couple to return to New Orleans in 1936. They moved into the French Quarter, and New Orleanians became the subjects for her artistic observations. She showed gospel shouters and streetwalkers, sassy cabaret singers and solemn nuns, a series of dragon-like society matrons, and pictures of genteel Creole ladies gossiping.

Mrs. Durieux also provided illustrations for "Gumbo Ya-Ya" and "The New Orleans City Guide," which was compiled by the Federal Writers' Project of the Works Progress Administration, which was part of the New Deal. The guide was regarded as a model for the rest of the series about states and cities, and it has become a collector's item.

In 1938, Newcomb College hired her to teach lithography. Four years later, she and her husband moved to Baton Rouge, and she lived there the rest of her life. She taught lithography at Louisiana State University until her retirement in 1963.

Pierre Durieux died in 1949. A year later, Mrs. Durieux launched into another phase of her career: making prints with an ink containing radioactive promethium. She called the results "electron prints," and the originals are stored in special containers at LSU's Nuclear Science Center because they are radioactive.

During her later years, Mrs. Durieux's lithographs became increasingly stark and somber.

"Her prints are amazing in their psychological implications," Zigrosser wrote of Mrs. Durieux in *The Artist in America*. "It is never an explosion of bitterness or hate; it is rather the detached probings of a surgeon stripping off layer after layer of protective tissue until the essential nature is revealed."

— November 30, 1989

Walker Percy

He wrote of people looking for answers

Walker Percy, the physician-turned-writer who lived on the Bogue Falaya River and wrote complex philosophical novels about people trying to find their way in a world gone haywire, died Thursday of cancer at his Covington home. He was 73.

His last major public appearance was in May 1989 in Washington, D.C., when he delivered the annual Jefferson Lecture of the National Endowment for the Humanities.

By geography, Mr. Percy was a Southern writer, since he grew up in Alabama and Mississippi and spent most of his adult life in Covington. But Mr. Percy resented the description, saying once, "You'd never call (John) Updike a 'Northern novelist,' and I don't know anybody who'd call (Saul) Bellow a 'Midwestern novelist.'"

Besides, Mr. Percy's six novels and two books of essays more closely resemble the works of the New England writer Nathaniel Hawthorne, dealing as they do with good and evil in the heart, Linda Whitney Hobson wrote in *Understanding Walker Percy*.

And, she said, his philosophical novels put him in the company of Herman Melville and Robert Penn Warren.

Although Mr. Percy achieved fame as an author, he was trained to be a physician, and he earned a medical degree from Columbia University in 1941. But while performing autopsies as an intern at Bellevue Hospital, Mr. Percy contracted tuberculosis. During his convalescence, he decided to abandon medicine and become a writer.

After working on book reviews, articles and two novels that never were published, Mr. Percy's first novel, *The Moviegoer*, appeared in 1961. The book, whose principal character is a movie-obsessed Gentilly resident named Binx Bolling, won the National Book Award in 1962.

Five other novels followed: *The Last Gentleman* (1966); *Love in the Ruins* (1971), which won the National Catholic Book Award; *Lancelot* (1975); *The Second Coming* (1980), which won the *Los Angeles Times* fiction prize; and *The Thanatos Syndrome* (1987). He also wrote two books of essays, *The Message in the Bottle* (1975) and *Lost in the Cosmos* (1983), as well as articles on philosophical, literary and medical topics, and limited-edition printings of some articles and speeches.

"The reconciliation of change and continuity, of loss and renewal, and of science and faith has given energy to Walker Percy's narratives from the beginning of his career to the present and has made him a persuasive moralist in troubled times," Hobson wrote.

"In some way," she said, "each of his works successfully probes—sometimes gently, sometimes in wrath—the disease of the American soul."

Mr. Percy, who was born May 28, 1916, in Birmingham, was orphaned in his teens. He and his two brothers were adopted by William Alexander Percy, their father's first cousin, whom Hobson described as a "bachelor poet, planter and social conscience" of Greenville, Miss.

Will Percy's house was a center of culture and a magnet for famous literary people. Carl Sandburg, Langston Hughes and Stephen Vincent Benet were house guests, and William Faulkner occasionally showed up to play tennis. Besides playing classical records continually, Will Percy read poetry aloud so the boys could appreciate the words, Hobson wrote.

While a student at Greenville High School, Walker Percy discovered a talent for composing sonnets. He sold some to less gifted classmates for 50 cents apiece.

While he enjoyed writing, "in the South, you didn't set out to become a writer," Mr. Percy said in 1980. Consequently, he earned a degree in chemistry from the University of North Carolina in 1937 and a medical degree from Columbia University College of Physicians and Surgeons in 1941.

But tuberculosis ended his medical career. Convalescing in a sanatorium in the Adirondacks, he started reading intensely—fiction and philosophy by such authors as Fyodor Dostoevsky, Jean-Paul Sartre, Gabriel Marcel and Soren Kierkegaard. The experience helped shape Mr. Percy's interest in the uniqueness and isolation of individual experience in a universe that he believed can be indifferent or even hostile.

From Kierkegaard, Hobson wrote, Mr. Percy learned to see man as free but, as a consequence of his liberty, burdened with a terrible responsibility for his acts.

In 1946, Mr. Percy married Mary Bernice Townsend, a nurse he had met in Greenville who was known by her nickname, Bunt. They moved into Will Percy's home in Sewanee, Tenn., to read and study religion for a year. At the end of that period, both converted to Catholicism.

"Belief and acting toward a belief were important to him," said Faust, the owner of Maple Street Book Shop. "He didn't care if you followed an organized religion. He just cared if you were looking as if you were questioning why you were on Earth."

The impact of his faith showed up in his literature. "It is . . . no coincidence that the Percy hero often makes a leap of faith at the end of a novel," Hobson wrote. "A Percy hero has to have a leap of faith, an act of will and a quest, during which he learns that the leap and act are available if he wants to bring himself out of despair."

The Percys moved to New Orleans in 1947, and Mr. Percy started writing. Two books followed—*The Charterhouse*, about a country club, and *The Gramercy Winner*—but neither was published. There are no plans to publish them, Faust said.

In 1950, they moved across Lake Pontchartrain to Covington. Four years later, Mr. Percy sold his first book review to Thought, a Fordham University quarterly.

His first novel, *The Moviegoer*, was published in 1961. On the surface, it is an account of the week before John Bickerson "Binx" Bolling's 30th birthday. But there's more to it. This book, studded with images of the Gentilly neighborhood and bygone motion pictures, is an odyssey of the soul in which Bolling realizes he's in a comfortable rut and ultimately decides to embark on a quest—in this case, a series of decisions that will shape the way he lives the rest of his life.

Five years later, his second novel, *The Last Gentleman*, appeared, and it was nominated for a National Book Award. It introduced the character of Will Barrett, a confused young Mississippian, who would reappear in *The Second Coming*, in 1980. Mr. Percy's third novel, *Love in the Ruins*, confused people when it was published in 1971. This satiric, frequently violent view of a sort of apocalypse in a polarized society opens with a sniper attack from a Howard Johnson motel near a city like New Orleans.

"It was a fun book to write," he said, "but the fun ended on a Sunday in January (1973) . . . when The Associated Press called me up . . . to ask if I was watching television. . . . There was a black sniper on top of the Howard Johnson's hotel in downtown New Orleans. . . ."

"It was an eerie thing. I was afraid they might find my book among his belongings. They didn't."

Less than a year later, the Arab oil embargo and its accompanying gasoline shortage made people remember another image from *Love in the Ruins*: automobiles running out of gas on freeways.

"I have absolutely no visionary powers," Mr. Percy said. "If I did, I'd have taken automobile mechanics in high school.... If I'd known I could become a successful writer, I'd have taken typing, too."

In his two works of non-fiction, *The Message in the Bottle* and *Lost in the Cosmos*, Mr. Percy mused about philosophy and language. Language was a topic of vital interest to him. "This is what makes man different from animals and what makes each person an individual self," Faust said. "It's a tool he uses to help define the self."

Because of their deep philosophical and religious underpinnings, Mr. Percy's books have touched off a torrent of books and monologues, elevating him to the status of such eminent and intensely studied writers as Faulkner, Flannery O'Connor, and Eudora Welty.

Mr. Percy could be reclusive, but for years, Faust said, he lunched regularly at restaurants every week with two select groups of friends—older companions on Thursdays and younger people on Wednesdays. Although admission to these groups was by vote, members could bring guests, and the actor James Mason showed up at one gathering. At these lunches, which could last for hours, participants talked about the fortunes of the New Orleans Saints, current events and occasional critiques of Mr. Percy's work, Faust said, but Mr. Percy cut off questioning about his work in progress.

Mr. Percy encouraged young writers and, in one memorable case, helped create a New Orleans legend.

In 1969, a New Orleans man committed suicide, leaving behind a manuscript that publishers had rejected. But his mother believed in it and got the book to Mr. Percy, who liked it and used his influence to get it published. The result was *A Confederacy of Dunces*, which astonished everyone by becoming a best seller and winning the Pulitzer Prize in 1981 for its author, John Kennedy Toole.

Mr. Percy was a fellow of the American Academy of Arts and Sciences and a member of the National Institute of Arts and Letters and the Fellowship of Southern Writers. Pope John Paul II named him the only American on the 14-member Pontifical Council for Culture, and he was the United States representative to the Vatican World Council in 1988. He received the University of Notre Dame's 1968 Laetare medal, the most prestigious award given an American Catholic.

Tulane, Loyola and Marquette universities, the University of North Carolina, the University of the South, and the College of St. Scholastica gave him honorary degrees. The 1976 citation from the University of the South hailed Mr. Percy as "novelist and essayist, gentleman first and last" and said, "Educated as a physician, you have enlarged the metaphysical dimensions of modern fiction and have invested language with a fresh idiom in our time."

— May 11, 1990

John Ognibene

An artist and passionate AIDS activist

John Joseph Ognibene Jr., a gay activist who lobbied—and frequently fought with—politicians to get more money for AIDS work, died Thursday at his New Orleans home of complications from acquired immune deficiency syndrome. He was 48.

Mr. Ognibene, who lived in New Orleans for 12 years, was born in New York City, where he received a bachelor's degree in fine arts from Pratt Institute and taught music and art at Fiorello H. LaGuardia High School. In New Orleans, he was an interior designer, and he designed the local television special "Christmas on Broadway."

Mr. Ognibene also painted, specializing in portraits and cityscapes that resembled the works of Edward Hopper.

Shortly after moving to New Orleans, Mr. Ognibene founded Crescent City Coalition, one of the city's first gay activist groups, said Jim Kellogg, a New Orleans lawyer.

The organization was established to protest one weekend's arrests of 103 gay men on charges of obstructing sidewalks, Kellogg said. The coalition claimed the arrests amounted to nothing more than police harassment, and all charges were dropped.

When AIDS hit Louisiana in 1982, Mr. Ognibene directed his energy to fighting the epidemic. Besides being concerned with channeling more money to AIDS research, he wanted to educate as many people as possible about the ways the illness is—and isn't—spread. His energy frequently turned to frustration and rage, Kellogg said, because he realized no state could afford the kinds of programs he wanted.

But Mr. Ognibene kept working with city and state officials because, he said, the need was clear.

"We're sitting on a time bomb," he said in 1985, "and nobody's doing anything about it."

He was fundraising director for NO/AIDS Task Force and a member of ACT UP New Orleans.

He also was a volunteer for the New Orleans People With AIDS Coalition and Friends of Charity Hospital C-100 Clinic. The latter organization refers to the hospital's outpatient clinic that has treated hundreds of people with AIDS, including Mr. Ognibene.

— *September 11, 1990*

Barbara Boggs Sigmund

She confronted cancer with courage

Barbara Boggs Sigmund, a daughter of U.S. Reps. Hale and Lindy Boggs and the mayor of Princeton, N.J., since 1984, died Wednesday of cancer at her Princeton home. She was 51.

Her mother and sister, Cokie Roberts of Washington, D.C., were with her, said Claude M. Crater, a funeral director. Mrs. Sigmund, the eldest of the Boggses' three children, had lived in Princeton since the early 1960s.

Her eight-year battle with cancer, and the courage with which she waged it, attracted nationwide admiration. Her illness was the reason Lindy Boggs did not seek re-election, although Boggs never mentioned it directly.

In discussing her plan to leave Washington to spend more time in Princeton, Boggs told an interviewer, "I can't hug Barbara from here."

Mrs. Sigmund confronted cancer in 1982, when melanoma was found behind her left eye. Doctors removed the cancer and the eye.

After surgery, Mrs. Sigmund wore a patch and turned it into a personal trademark that captured the pluck with which she faced the disease. She wore bright patches that matched her clothing, including a spangled patch for evening wear, and she handed out eye patches last year during an unsuccessful campaign for governor.

Shortly after that race, doctors discovered that Mrs. Sigmund's cancer had reappeared and spread, but she continued to live with her characteristic verve, puttering about Princeton on a small scooter friends bought for her.

Her attitude in the face of cancer was evident early on. The day she was released from a hospital after her eye was removed, she went to a fundraiser where she said, "You all are a sight for a sore eye."

During her second bout with cancer, Mrs. Sigmund became philosophical about the battle she was waging and the role she felt she had to play.

"If you're in a public situation, you do feel responsible to demonstrate to people that diseases that are so terribly feared like cancer don't have to be an immediate death sentence and that one can continue to live life to the fullest for a long time after the diagnosis is made," she said earlier this year. "The fact that you might die . . . does not mean you give up hope."

By her example of candor, Mrs. Sigmund said, she hoped to help others. "The one journey we can't cash in the ticket for is the journey towards our own death," she said. "I think that one of the gifts maybe I'm still able to give people is to give them a little sense of what the journey is like."

Last month, the Arts Council of Princeton published "An Unfinished Life," a compilation of Mrs. Sigmund's essays and poems. Many pieces dealt with her illness, and they covered a broad range of emotions, including anger, resentment, resignation, grit and bafflement at having contracted a terminal illness.

Mrs. Sigmund, who grew up in an environment suffused with politics, was president of the student body at Manhattanville College of the Sacred Heart in Purchase, N.Y., where she received a degree in politics in 1961.

After working as a recruiter for National Extension Volunteers, a domestic version of the Peace Corps sponsored by the Catholic Church, she joined the White House staff, and she served on an advisory committee that helped form VISTA.

She married Paul Sigmund, now a professor of politics at Princeton University, in 1964. They had three sons.

Encouraged by her father, the House Majority leader, shortly before his plane was lost over Alaska, she won a seat on the Princeton council in her first race for public office, in 1972. Four years later she won a seat on the Mercer County Board of Freeholders, the county's governing body, and in 1979, she became its first woman president.

She established a shelter for the county's battered women that became a model for similar shelters throughout the state. Earlier this year, she said it was the political accomplishment she was proudest of.

In 1984, she was elected Princeton's mayor. Besides those local contests, Mrs. Sigmund ran unsuccessfully for the U.S. Senate in 1982—the campaign began a month after her left eye was removed—and for the New Jersey governorship last year.

Manhattanville College named her a distinguished alumna, and she received honorary degrees from Chestnut Hill College, Caldwell College and St. Elizabeth's College.

She received an award from the New Jersey Division of the American Cancer Society, and the Washington, D.C., division of that national organization gave her its Hubert Humphrey Courage Award.

"Courage is a verb, not a noun," she said in 1983. "It's a word of action. Courage is a leap into the void. Courage is not static."

— October 11, 1990

Phyllis Dennery

A federal law crediting volunteering bears her name

Phyllis Dennery, a volunteer who poured time and energy into a host of civic and religious projects, including the founding and development of PBS affiliate WYES-TV, died Wednesday at Touro Infirmary of lingering effects of a stroke. She was 71.

Mrs. Dennery, who was president of the public television station's board of trustees in 1966 and 1967, gave her surname to a provision of federal law—the Dennery Amendment to the Telecommunications Act of 1978—governing such stations.

The Dennery Amendment was the result of a conversation with her husband, who had asked her why public broadcasting didn't get any credit for her volunteer work. The amendment, which Congress passed unanimously, put a monetary value on the time volunteer workers put in public stations and let stations use that "income" in applying for federal matching money.

The year after it was passed, public-broadcasting officials estimated the amendment qualified them for an additional $20 million in federal revenue.

Mrs. Dennery also established La Fete, an annual series of summertime activities designed to rouse New Orleans area residents from their hot-weather torpor and lure visitors to the city during what traditionally is a slack season.

Since its founding in 1980, La Fete has presented fireworks, cooking programs and a variety of entertainment, including a 1983 performance by the ballet star Mikhail Baryshnikov and his troupe.

La Fete's focus turned to food, and Mrs. Dennery compiled a cookbook, *Dining In—New Orleans*, and a sequel, both of which feature recipes from New Orleans restaurants.

In organizing activities "she was always very, very professional—very demanding, very exacting," said Dot Shushan, a longtime friend. "That's what she gave, and that's what she thought other people should."

Mrs. Dennery was born in New York City in 1919. She moved to New Orleans in 1941 when she married Moise W. Dennery, a lawyer who also has been extensively involved in civic causes and honored for his work.

"She came into a situation where she was an outsider and wanted very much to be a part of the community, a part of Moise's life and his circle of friends and family members," said former U.S. Rep. Lindy Boggs, another close friend. "I think she wanted to pull her oar and feel she had something to offer and do it very well and be respected for it."

Mrs. Dennery was president of the New Orleans section of the National Council of Jewish Women and the Friends of the New Orleans Public Library, and she was elected vice chairman of the National Friends of Public Broadcasting, which builds community support for public stations.

When she worked for these organizations, "she motivated a lot of people into volunteering, including me," Shushan said. "She had a happy knack of being able to find the right kind of volunteers and motivate them by selling the particular thing she was involved in and getting them enthusiastic, too."

In 1979, she was one of six national winners of the National Volunteer Activist Award for her work in behalf of the Dennery Amendment. In its citation, the National Center for Voluntary Action said she "has demonstrated that one citizen with a good idea, commitment and energy can work effectively with Congress to create new, needed legislation."

— February 21, 1991

Alvin B. Rubin

A judge who combined reasoning and compassion

Alvin B. Rubin, a federal judge known for his lucid, thoughtful opinions in cases involving civil liberties, died early Tuesday of liver cancer at Our Lady of the Lake Hospital in Baton Rouge. He was 71.

In 24 years on the U.S. District Court in New Orleans and the 5th U.S. Circuit Court of Appeals, Judge Rubin wrote more than 700 opinions. They included rulings that ended Louisiana's exemption of women from juries, applied the Voting Rights Act to local elections and upheld government employees' rights to criticize their superiors and organize unions.

"I can't think of a better judge," 5th Circuit Judge John Minor Wisdom said. "He combines solid reasoning power with being a warm, compassionate person."

Judge Rubin's tenure on the federal bench began in 1966, when President Lyndon Johnson picked him to be a district judge in New Orleans. Eleven years later, President Jimmy Carter nominated him to succeed Wisdom on the appeals court. Wisdom had taken senior status, a position that lets judges lighten their workloads while continuing to hear cases and write opinions.

In 1989, Judge Rubin took senior status, to the disappointment of civil rights lawyers for whom he represented the last vestige of the activist appellate court that desegregated schools and fought job discrimination.

By then, he knew he had cancer, but he remained active, Jack Weiss, a New Orleans lawyer, said. Last month, he attended the American Law Institute's annual meeting in San Francisco.

Alvin B. Rubin was born in Alexandria, La., and received undergraduate and law degrees from Louisiana State University, where he was in the same law school class as former U.S. Sen. Russell Long.

Judge Rubin, editor of the *Louisiana Law Review*, graduated at the top of the class of 1942; Long, the law review's associate editor, was No. 3.

The men were lifelong friends, and Long said he frequently called Judge Rubin for advice. It was Long who, as Louisiana's senior senator, backed his old friend for the appellate court.

"I happen to think he's the most talented judge on the federal judiciary," Long said in an interview last year. "He has that rare combination of being practical and brilliant. . . . My impression is he's been right about everything he's done."

Judge Rubin served in Europe during World War II. After his discharge in 1946, he went into private practice in Baton Rouge until his appointment to the federal bench.

"He was the finest lawyer at the bar," said retired U.S. District Judge Fred Cassibry.

Cassibry could attest to Judge Rubin's skill because when Cassibry was a Civil District Court judge, Judge Rubin argued cases in his court.

"He was very effective, very bright, always prepared," Cassibry said.

On the bench, Judge Rubin made people aware that he held high standards in his courtroom and had no tolerance for mediocrity, U.S. District Judge Martin L. C. Feldman said.

One day, when it became obvious that the lawyer appearing before Judge Rubin was unprepared, "he was very tough on the guy, but he did it in an instructive way," Feldman said. "He made the guy feel bad about being unprepared . . . in a way that he never walked into Judge Rubin's court unprepared again."

Judge Rubin was "a stickler for the law," Cassibry said, "but he was also very imaginative and added a lot to the law. I don't think he ever tried to make law himself, but he was very innovative in his interpretations of the law."

Among Judge Rubin's innovations was a 1980 decision in which he applied the federal Voting Rights Act to a school board election in Texas, saying the at-large system diluted the Mexican-American vote.

Moreover, Judge Rubin occasionally wrote his opinions in distinctive ways. For instance, in striking down a Texas fire department rule that let a chief suspend the union president for criticizing him, Judge Rubin began his opinion with this passage from Dr. Seuss' children's book *Yertle the Turtle*: "'Silence,' the king of the turtles barked back. 'I'm king, and you're only a turtle named Mac.'"

"Those in authority do not readily accept public criticism by their subordinates," Judge Rubin then wrote.

In deciding a case, Judge Rubin used his "rare ability to blend theory and practice," Feldman said. "He also had a rare ability to take a concept that was extremely complex and intricate and make it seem uncomplicated and understandable."

This gift is something "you can't learn or practice," Feldman said. "You have this by instinct or you don't."

Judge Rubin kept up an active schedule as a teacher, lecturer and moot-court judge at schools in the United States and Europe; a list of his books and articles fills four pages of his résumé. The co-author of one book, *Louisiana Trust Handbook*, was his wife, Janice G. Rubin.

"He made me feel guilty all the time because he worked all the time. Prodigiously," Cassibry said. "We drove to a conference in Atlanta, and he sat in the back seat with Janice, his wife, and dictated on the damn Dictaphone the entire time."

He was a member of the Board of Editors of the American Bar Association Journal and the ABA's House of Delegates, the association's policy-making organization. He also was the first alumni member of LSU's chapter of Phi Beta Kappa.

In 1989, he was elected to the American Academy of Arts and Sciences, an organization that honors a select number of scholars and national leaders.

In December of that year, he received the Benjamin Smith Civil Liberties Award from the American Civil Liberties Union of Louisiana. The award was named for a New Orleans lawyer who represented people and causes no one else would champion.

In the program for the dinner where Judge Rubin received the award, Shirley Pedler, the executive director of the ACLU Louisiana chapter, said his "evenhanded and righteous application of constitutional principles represents the best of American tradition, the promise that the necessary vagaries of democracy will not be allowed to stamp out guarantees to individual liberty, and that the least among us stand as equals to the powerful before the law."

— *June 12, 1991*

Thomas Bloodworth Jr.

I helped Churchill decide where to deliver his "Iron Curtain" speech

Thomas S. Bloodworth Jr., a former member of the diplomatic corps who helped an inquiring Winston Churchill decide where to deliver his historic "Iron Curtain" speech, died Thursday night of an aortic aneurysm at his Gentilly home. He was 69.

Relatives found him during the weekend.

Mr. Bloodworth retired in February 1987 as a *Times-Picayune* copy editor with a reputation for erudition in many fields, including antique porcelain, foreign policy, Carnival lore, obscure battles, and the grammar of several languages.

Mr. Bloodworth was born in Natchez, Miss., and grew up in New Orleans. He was valedictorian of Warren Easton High School's Class of 1938. At Tulane University, where he graduated in 1942 with a major in history, Mr. Bloodworth was elected to Phi Beta Kappa.

He was doing graduate work at the University of Virginia when he was drafted into the Army Air Forces, in which he served until September 1946.

He was in the foreign service from 1946 to 1952, and was posted in India and Israel when both countries won their freedom. As a consular official in London in 1946, he took a call from Churchill's secretary, who needed information about Westminster College in Fulton, Mo., which had offered Churchill an honorary degree, said John Bloodworth, a nephew.

Based on the information Mr. Bloodworth supplied, Churchill came on the line and said he would accept the degree. His speech warned of the Soviet domination settling over Eastern Europe and popularized the term "Iron Curtain."

After leaving the diplomatic corps, Mr. Bloodworth worked in book and record stores in New Orleans, then joined the newspaper as a proofreader in 1960.

"His legacy was a legacy of accuracy," said Tom Gregory, the associate editor for news of the *Times-Picayune*.

With his thrown-together appearance and his ability to cite authors and periodicals most people had never heard of, Mr. Bloodworth seemed anachronistic, Gregory said, like a character in a Graham Greene novel.

Mr. Bloodworth, who counted Tennessee Williams among his friends, was an authority on Southern literature, especially works pertaining to New Orleans.

In retirement, his nephew said, he proofread menus for friends' restaurants and was a consultant on antique porcelain and silver patterns. He died while doing a crossword puzzle—appopriately, in ink.

He also maintained a meticulously labeled herb garden which included his own strain of tarragon and about a dozen types of peppers he would grind and bring with him to restaurants.

— *October 15, 1991*

William J. "Buzzy" Fanning

He let AIDS patients know that people cared

William J. "Buzzy" Fanning, a retired maitre d' who devoted the past five years to improving the lives of Charity Hospital's AIDS patients, died Thursday of intestinal gangrene at Southern Baptist Hospital. He was 71.

Mr. Fanning started visiting Charity patients in 1985. A year later, as staffs at gay bars heard about his visits, they began giving him their tips to buy gifts for "Buzzy's Boys"—later "Buzzy's Boys and Girls."

The gifts were usually minor—pajamas, milkshakes and stuffed animals, for instance.

"It's the little things that count," Mr. Fanning said. "It gives them a little dignity."

The donations were never huge, but they were enough for Mr. Fanning to start two funds: one to pay for expensive prescriptions, another for hospital equipment for home care.

"I don't ever solicit money," he said in his trademark raspy voice. "They come to me."

Mr. Fanning was born in Brooklyn, N.Y. During World War II, he served on the *Gripsholm*, a cruise ship that had been converted to a prisoner-exchange hospital ship. After the war, he started working in restaurants—as a dishwasher, busboy and waiter—in California and Florida before winding up in New Orleans around 1950, his half-brother, Frank Mancini, said.

Mr. Fanning worked at several restaurants before joining the staff at Brennan's, where he stayed for about a quarter-century. He became maitre d' and got to know politicians and celebrities who ate there. He also befriended students, and sometimes helped them pay college tuition, said Brian Eschette, a friend.

"I knew him when I was a freshman medical student," said Dr. Brobson Lutz, director of New Orleans' Health Department. "He used to slip me into Brennan's and slip me milk punches."

One of Mr. Fanning's friends was Clay Shaw—a Brennan's regular—who was arrested, tried and acquitted during Jim Garrison's investigation of President Kennedy's assassination. Because Mr. Fanning had known Shaw, he was asked to be a consultant for "JFK" scenes filmed at the French Quarter restaurant.

Mr. Fanning retired in 1983, as AIDS began making inroads in New Orleans. He began visiting patients at Charity Hospital after seeing a friend suffer from Kaposi's sarcoma, a cancer associated with AIDS.

Despite the psychological drain, he kept up his rounds. "He touched so many people's lives," Mancini said. "He always said he was a very lucky boy. He had a remarkable life."

— November 15, 1991

Victor H. Schiro

"I'm just a little guy . . . who loves his city"

Victor H. Schiro, the irrepressibly optimistic two-term mayor of New Orleans who was as celebrated for his personal style as for his politics, died Saturday night at his home. Mr. Schiro, who had been in poor health since a 1988 stroke, was 88.

According to Dawne Orgeron, administrator of City Health Department's Emergency Medical Services, Mr. Schiro's wife said she had gone to check on him shortly after 10 p.m. and found him dead.

Mr. Schiro was a city councilman when he was named interim mayor in 1961 to succeed deLesseps S. "Chep" Morrison, whom President Kennedy had appointed ambassador to the Organization of American States.

A year later he won election and served another eight years as the city's chief executive. In 1970, when the City Charter kept him from running again, Mr. Schiro went back to selling insurance at the agency that bore his name.

A dapper man known for his trim mustache and constant smile, he kept working—and glad-handing people wherever he went—until he suffered a stroke in 1988.

During his administration, Mr. Schiro's stock statement was "If it's good for New Orleans, I'm for it."

He championed the widening of Poydras Street, which was a first step toward lining that thoroughfare with high-rises and big businesses to rival Canal Street. And during his re-election campaign, he announced plans for a domed stadium.

But he faced problems, too. The civil rights revolution seethed in the 1960s, and in September 1965, Hurricane Betsy swept through.

That killer storm led to an enduring Schiro image that has become part of the city's lore: a man in a yellow slicker and a Civil Defense helmet, giving his constituents televised advice on surviving the calamity as the storm bore down on the city. Cautioning viewers not to panic, Mr. Schiro solemnly warned: "Don't believe any false rumors unless they come from me."

Another time, in an attempt to be philosophical, Mr. Schiro said, "That's the way the ball crumbles."

"I had my share of bloopers because I speak freely," Mr. Schiro said in a 1984 interview. "I don't take a script. I just say whatever comes out. I'm a human being. I'm entitled to have a few bloopers. Who cares? They understood me, and when I gave an order, they acted—beautifully."

When he left office, Mr. Schiro said voters probably liked him because "I'm just a little guy . . . who loves his city. . . . I think people know that. They want people to be sincere about the job. You can put up with a lot if a person is sincere."

Despite Mr. Schiro's zeal, he probably was the least dynamic of New Orleans' post–World War II mayors, said Ed Renwick, director of Loyola University's Institute of Politics.

"Since the end of the war, Schiro probably is the mayor who did the least number of things to change the city," Renwick said. "But he was also mayor during that turbulent desegregation period, which was a very difficult period to govern."

Mr. Schiro, who was named for the French novelist Victor Hugo, was born in New Orleans, but he spent his early years in Honduras and California before returning to the city.

In the mid-1920s, Mr. Schiro forsook his night-school pre-law course at Loyola University to go west once more. He found work as a movie extra and, during breaks in film jobs, as co-manager of an unsuccessful Nevada gold mine in the Rocky Mountains.

Eventually, he bluffed his way into a job as an assistant cameraman and was assigned to work with the fledgling director Frank Capra, who would eventually win three Academy Awards.

Everything went smoothly until the company went on location in the California desert. As shooting was about to begin, Mr. Schiro felt he had to tell Capra the truth: He knew nothing about movie cameras.

"Capra jumped three feet," Mr. Schiro said, "and I thought he was about to hit me over the head. Instead, he started smiling, put his arm around me and said, 'Son, you sure got guts.'"

Mr. Schiro returned to New Orleans in 1928 and took a job as an announcer at WJBO-AM. In 1932, he married Mary Margaret Gibbes, a woman known by her nickname, Sunny. They had no children.

He also started work as an agent for Metropolitan Life Insurance Co., but he didn't leave broadcasting. From 5 a.m. to 8 a.m., he was an announcer at WWL-AM. In 1948, he founded the Vic Schiro Insurance Agency.

A year later, he got into politics when Morrison asked him to join his ticket as a candidate for the city's Commission Council. At first, he declined. Then Morrison told him that another candidate for the council seat had said Mr. Schiro probably was too wishy-washy to make the race.

"That made me want to get into the fight," Mr. Schiro said. "I like a good fight once in a while."

He won.

In 1952, New Orleans voters approved the Home Rule Charter, which replaced the Commission Council with the City Council.

The charter took effect in 1954. That year, Mr. Schiro was elected to an at-large post on the new governing body, and he was re-elected in 1958. Three years later, when Morrison left office, the City Charter said the five district council representatives had to pick one of the two at-large members to be interim mayor to serve the remaining months of Morrison's term.

The candidates were Mr. Schiro and James A. Comiskey, a Morrison foe, and the politicking to succeed Morrison was intense.

"I've always thought of myself as a salesman," Mr. Schiro said. "I was fighting for my political career, and I certainly did the best selling job of my life."

After a series of meetings, including one legendary session at Assessor Henry Heaton's Lakefront boathouse, and hours on the telephone, Mr. Schiro won all five votes of the district councilmen, and he later won citywide election to two full terms.

Throughout his administration, Mr. Schiro turned up at all sorts of events, making speeches, shaking hands, handing out proclamations and keys to the city, and cutting ribbons.

There were tangible achievements, too. Lower Algiers, a community across the Mississippi River from downtown New Orleans, got running water; the city got three overpasses; and twin regional libraries were built in Algiers and eastern New Orleans.

But when Mr. Schiro was running for re-election in 1965, polls showed he was trailing James E. Fitzmorris Jr. And an attack of appendicitis kept him from campaigning as actively as he would have liked.

But Mr. Schiro had an ace to play. On the night before the election, he appeared on television wearing pajamas and a bathrobe to announce plans for a domed stadium in eastern New Orleans.

At the time, Mr. Schiro denied this statement had anything to do with politics. But in a later interview, he said, "I have to admit it may have been the least bit political."

The next day, he won a first-primary victory. The arena, which became the Louisiana Superdome, eventually was built on former railroad property across Poydras Street from City Hall.

"I think I did the best I could," Mr. Schiro said. "I'm not a genius or an extraordinary person. I'm just an average guy. . . . I did my duty, and I did it well. I'm proud of what I did. I make no apologies to anybody."

In reviewing his years in municipal government, he said: "I wanted to always be useful. I wanted to do a job, and I figured that I would then have the big job and then retire. And that's what happened."

It didn't quite work out that way. In 1975, Mr. Schiro ran for state insurance commissioner. He placed second in a field of seven but withdrew from the runoff, saying, "I have no intention of running for public office again. I have no political future. . . . My future is my job."

— August 30, 1992

Jim Garrison

He had a theory about John F. Kennedy's assassination

Jim Garrison, the former New Orleans district attorney who attracted worldwide attention with his sensational but ultimately fruitless investigation of President Kennedy's assassination, died Wednesday at his home, Coroner Frank Minyard said. He was 70.

The cause of his death was not immediately known. Although he never publicly disclosed the nature of his illness, Mr. Garrison had been sick for more than a year, and for much of that time remained in bed at his Gentilly home, Minyard said.

Mr. Garrison, who had been on the state 4th Circuit Court of Appeal from June 1978 until his retirement last November, died 10 months after the opening of *JFK*, Oliver Stone's largely favorable account of the assassination inquiry, which introduced Mr. Garrison, portrayed by Kevin Costner, to a generation of Americans.

Mr. Garrison played a small role as Earl Warren, the chief justice of the United States, who led the federal commission that investigated the assassination. The casting was not without irony: Throughout his inquiry, Mr. Garrison attacked the Warren Commission's conclusion that Lee Harvey Oswald acted alone when he killed Kennedy in Dallas on Nov. 22, 1963.

Mr. Garrison began his assassination investigation in the fall of 1966, determined to uncover what he claimed was an elaborate conspiracy hatched in New Orleans.

In interviews with the *Times-Picayune* in 1983, some of Mr. Garrison's former staff members described it as a project doomed from the beginning. Theories about shadowy groups were vague and frequently in conflict, they said, and they never could prove anything.

"Most of the time, you marshal the facts, then deduce the theories," said Charles Ward, a Garrison aide who later served with him on the 4th Circuit Court of Appeal. "But Garrison deduced a theory, then he marshaled his facts. And if the facts didn't fit, he'd say they had been altered by the CIA."

On March 1, 1967, Clay Shaw, the retired director of the International Trade Mart, was arrested. Exactly two years later, after a tumultuous trial that attracted worldwide attention, a jury acquitted him of conspiracy charges after deliberating less than an hour. Mr. Garrison quickly arrested Shaw for perjury, but the federal courts blocked that prosecution, saying it amounted to harassment.

No one else was tried as a result of the investigation. At various times, Mr. Garrison claimed the FBI, the CIA, and the Johnson administration were trying to derail his work, and in a 1970 interview with the *States-Item* newspaper, he flatly accused the CIA of killing Kennedy. Despite his defeat in the Shaw trial, Mr. Garrison won re-election in 1969 with 53 percent of the vote.

In 1973, Mr. Garrison was in court as a defendant—one of three men tried on charges of accepting bribes and conspiring to protect illegal pinball gambling.

He acted as his own attorney, and he was acquitted.

But three months later, he lost his bid for a fourth term to Harry Connick. Mr. Garrison ran unsuccessfully for the state Supreme Court, set up a private practice and wrote two books, *A Heritage of Stone* and *The Star-Spangled Contract*, before being elected to a seat on the 4th Circuit Court of Appeal in 1978.

He won re-election and had planned to stay on the bench until he turned 70 last November, but failing health forced him to step down three weeks early.

Some lawyers and fellow judges criticized Mr. Garrison's performance as a judge, saying he was aloof and lazy. While James Gulotta, a fellow appellate judge and close friend, conceded that Mr. Garrison relied more on his staff than the other 11 members of the court, "I don't think he's lazy," he told the *New York Times*. "He will do those things that interest him. In cases involving complicated legal principles, he will get into it tooth and nail. The mundane things don't interest him. . . . He has no small talk at all."

Mr. Garrison was born Nov. 20, 1921, in Dennison, Iowa, the grandson of a lawyer who once worked with Clarence Darrow. He grew up in New Orleans, and, after serving as a fighter pilot during World War II, he received his law degree and a master's degree in civil law from Tulane University and worked briefly for the FBI in the Seattle area.

Back in New Orleans, he opened a law practice, specializing in civil and domestic cases. He was an assistant district attorney under Richard Dowling from 1954 to 1958 and, later, an assistant city attorney.

In 1961, when Dowling ran for re-election, Mr. Garrison was one of his five opponents. Running as an independent who used television extensively, Mr. Garrison made the runoff and, eventually, won.

During his first term, Mr. Garrison attracted a great deal of attention as a reformer intent on cracking down on Bourbon Street's raunchier establishments.

"I didn't make the laws against B-drinking, prostitution, and drunk-rolling," he told the *Saturday Evening Post*. "But those are the laws, and I'm supposed to prosecute violations, and I'm going to do it. I'm going to end the rackets here, and the only way anyone can stop me is to kill me."

Mr. Garrison ran afoul of Criminal District Court judges over the management of the fund he used to finance these forays. The money, which came from bond forfeitures, could be spent at his discretion, but it required the signature of at least one judge.

Getting authorizations was difficult when the judges took summer vacations, but it wasn't any easier when they returned, he said. The judges countered that he wouldn't explain some of his expenses to them.

"This raises interesting questions about the racketeer influences on our eight vacation-minded judges," Mr. Garrison said. With that, the judges charged him with criminal defamation.

He was convicted in February 1963, but the U.S. Supreme Court unanimously threw out that verdict 21 months later, declaring unconstitutional the state law under which Mr. Garrison had been prosecuted.

During his second term, Mr. Garrison launched his assassination investigation. Rosemary James, one of the *States-Item* reporters who broke the story of the inquiry, said Mr. Garrison's interest probably began during a 1966 conversation on an airplane with Sen. Russell B. Long.

"Long dissented with the Warren Commission," James said. "That whetted Garrison's appetite." Shaw was arrested in 1967, but nearly two years of legal wrangling ensued before the trial began.

During that time, Mr. Garrison received worldwide attention. "I think he got to like all those headlines," James said. "He could see himself as a U.S. senator, a federal judge. Every time the national media left town, he'd invent a new theory to get them back."

Mr. Garrison claimed that, minutes after the assassination, mysterious men fled the Texas School Book Depository, where, the Warren Commission said, Oswald fired the fatal shots.

He also implicated, at one time or other, shadowy gunmen who reportedly were on the famous grassy knoll in front of the Kennedy motorcade, armed Cuban-Americans, militant homosexuals and men firing from storm drains.

The witnesses he presented at the trial were just as bizarre. They included Charles I. Spiesel, who testified that someone—he didn't know who—was trying to hypnotize him; Vernon Bundy, a narcotics addict who said he saw Shaw and Oswald while he was preparing to inject himself with heroin on the lakefront; and Perry Raymond Russo, who changed his story under cross-examination.

In 34 days of testimony, Mr. Garrison's office never summoned anyone who offered compelling proof that Shaw was part of a plot to kill the president. After deliberating 53 minutes, a Criminal District Court jury unanimously acquitted him.

"Garrison has a right to his opinion about the government and the Warren Commission," juror David L. Powe said, "but I just don't feel his opinion is enough to convict a man."

— *October 22, 1992*

Carlos Marcello

A "little man" who ran the Gulf Coast mob

Carlos Marcello, a squat, taciturn man who occasionally described him-self as a tomato salesman but was actually the Mafia boss of New Or-leans and the Gulf Coast, died Tuesday in his sleep at his suburban home in Metairie. He was 83.

The cause of death was not disclosed, but Mr. Marcello had been in fail-ing health for several years. He suffered from Alzheimer's disease.

Mr. Marcello, who stood 5 feet 3 inches tall and was known as "The Little Man," had lived quietly in Metairie since his 1989 release from federal pris-on, his fourth term behind bars in a lifelong contest with law enforcement authorities.

When Mr. Marcello returned home, he was engulfed by children and grandchildren bearing platters of cakes and sandwiches, and bottles of red wine.

Despite the image he liked to project of a kindly man preoccupied with family gatherings and his Grand Isle fishing camp, Mr. Marcello had a much darker side.

According to sources familiar with his career, he was named the local Mafia boss in May 1947 in a ceremony in a back room of the Black Dia-mond nightclub at Conti and North Galvez streets.

By that time, federal authorities said, he was heavily involved in illegal gambling in suburban Jefferson Parish, with the cooperation of local of-ficials there.

By the early 1960s, Marcello was moving out of gambling, fighting a run-ning battle with federal authorities constantly trying to deport him.

And in the late 1970s prosecutors finally secured their most important conviction as a result of the Brilab investigation into kickbacks for state insurance contracts.

Throughout his life, Mr. Marcello denied any connection with organized crime. In one of his more famous self-characterizations, he told immigration officials he was merely a tomato salesman for Pelican Tomato Co.

Unlike other Mafia dons, Mr. Marcello was not a snappy dresser, nor did he call attention to himself by quipping to columnists, showing up at smart restaurants and nightspots, or being photographed with celebrities.

Instead, Mr. Marcello, a poorly educated man whose command of English was never firm, kept his office in a decidedly downscale motel on Airline Highway, and he seemed to enjoy spending his free time with his family.

And, unlike other organized-crime leaders who murdered their way to power, Mr. Marcello seemed to eschew violence.

However, some authorities still suspect he might have played a role in President Kennedy's assassination—an outgrowth of his hatred of Attorney General Robert F. Kennedy, who launched a war on organized crime and roughly deported Mr. Marcello in 1961.

"We found, much to our surprise, that major figures in organized crime discussed the president and Robert Kennedy and killing them," said G. Robert Blakey, who was chief counsel and staff director of the House Select Committee on Assassinations from 1977 to 1979.

The committee officially limited itself to the conclusion that it could not rule out Mafia involvement in the Kennedy assassination.

"My own judgment is a little more affirmative," said Blakey, a law professor at The University of Notre Dame. "Far from being able to indicate that they didn't do it, we found national surveillance (that shows) that they were thinking about it, that they had motive, opportunity and means."

But as far as the public was concerned, Mr. Marcello was carrying on a consuming fascination with real estate—specifically, buying up hunks of St. Charles and Jefferson parishes.

"What he really liked was making the deal. That's what made him run," said Harold Hughes, who was assigned to Mr. Marcello when he was an FBI agent in New Orleans.

When Mr. Marcello was released from jail the final time, John Volz, who prosecuted him in the Brilab case, said, "I hope he is resigned to finishing out his lifetime in peace, and I wish him well in that."

Volz's statement amounted to a sort of benediction for a man whose tumultuous life began on Feb. 6, 1910. Mr. Marcello was born in Tunisia while his father was working on a sugarcane plantation downriver from New Orleans to earn enough money so he could send for his family.

Mr. Marcello, who was born Calogero Minacori, and his mother, Luigia Farrugia Minacori, joined Giuseppe Minacori eight months later.

Their surname was changed several years later because Giuseppe Mina-cori's boss, who also was named Minacori, resented being confused with an employee.

The boss suggested Marcello. The couple liked it, so they Anglicized their first names, becoming Joseph and Louise, and changed the baby's first name to Carlos.

The family settled in Algiers, a neighborhood across the Mississippi River from downtown New Orleans, where Joseph Marcello raised vegetables.

Carlos Marcello stayed in Algiers until he was 18, when he moved to the French Quarter. While living in a $2-a-week room on Conti Street, he plotted a bank robbery that would be financed with loot from a grocery-store holdup that had occurred in January 1930.

In preparing for the bank robbery with boys who were 13 and 16, Mr. Marcello and the older youth stole a getaway car.

The boys, who stole $65 from the grocery store, were arrested before they could rob the bank, and they told police of Mr. Marcello's plot.

Based on that story, police arrested Mr. Marcello, whom newspaper reports described as a "Fagin" and the "alleged holdup teacher" of "baby bandits."

He was the only one of the three to be convicted, and he was sentenced to nine to 14 years at the Louisiana State Penitentiary at Angola.

He entered Angola in May 1930, but Gov. O. K. Allen paroled and pardoned him four years later, reportedly at the request of a legislator who knew the Marcellos.

Mr. Marcello returned to work with his father, but that lasted only a year.

In 1935, he bought a bar in Gretna, which he named the Brown Bomber, the nickname of the heavyweight boxer Joe Louis. He also opened a liquor store on Teche Street in Algiers.

In September 1936 he married Jacqueline Todaro, a close friend of his sister Mary. She helped him run the liquor store, and they lived in back.

Four years after his release from Angola, Mr. Marcello was arrested in March 1938. This time, he and four other men were charged with selling 23 pounds of marijuana to a federal undercover agent.

Mr. Marcello pleaded guilty and was sentenced to a year and a day in the federal penitentiary in Atlanta. After his release, Mr. Marcello went to work for the Jefferson Music Co., a suburban-based distributor of jukeboxes, pinball machines, pool tables—and illegal slot machines.

When the New York City mobster Frank Costello was banished from New Orleans as a result of pressure from teachers and ministers, he looked to the suburbs as an area of expansion.

A lieutenant recommended Mr. Marcello to manage 250 of Costello's slot machines in Algiers.

Mr. Marcello, whose new job let him make extensive contacts with West Bank tavern keepers and politicians, was allowed to keep two-thirds of the machines' grosses. Costello's company kept the rest.

In an FBI tape made without his knowledge during the Brilab investigation, Mr. Marcello spoke of filling a suitcase with wads of money for public officials.

One recipient allegedly was Beauregard H. Miller Sr., a suburban police chief, who, Mr. Marcello said, would get $50,000 from Mr. Marcello while denying that gambling existed in his city.

In 1945, when Costello opened the Beverly Country Club in a suburb, Mr. Marcello was brought in as a 12.5 percent partner.

The club offered roast prime rib, such stellar performers as Sophie Tucker and Joe E. Lewis, and three dice tables, three roulette wheels, and slot machines that lined the walls.

Three years after the Beverly opened, Mr. Marcello and his partner, Victor Trapani, bought the Old Southport casino just across the parish line from New Orleans.

While gambling flourished, Mr. Marcello was moving up in the ranks of the underworld.

On April 30, 1947, Silvestro "Silver Dollar Sam" Carollo, believed to be the Mafia boss of New Orleans, was deported to Sicily. With Costello's blessing, Mr. Marcello was named Carollo's successor five days later, according to sources familiar with Mr. Marcello's career.

Mr. Marcello was one of a host of local gambling figures summoned before Sen. Estes Kefauver's famous organized-crime hearings in January 1951, but he refused to say anything more than his name, address, and this statement, which he repeated after every question: "With due respect to the committee, I am going to refuse to answer any and all questions on the grounds that they might tend to incriminate me."

Mr. Marcello was found guilty of contempt of Congress and sentenced to six months in prison. An appeals court reversed that ruling, but Mr. Marcello wasn't free.

A 1952 law made his marijuana conviction a deportable offense, and at the end of the year, immigration officials warned Mr. Marcello that he was subject to being forced out of the United States. But more than eight years elapsed before they succeeded.

On April 4, 1961, less than three months after Robert Kennedy had been sworn in as attorney general and begun a war on organized crime, federal officials informed Mr. Marcello that he was a citizen of Guatemala and roughly put him on a plane for that Central American country.

The reason they chose Guatemala: The Justice Department said a birth certificate bearing Mr. Marcello's name was found in the Guatemalan village of San Jose Pinula.

After a month in Guatemala, Mr. Marcello moved on to San Salvador, then Honduras.

He was eager to return to the United States. Less than two months after his deportation, he did so, to the consternation of federal authorities. The details of his re-entry have always been a mystery.

In the fall of 1966, Mr. Marcello was one of several reputed Mafia leaders arrested at a restaurant over lunch in the New York City borough of Queens. Among the 12 others were Carlo Gambino, Santo Trafficante and several members of the Colombo and Genovese families. All were charged with consorting with known criminals, but all were acquitted.

When Mr. Marcello returned from New York, a crowd of relatives and reporters was waiting for his plane.

In that group was Patrick Collins, an FBI agent. Collins approached Mr. Marcello, and what happened next became a matter of intense dispute. The FBI agent claimed Mr. Marcello hit him, but Mr. Marcello claimed he was gesturing for Collins to move away.

A federal grand jury charged Mr. Marcello with assaulting a federal agent. After one mistrial, Mr. Marcello was convicted in 1969 and sentenced to six months imprisonment. He served his term at the Federal Medical Center in Springfield, Mo., and later said that he needed the rest.

By that time, illegal gambling in suburban Jefferson Parish had been eradicated, but Marcello was adapting well, having become a major land-holder in St. Charles and Jefferson parishes.

The Marcello family has bought and sold vast acreage on the West Bank of Jefferson Parish over the years, and still owns large amounts of property that include an undeveloped tract called Churchill Farms between West-wego and Avondale.

Mr. Marcello lived relatively quietly until prosecutors enmeshed him in Brilab. Marcello and former state Commissioner of Administration Charles Roemer were convicted in 1981 of conspiracy to obtain kickbacks for a state insurance business.

Later that year, Mr. Marcello was found guilty of conspiring to bribe a federal judge who was about to preside over a mob trial in California. He was sentenced to 10 years in prison.

But four years after Mr. Marcello entered prison, the U.S. Supreme Court limited the use of a mail-fraud statute that the government had used to convict Mr. Marcello and Roemer.

In June 1989, the 5th U.S. Circuit Court of Appeals cited that ruling in throwing out Mr. Marcello's and Roemer's convictions. That decision took seven years off Mr. Marcello's sentence. By the time the appellate court ruled, Mr. Marcello had served enough of his 10-year sentence to be released for good behavior, and he was freed in October 1989.

By the time Mr. Marcello went to prison, his wealth from business interests and real estate holdings in St. Charles and Jefferson parishes amounted to about $30 million, federal authorities estimated. Consequently, he was able to live comfortably and quietly after his release.

"I'm retired," he said in a 1990 interview. "I'm happy. Everybody's been nice to me."

— March 3, 1993

Ted Wisniewski

He pushed limits to help people with AIDS

Dr. Ted Wisniewski, a physician who shaped Louisiana's AIDS policy and set up a statewide network of services for people with acquired immune deficiency syndrome, died of AIDS complications Monday night at his New Orleans home. He was 37.

Even though he had been a physician for only a decade, Dr. Wisniewski attained a position of respect in the community of people with AIDS and those who fight the disease.

He was administrator and medical director of the outpatient AIDS clinic at Charity Hospital, where he treated people infected with the human immunodeficiency virus, or HIV, which causes AIDS. Dr. Wisniewski also was director of the HIV program office in the state Department of Health and Hospitals. He was chief of the HIV section at Louisiana State University Medical Center, and he led the state committee that recommended setting up treatment centers around Louisiana.

The establishment of Charity's outpatient clinic was, arguably, Dr. Wisniewski's major local achievement because poor people could be treated for HIV-related infections there without having to check into Charity Hospital.

Dr. Wisniewski also was leader of a group that drafted a statewide plan for treating people infected with HIV. The report recommended early-intervention clinics around the state to treat people as soon as possible so they can live longer.

"There's a belief that early intervention will be the biggest cost-saver down the road," he said when the report was published. "It not only keeps people well, but keeps them working."

By the time Dr. Wisniewski died, such clinics had been established in New Orleans, Alexandria, Natchitoches, Monroe, Opelousas, and Lake

Charles, said Donna Williams, the state HIV program's quality-assurance officer.

As a result of the team's recommendations, Louisiana established eight regional organizations to review services around the state for HIV-infected people, as well as programs to continue their health insurance and treat them at home, Williams said.

"If he had never been born, where would we be in terms of HIV services, not only locally but throughout the state?" said Harlee Kutzen, the New Orleans outpatient clinic's director. "He pushed limits to improve services."

Dr. Wisniewski's involvement began in the mid-1980s, when the epidemic was only a few years old, said Louise McFarland, chief of the epidemiology section in the state Office of Public Health. Besides treating patients, he went with her to gay bars to tell people how HIV is spread.

"If anyone was really committed to working against this disease, it was Ted," McFarland said.

Starting in May 1992, his battle became personal when Dr. Wisniewski's physician diagnosed an intestinal infection that signaled the onset of AIDS.

Instead of hiding, Dr. Wisniewski announced his condition in a letter to friends and colleagues and at the first meeting of the state AIDS commission.

When he resigned, six people were needed to replace him, said Kim Mathisen, the Charity outpatient clinic's office manager.

One of Dr. Wisniewski's last public appearances was Sept. 27 at the NO/AIDS Task Force's annual pledge walk. Too weak to stand, he rode the 6.2-mile route in a wheelchair, surrounded by marchers carrying banners of AIDS-related organizations, many of which he had helped create.

He was born Thaddeus Louis Wisniewski Jr. in Milwaukee in January 1956. After finishing high school, he enrolled at Marquette University, where his record was so good that the Medical College of Wisconsin accepted him after his junior year.

In 1977, he joined the Glenmary Home Missioners in Cincinnati as a brother. He left the Catholic order in 1983, the same year he finished medical school.

Dr. Wisniewski came to LSU Medical Center for his family-practice residency in 1983, about a year after the first AIDS case was recorded in Louisiana. During the 1985-86 term, he was chief resident, signifying that the faculty regarded him as the best in his class.

Even though he was a layman, friends said Dr. Wisniewski maintained a spiritual dimension in his work. "He . . . always viewed the care of individuals with HIV as a ministry and not just a job," said Brother Howard Piller of New Orleans, a nurse practitioner in the outpatient clinic.

— *June 16, 1993*

Sam Wilson

He was the dean of New Orleans preservationists

Sam Wilson, a New Orleans architect who became the dean of historic preservation in a city that cherishes its past, died Thursday at his Garden District home. He was 82.

Mr. Wilson, who apparently suffered a stroke, had planned to attend the City Council meeting that day to speak out against the demolition of The Rivergate exhibition center to make way for a casino, said Sally K. Reeves, archivist at the New Orleans Notarial Archives.

"He certainly died in the traces," she said. "He was planning to speak for architectural excellence—not of an old design but of an Eero Saarinen-style building of the mid-20th century, for fine architecture is to be found in any era."

[The Rivergate was demolished in 1995.]

While Mr. Wilson championed fine architecture wherever he could find it, his heart belonged to the buildings of the French Quarter, the original city of New Orleans, which he studied throughout his 60-year career.

He also restored many of its structures, including Gallier House, the Hermann-Grima House, Le Petit Théâtre du Vieux Carré, and the Cabildo, which he worked on twice—in the late 1960s and after a fire in 1988. The Cabildo, a building overlooking Jackson Square that is one of New Orleans' iconic structures, was not only a seat of government but also the place where the transfer of the Louisiana Purchase territory occurred in 1803.

In each project, Mr. Wilson's goal was to bring back every bit of a building's original glory.

"They felt they were building important buildings then—the church and the convent and all kinds of things," he said in a 1989 interview. "When Adrien de Pauger laid out the streets of New Orleans, you know, he said this would some day be a great city."

Mr. Wilson never stopped reading, writing, and lecturing about—and exploring—the Vieux Carré, another name for the French Quarter.

In 1938, he spent weeks in Parisian archives plowing through boxes of musty papers that told the story of the founding and settlement of the city he loved.

Mr. Wilson's Paris research "raised research on local subjects to a new plateau," said Malcolm W. Heard, an associate professor of architecture at Tulane University. "He maintained his work on the subject to the end of his life."

Mr. Wilson's passion for the buildings wasn't confined to archival research; as a young man, he studied the French Quarter on his hands and knees.

During the Depression, when jobs for architects were sparse, he joined a team to measure many of these buildings—the Cabildo, the Presbytere, the Beauregard-Keyes House, and the Ursuline Convent among them—for a series of schematic drawings that were part of a project for the Works Progress Administration, which was part of the New Deal.

That work helped him appreciate not only the majesty of the buildings but also their detail—probably his greatest contribution, said Lynda Friedmann, a former executive director of the Vieux Carré Commission.

"A lot of the value of his architecture is in the fine-tuned precision measurement of moldings and other architectural elements," she said. "You take one inch at a time away, and you lose it. He didn't take that first inch, and it was very important to draw the line."

"As a result, historic renovations in the French Quarter are historic renovations and not progressions toward an ersatz Metairie," Friedmann said, referring to a suburban community.

Mr. Wilson's knowledge of such small details could be astonishing, said Ann Masson, a preservationist and the executive director of Gallier House.

"He could look at shutters or baseboards or millwork trim and say, 'This is obviously a replacement,'" she said. "Each of the periods had its own style, even in small details, and Sam had this ability. Of course, there's a whole specialty in historic architecture, but you didn't need that if you had Sam looking at your building."

Samuel Wilson Jr. was born in New Orleans and grew up in the Carrollton neighborhood, where he built villages in his back yard. The houses were of colored paper, and they stood around a lake that flowed from a rusty pipe he had rescued from a junkyard, but they were early indicators of talent.

Mr. Wilson entered Tulane University at 15 and received his degree in architecture in 1931. Moise Goldstein, a New Orleans architect, hired him, and he set to work on such projects as Dillard University and the Sears building at Baronne and Common streets.

In 1934, he formed a partnership with Richard Koch, a tie that lasted until Koch's death in 1971. The two men became leaders of the fledgling architectural-preservation movement.

"Sam was everything to this preservation and historical community," Masson said. "He was more than just the leader; he was the heart, the driving force. Everyone always turned to Sam for information, for encouragement. . . . I don't know anyone who could fill his shoes. No one even comes close."

The American Institute of Architects named Mr. Wilson a Fellow, its highest honor, and the French Ministry of Culture declared him a Chevalier de l'Ordre des Arts et des Lettres. He received awards from a long list of organizations, including the National Trust for Historic Preservation, the Louisiana Architects Association, the Louisiana Landmarks Society, the American Association of State and Local History, the Vieux Carre Commission, the Louisiana Preservation Alliance, and the Boy Scouts of America.

For 40 years, he taught a Tulane course on Louisiana architecture. Tulane gave him an honorary doctorate in 1990. He wrote more than 55 books and articles, which, like everything else in his life, were notable for the depth of research, said Phares Frantz, the president of Koch and Wilson.

Among his academic exploits was a decades-long study of the life and work of Benjamin Latrobe, the architect of the U.S. Capitol and the White House, who came to New Orleans in 1812 to build the city's first waterworks. Mr. Wilson edited a volume of Latrobe's New Orleans journal.

Mr. Wilson's interest in the Latrobes had a personal angle, too: He married Latrobe's great-great-granddaughter, Ellen Elizabeth Latrobe, in 1951. She died in 1991.

— *October 22, 1993*

John Schwegmann

He pioneered supermarket development

John Gerald Schwegmann, the son of a 9th Ward grocer who became a local pioneer in the development of the modern supermarket, died Monday at Touro Infirmary. He was 83.

He had been in poor health for several years after suffering a series of strokes, corporate spokeswoman Sue Burge said.

Mr. Schwegmann, who was born above his father's small grocery store at Burgundy and Piety streets, joined two of his brothers in 1946 to open the first Schwegmann Brothers Giant Super Market at Elysian Fields and St. Claude avenues.

By the time of his death, the empire, whose name had been changed to Schwegmann Giant Super Markets, had grown to 18 stores with 5,000 employees, and his surname had become synonymous in New Orleans with the massive modern supermarket that sells everything from gourmet food to garden supplies. [The chain was sold a year after his death.]

Although his principal activity was marketing groceries, Mr. Schwegmann also was intensely involved in politics. He spent 12 years in the Legislature and nearly five years on the state Public Service Commission, and he ran for governor in 1971.

Mr. Schwegmann used his positions as an elected official and a businessman to speak loudly on such diverse issues as price-fixing, the Pentagon Papers, taxes, and the Superdome. He espoused his opinions in mini-editorials that were part of his newspaper ads, and he had the names of candidates he supported printed on the supermarket chain's shopping bags.

"Everything he's touched has turned to money," said Saul Stone, one of Mr. Schwegmann's attorneys, in a 1979 interview. "He's some lucky kind of guy."

Mr. Schwegmann was born Aug. 14, 1911, above Schwegmann's Grocery and Bar, which his German-born grandfather had founded in 1869. The store was later commemorated by Schwegmann's Old Piety & Burgundy Whiskey.

He recalled that the store "in the early years had no heat in the winter, and the front doors . . . were always open, allowing the cold wind to blow in.

"If the clerks complained, they were told the heat would make them drowsy and that it would take the bloom off the fruits and vegetables, even though (olive oil) was freezing and breaking on the shelves. However, the real reason for keeping the doors open was to show that the store was open and ready for business."

Mr. Schwegmann's education was limited to grammar school, a year of high school and six months at a business college. After a series of jobs, he went to work in his father's store in 1939.

In that store, the Schwegmanns introduced New Orleanians to self-service shopping, a novelty that eventually became an ordinary feature of American life, largely dooming the smaller stores in which proprietors filled each customer's order.

"Some of the old-time customers were very put out about it and asked, 'Where is the counter where I can get waited on?'" Mr. Schwegmann said years later. "My father said, 'Here is a basket. Shop for yourself.'

"One customer replied, 'If you think I am going to run all around this puzzle garden, you are out of your mind. I will stay right here and get served.' My father took the basket, went around the shelves and filled her order. When he added it up, he used the old prices in the days of service, which were 10 percent higher.

"She said, 'You are not charging me 10 percent more. I will go and pick up my own groceries,' and that was the beginning of Schwegmann's self-service stores."

On Aug. 23, 1946, John G. Schwegmann and his brothers, Anthony and Paul, opened the first supermarket in the family chain.

In 1948, Mr. Schwegmann entered a new field of activity: litigation. The Legislature had passed a law requiring a minimum markup on alcoholic beverages at all levels of the merchandising chain. The grocer, convinced stores should be able to set their own prices, volunteered to be a guinea pig in a test case opposing the law, and Stone agreed to represent him. The state Supreme Court declared the law unconstitutional.

Mr. Schwegmann next took on the state's fair-trade law, which let manu-facturers set retail prices for an entire area by entering into a contract with just one retailer in that region. He was successful in federal district court, the 5th U.S. Circuit Court of Appeals and the U.S. Supreme Court. The nation's highest tribunal did not declare the law unconstitutional, Stone said, but it did rule that merchants could not be forced to charge certain prices.

Perhaps Mr. Schwegmann's best-remembered fight was his battle against milk price-fixing. It pitted him against the state agriculture commissioner and, later, the state Milk Commission, which could set milk prices at the processing and retail levels, said Michael R. Fontham, one of Mr. Schwegmann's attorneys.

The federal suit, which grew out of Mr. Schwegmann's attempts to import cheaper out-of-state milk, was in litigation for eight years, Fontham said. Finally, a three-judge panel said Mr. Schwegmann could not be barred from buying cheaper milk.

One out-of-state company from which he bought milk was Dairy Fresh Corp., an Alabama company with a processing plant in Hattiesburg, Miss. State health officials tried to impound the milk, Fontham said, "but eventually, he was able to bring it in."

Such battles were "just altruistic," Stone said. "He favored unrestricted, free competition. It's principle, nothing personal with it. He had nothing to gain at all."

Mr. Schwegmann's last court battle involved a $30 million suit filed in 1979 by Mary Ann Blackledge, a former clerk in a Schwegmann's store, who claimed she and the supermarket magnate had lived as husband and wife for 12 years. She said $30 million was her share of the wealth they accumulated while they were together.

In 1982, a state judge ruled that Blackledge could not file such a suit unless she had a written contract. He said she could sue to recover money she might have spent in business relationships with Mr. Schwegmann, but she didn't file such a suit.

Mr. Schwegmann's political career began in 1955 with an unsuccessful race for a Jefferson Parish seat in the state Senate. He won a seat in the state House in 1961 and, seven years later, he was elected a seat in the state Senate. In 1975, he was elected to the Public Service Commission.

After suffering strokes in 1977 and 1978, he resigned from the commission in October 1980. His son was elected to the same seat seven months later.

In the Legislature, Mr. Schwegmann declared his independence early and acquired the reputation of a maverick. Because of his crusades and feuds, he failed to get many of his bills passed. In a 1962 speech, he said, "How can you win with a stacked house? I came out fighting, and at least I was loyal to the people."

He was a persistent critic of the Superdome, saying it should not be built with state bonds.

It was one of Gov. John McKeithen's pet projects, and he tried to use his charm to win Mr. Schwegmann over to his side.

During one exchange, McKeithen said: "Now, John's going to be reasonable about this. After all, we can help him. John, what can we do for you?"

This was his reply: "Governor, you can't do nothin' for me."

— *March 7, 1995*

Jules L. Cahn

A jazz devotee who always carried a camera

Jules L. Cahn, an elfin jazz aficionado whose shock of white hair, wardrobe of Mexican wedding shirts, and ever-present camera were familiar sights at New Orleans musical events, died Saturday night of a heart attack at his New Orleans home. He was 78.

Mr. Cahn could be expected to show up at jazz funerals, jazz concerts and the New Orleans Jazz and Heritage Festival, where he always had a photo pass to let him get close to the stage, and to the music he loved. Last year, as part of the festival's 25th anniversary, some of his thousands of photographs were enlarged and hung inside music tents.

"He had more footage on film and videotape than anyone else I know of outdoor New Orleans musical activity, whether it was the [Mardi Gras] Indians or a funeral or a parade," said Richard B. Allen, a former director of Tulane University's jazz archive. "He had all those things covered. He never let anything stop him."

The rumpled appearance he seemed to cultivate belied Mr. Cahn's status as a businessman and property owner. He was vice president of Dixie Mill Supply Co., an industrial distributor of pipes, valves, fittings and machine tools, and he owned about 100 pieces of property in the French Quarter.

One of his holdings was a building at 1117 Decatur St., which he donated to help the saxophonist Earl Turbinton create The Workshop, a living exhibition of modern jazz in performances and photographs.

The Workshop, which opened in 1969, lasted just a year but had a strong influence on such artists as Cannonball Adderley and Joe Zwainul.

In a much less public way, Mr. Cahn backed people trying to make their way in music, said Johnny Donnels, a French Quarter photographer who was a longtime friend.

"He was really nice to all kinds of young people who were interested in the arts," Donnels said. "People would walk up to him when I was with him and just say, 'Thanks.'"

— March 13, 1995

Hazel Guggenheim McKinley

A painter whose work was "full of life and color"

Hazel Guggenheim McKinley, a member of an illustrious New York family who was determined to make a name for herself as a painter, died Saturday of cancer at Mercy + Baptist Medical Center in New Orleans. She was 92.

Mrs. McKinley, whose uncle Solomon Guggenheim endowed the Fifth Avenue museum bearing his name, had lived in New Orleans since 1969.

She painted in watercolors, "whimsical things, usually, mostly people in action, having fun," said Naomi Marshall, whose Downtown Gallery was the site of Mrs. McKinley's first New Orleans show. "They weren't overpowering, just pleasant, nice to be around."

Critics agreed. "If anyone ever had fun painting watercolors, that person is Hazel McKinley," Helen Carson wrote in the *New York Sun*. "Her paintings are full of life and color and as capricious as a spring breeze."

Her works were shown in museums in the United States and Europe, and they were in the collections of such people as Greer Garson, Benny Goodman, and Jason Robards.

Mrs. McKinley was born in New York. Shortly before her ninth birthday, her father, Benjamin Guggenheim, went down with the Titanic. Survivors said he donned formal wear before the liner slipped beneath the waves.

"Because of the death of her father when she was so young, she was basically a lonely person," said her son, John King-Farlow. "After trying to be a writer for several years, she finally found her niche in painting."

After two years at New York University, she headed for Europe, where she spent most of the 1920s and 1930s studying painting and meeting such luminaries as Ernest Hemingway, Ezra Pound, and Max Ernst.

Her second husband, Milton Waldman, an English writer and editor, "introduced her to the joys of bohemia and literature and art and got her going on her way," King-Farlow said.

Her flamboyant sister, Peggy, was in Europe, too, meeting some of the foremost creators of 20th-century art and buying their creations. The attention Peggy received helped drive her sister into art, Marshall said.

"She felt she had been left behind by her sister and everybody had forgotten about her," Marshall said.

After World War II erupted in Europe in 1939, she returned to America with her two children and came to New Orleans, where her fourth husband, Lt. Charles McKinley Jr., was stationed, her son said.

"She developed a great love for it," he said, "so when she came back from Europe in 1969, she made New Orleans her home for the rest of her life."

— June 13, 1995

Pierre Clemenceau

A Frenchman who made New Orleans his home

Pierre Clemenceau, a grandson of the legendary French Premier Georges Clemenceau who became celebrated as a wit and bon vivant in his adopted home of New Orleans, died Friday at Ochsner Foundation Hospital. He was 91.

He had suffered a brain tumor and his heart failed, said Dr. George Porter III, Mr. Clemenceau's doctor and friend.

"He was a truly beloved figure," Porter said. "He had a personality so devoid of any meanness or cant or smallness. He had true Gallic charm in the Maurice Chevalier manner."

His grandfather, the French premier from 1917 to 1920, was known as "The Tiger" for exhorting his countrymen to fight on during the final years of World War I.

Mr. Clemenceau, a New Orleanian since 1947, grew up accustomed to the company of famous and powerful people. A family album was filled with pictures of such famous friends as Chevalier and Ernest Hemingway.

Young Pierre once breezed into his grandfather's office while Alexander Kerensky, the exiled head of the provisional Russian government overthrown by the Bolsheviks in 1917, cooled his heels.

As a teenager, Mr. Clemenceau often accompanied his grandfather to Giverny to see the impressionist master Claude Monet. While the men spoke of art and politics, young Pierre roamed the gardens that Monet immortalized on canvas.

"A boy of 14 is not prepared to understand such a man. . . . I was more interested in going into the garden and looking from the little bridge at the frogs," Mr. Clemenceau said when an exhibit of Monet's paintings opened at the New Orleans Museum of Art.

Mr. Clemenceau, who was born in Paris, met his wife, Jane Louise Grunewald of New Orleans, while she was in school at Fontainebleau. They fled France during World War II and moved to the United States after spending a year or so in northwest Africa, Porter said.

They lived first in Washington, then in New Orleans, where he became president of Grunewald Music Co., his wife's family's business.

Mr. Clemenceau was Haiti's consul general in New Orleans, wrote poetry and short stories in his native tongue, and created paintings that combined elements of romanticism and impressionism.

"He was very, very creative in more than an amateur way," Porter said.

Despite the passage of time and his own accomplishments, Mr. Clemenceau could not escape the legend of his grandfather. In 1989, France invited him and the grandsons of three other wartime leaders—President Woodrow Wilson, British Prime Minister David Lloyd George and Italian Premier Vittorio Orlando—to Versailles to celebrate the 70th anniversary of the signing of the treaty that ended World War I.

— December 14, 1995

Brenda MacBeth

Colleagues were inspired to give her their sick time

Brenda MacBeth, the City Hall employee whose battle with breast cancer inspired colleagues to sign over their sick leave to her, died of the disease Saturday at East Jefferson General Hospital. She was 52.

Her cancer was diagnosed in 1991. Because Ms. MacBeth had to spend so much time in treatment—at East Jefferson and the National Cancer Institute—she used up all her sick days, meaning she faced losing pay for living expenses, including her health-insurance premium.

But Connie Thomas, Mayor Marc Morial's executive secretary, remembered a 1991 provision that lets city workers sign over sick time to a fellow worker. Each municipal employee gets about 25 sick days per year, and Thomas encouraged workers to give Ms. MacBeth some of the time they knew they never would use.

City workers responded, giving her a total of 47 days within a week after the drive began.

The donations kept up. When Ms. MacBeth died, she still had slightly more than two weeks of donated time, said Michele Moore, director of the city Office of Communications.

"I've been very, very fortunate," Ms. MacBeth said last year. "I thought this was a setback, but it brought out all these wonderful things in people. You just never know."

"She was highly respected among her colleagues, and she will be missed, both for her sense of humor and her commitment to excellence," Morial said Saturday.

Ms. MacBeth was born in Victoria, British Columbia, and graduated from the University of British Columbia. In 1977 she moved to New Orleans, where she was a secretary at the Royal Sonesta Hotel and an administrative assistant to the architect August Perez III during the 1984 world's fair.

In 1986, Kurt Steiner, Mayor Sidney Barthelemy's chief administrative officer, hired her as his executive secretary. She later was director of the Mayor's Office of International Trade and Development and an administrative assistant to Joseph I. Giarrusso when he was a City Council member and, more recently, the city commissioner of criminal justice.

— January 7, 1996

Charles L. "Pie" Dufour

A columnist and historian who loved Mardi Gras

Charles L. "Pie" Dufour, a newspaperman and historian whose work was a touchstone of New Orleans journalism for more than half a century, died Sunday. He was 93.

Besides turning out more than 9,700 installments of "Pie Dufour's a la Mode," his daily column, Mr. Dufour wrote 20 books and more than 50 scholarly articles, taught history at Tulane University, and lectured to countless clubs and conventions.

During the summers, he led what he called "drip-dry tours" through Europe, and they provided fodder for his columns.

He wrote his 20th book, *Louisiana Yesterday and Today*, with Walter G. Cowan and John Wilds.

"I think he was one of the leading historians of Louisiana," said Cowan, a former editor of the *States-Item*. "His work on the Civil War and the history of New Orleans and Louisiana is so thoroughgoing that I don't know of any other single author who could touch him."

Mr. Dufour wrote on subjects as diverse as classical music, Carnival and Tulane football. He heard such opera legends as Enrico Caruso and Rosa Ponselle, and the people he interviewed ranged from Arnold Toynbee, the renowned British historian, to "Oyster Joe" Martina, the New Orleans Pelicans' pitcher.

He did all his work on an ancient manual typewriter that he steadfastly refused to swap for an electric model. When Mr. Dufour retired from the *States-Item* at the end of 1978, as computers were making inroads into the newsroom, he was one of the few staff members still using a manual typewriter.

Mr. Dufour, whose nickname was bestowed in childhood, came from a family with deep roots in New Orleans and journalism.

His great-grandfather brought his family to the city in 1809, six years after the Louisiana Purchase and three years before Louisiana became a state. A great-uncle published *L'Abeille* (The Bee), a French-language newspaper printed in New Orleans from 1857 to 1921.

He was born in New Orleans in 1903, the son of state appeals court Judge Horace L. Dufour. He enrolled at Tulane in 1921 in a pre-law curriculum; as second baseman for the baseball team, he once hit a triple that gave Tulane a 2–1 victory over Louisiana State University.

He also started working part time as a reporter for the *New Orleans Item*. He continued this double life until his dean told him he would have to choose between getting an education and earning a living.

"I told him I was just trying to keep alive," Mr. Dufour recalled in a 1974 interview. "Since my appreciation of Louisiana jurisprudence was at irreparable variance with the legal doctrines then promulgated by the state legislative and judicial authorities, I could make no valuable contribution to the existing body of law. I quit."

On June 30, 1924, he started full-time reporting for the *Item*. From then until 1940, he was a reporter, a sports writer and music critic for the paper.

He left the *Item* in 1940 to do a radio sports show. That lasted until 1942, when he joined the Army and was assigned to be an airplane mechanic. Since he knew nothing about that line of work, Mr. Dufour jokingly referred to himself as "Hitler's secret weapon."

He was commissioned a second lieutenant in August 1943 and assigned to military intelligence in Washington, then to Beirut, Lebanon, as an assistant military attache to Syria and Lebanon. He left the Army as a major in July 1946.

When he returned to civilian life, Mr. Dufour did public relations for Jackson Brewing Co. and, later, New Orleans Public Service Inc., which not only provided electricity to New Orleans but also operated the buses and streetcars. For transit riders, Mr. Dufour founded *Rider's Digest*, a free weekly newsletter containing quips, sports news, Hollywood gossip, and essays on New Orleans history.

He returned to newspapering in November 1949 with a daily column that ran Mondays through Saturdays in the *New Orleans States*—later in the *States-Item*—and Sundays in the *Times-Picayune*. He also wrote music criticism.

Besides his newspaper output, Mr. Dufour wrote history books, including *Ten Flags in the Wind*, a history of the Louisiana territory; three Civil War books; and *Women Who Cared*, a history of the Christian Woman's

Exchange on its centennial in 1981. In gratitude for *Women Who Cared*, the service organization made him an Honorary Christian Woman.

He also wrote about Carnival. Each year, on the day one of the older organizations was scheduled to parade, he devoted his column to that krewe.

In the newsroom, he was an arbiter of Carnival style, inveighing against infractions such as "King Rex," which, he hastened to point out, is redundant. Mr. Dufour wrote centennial histories of two old-line Mardi Gras organizations, the Knights of Momus and the Krewe of Proteus. With Leonard V. Huber, he wrote *If Ever I Cease to Love: One Hundred Years of Rex, 1872–1971*, a privately published history of the Rex organization.

He was steeped in Carnival, and his devotion to the annual observance was legend. On Mardi Gras morning, the diminutive Mr. Dufour could be spotted on St. Charles Avenue, wearing the Rex organization's tie—black with thin stripes of purple, green and gold, the Mardi Gras colors—and standing on tiptoe on the curb, peering Uptown as eagerly as a child, straining for the first glimpse of the Carnival king's parade.

"Huey Long spoke of every man a king," Mr. Dufour told an interviewer, "and that's what Mardi Gras does. It's democratic in that everyone can be a king."

There was a rumor that Mr. Dufour once was Comus, the monarch of the oldest krewe who reigns in masked anonymity, wielding a goblet instead of a scepter. It seemed obvious, even when he was masked and in costume, but when an interviewer asked him about it, Mr. Dufour quickly changed the subject, saying, "That's a military secret."

For a quarter-century, Mr. Dufour taught a New Orleans history course at Tulane with John Chase, a local editorial cartoonist.

In 1953, he finally finished his bachelor's degree at Tulane. In November 1978, the university gave him an honorary doctorate of humane letters.

At the ceremony where that degree was conferred, Mr. Dufour brandished the diploma and academic hood and said, "I want to show you that I'm making progress. It took me 32 years to get my first degree and only 25 years to get this one."

In its citation accompanying the honorary degree, Tulane summed up Mr. Dufour: "He is, himself, a New Orleans tradition."

— May 28, 1996

Harry Bartlett Kelleher Sr.

He rallied support for public education

Harry Bartlett Kelleher Sr., a leader of one of New Orleans' most prominent law firms who devoted his life to civic works and racial peace, died Saturday at Memorial Medical Center. He was 87.

Mr. Kelleher, a founder of the Lemle & Kelleher law firm and former chairman of Tulane University's board of administrators, was Rex, king of Carnival, in 1965, an honor he called "the most soul-satisfying experience that anyone could have."

His selection as Rex was an accolade for years of quiet, understated civic activity, not only in such traditional activities as board memberships and fundraising drives but also in a movement to keep New Orleans' public schools open during the desegregation crisis of the early 1960s.

The Orleans Parish School Board was under fire then, and a group of doctors approached Mr. Kelleher to see if he would lend his prestige as a community leader to rally support for the board and public education in general.

"They thought the School Board was so badly besieged that it was time for responsible people to stand up and take a position on how they felt about public education," Mr. Kelleher said in an interview years later. "They had in mind to have a testimonial dinner for the members of the School Board."

About 1,800 people, more than the capacity of the ballroom of the Roosevelt Hotel, showed up.

"Everybody was forced to recognize that public education was the foundation stone of democracy, and without decent public education, New Orleans just couldn't survive as a community," he said.

Even though the objective was to get the races to work together, there were two committees—one black, one white—to solve a range of problems, ranging from desegregating lunch counters to getting nonmenial jobs for black people in major stores.

"Each side would work on the problem from its respective point of view, behind the scenes, without publicity, without notoriety and very quietly, in an effort to get pragmatic solutions that could and would work," Mr. Kelleher said. "It worked surprisingly well. The whole program did.

"I believe now, in retrospect, it was because the black committee was able to make commitments on behalf of its constituency and deliver upon them. And the white committee demonstrated its ability to do that, too."

In recognition of such work, he was one of the first members of the Louisiana Commission on Race Relations that Gov. John McKeithen set up in 1965. In 1967, Mayor Victor Schiro appointed Mr. Kelleher to an advisory committee that resulted in the New Orleans Human Relations Committee.

The next year, he received the Weiss Award from the New Orleans chapter of the National Conference of Christians and Jews for "distinguished service in the field of human relations."

Mr. Kelleher also was an attorney for the city's Board of Liquidation, City Debt and for the Superdome Commission. In the latter capacity, he represented the commission in a series of suits that challenged its authority. His success in those cases helped pave the way for construction of the Mercedes-Benz Superdome. He also worked as an attorney for the Saints football team.

Mr. Kelleher was born in New Orleans in 1910 and earned bachelor's and law degrees at Tulane University. The law school named him its distinguished alumnus in 1984, and he was named the university's distinguished alumnus in 1990.

Mr. Kelleher never held public office, but he was the object of a drive to get him to run for mayor in 1968. Although flattered, he said he would not consider becoming a candidate.

Because he excelled in persuading people to get along, "you always felt that he had transcended New Orleans and Louisiana and had a national perception," said William Borah, a lawyer and longtime friend. "He understood the dynamics of New Orleans and Louisiana, but he was never limited."

— August 17, 1997

Nellie May "Jack" Kelleher

A volunteer who taught art and fought racism

Nellie May Bartlett "Jack" Kelleher, a volunteer whose activities included designing nursery-school furniture, teaching etiquette and art, and fighting racism, died Monday at her New Orleans home. She was 89.

During six decades of volunteering, Mrs. Kelleher was president of the Junior League of New Orleans, president of the Family Service Society board and co-chairwoman of the board of Community Chest, the forerunner of United Way.

During the 1940s, she joined a drive to get clothes to Russians, whose country had been devastated by World War II, and she was a member of New Orleans' first interracial committee, an organization started by the Council of Social Agencies as a forum to discuss race-related problems.

The committee was formed because, at that time, there was no place where black people and white people could talk about these issues and try to resolve them, Mrs. Kelleher said in a 1990 interview.

"Our efforts were very helpful, and we noticed a difference," she said. "I can remember walking down the street in the rain to the local newspapers to ask them not to play up the color of criminals in articles."

As a board member of the New Orleans YWCA, she organized the first integrated meetings of public- and private-school teachers to discuss problems facing educators.

But Mrs. Kelleher's chief joy as a volunteer came from introducing children to art. A 1930 Newcomb College graduate who majored in the subject and won a first prize for a watercolor painting, she taught at Kingsley House, a New Orleans settlement house, and the Junior League Community Center.

"I'm crazy about teaching children, making them want to draw and showing them things they have never seen before," she said.

She established the photography department at Newcomb, and she was a fixture at the college's annual pre-Christmas art sale.

Mrs. Kelleher, a New Orleans native and Louise S. McGehee School graduate, was a child when she acquired the nickname by which everyone came to know her. For reasons nobody remembers, the girls with whom she played gave each other boys' nicknames.

"Hers was the only one that stuck, much to my grandparents' horror," said Mrs. Kelleher's daughter, Jackeen Kelleher Churchill.

After graduating from Newcomb, she went to work as the only staff member at the Arts and Crafts Club, a French Quarter art school and gallery on Royal Street.

She stayed there until 1936, when she married Harry B. Kelleher, a New Orleans lawyer and civic leader. He died last month.

When she married, Mrs. Kelleher became a full-time volunteer. She designed and bought furniture for Newcomb Nursery School, served two terms on the Metairie Park Country Day School board and was active at Christ Church Cathedral.

She also set up ballroom-dance classes for debutantes and members of Carnival courts, and she taught etiquette to seamen.

Years later, she said, "Whenever I shake hands with a young man, I know whether I taught him dancing."

A member of the first Total Community Action board, Mrs. Kelleher also was a member of the Citizens Committee for Juvenile Court and of the Newcomb alumnae board.

For work at her alma mater, including membership on committees that interviewed candidates for the deanship and organized the celebration of the college's centennial, Mrs. Kelleher received the 1989 Alumnae Award for Service and Loyalty.

— September 16, 1997

Marjorie Roehl

She wrote about murders and Mother Teresa

Marjorie Roehl, an award-winning journalist who wrote about such diverse topics as crime, haunted houses and Mother Teresa for newspapers in New Orleans and New Jersey, died Sunday of pneumonia at Memorial Medical Center. She was 78.

Miss Roehl, who retired in 1990, was an armchair expert on murders, which she chronicled with enthusiasm, and she won the Alex Waller Memorial Award, the Press Club of New Orleans' highest award, for a 1981 series she and a *Times-Picayune* colleague wrote on Charity Hospital.

"She covered a range of assignments and did her job very competently," said Walter Cowan, a colleague, boss and longtime friend. "She became quite a star."

She often told stories on herself, generally those that stressed her sheltered upbringing and education in convent schools.

Early in her career, she said, she was sent on a police raid of a French Quarter house of dubious reputation. When she returned to the office, she told colleagues she was amazed that, in the early afternoon, the women in the house "were all wearing kimonos and they all had red hair."

"It was a brothel, Marjorie," someone said.

"What's that?" she replied.

"She was a very naive young lady, I know that," Cowan said. "She was the pet of the staff, being so young and impressionable."

Miss Roehl was born in New Orleans and graduated from Holy Name of Jesus School and Ursuline College.

As she grew up, she nursed one ambition. "She wanted to be a reporter from the time she was 10," said her daughter Beth Millbank.

She fulfilled that dream by working part-time for a newspaper while in college. Within weeks of graduation, she joined the staff of the *New Orleans Tribune*, moving over to the *New Orleans Item* when it bought the *Tribune*.

During the next decade, she wrote tirelessly about crime and interviewed many celebrities who came through New Orleans. Walt Disney talked with her while wearing a bathrobe, but an uncooperative Katharine Hepburn shut the door in her face. Theater luminaries Alfred Lunt and Lynn Fontanne were extremely gracious, she said, as were Barbara Stanwyck and Robert Taylor, and she treasured this letter from Kirk Douglas: "Dear Marjorie: Thanks for the wonderful weekend."

The weekend in question, she added, was the one when Douglas was married in the New Orleans studio of sculptor Angela Gregory, a close friend of hers and the actor's.

In the late 1940s, Miss Roehl married Karl Kaschewski and moved to New York City, where she became a technical writer for General Electric and Bell Laboratories. One of her assignments at Bell was to write about development of the Minuteman missile, but because of the tight security surrounding the project, she never was told what the overall program was.

She also did long freelance stories about murders for the *New York Daily News*. Despite her sheltered upbringing and innate kindness and gentility, she couldn't get enough of crime.

"We were raised on murders," Millbank said. "Mom loved murder."

In 1963, Miss Roehl joined the staff of the *Daily Record* of Morristown, N.J., where she and her family had moved in 1955. She started as a columnist, writing a weekly feature called "The Woman's Angle."

"We always had to be very careful about what we did because if we didn't, we'd wind up in the next week's 'Woman's Angle,'" Millbank said.

The *Record* published two of Miss Roehl's books: *Hosts of Ghosts*, about haunted houses in the area, and *The Quiet Millionaires*, about the many rich people who had lived in Morristown at the turn of the century.

After her marriage ended in divorce, she returned to New Orleans in 1975 and joined the *States-Item*, continuing on the *Times-Picayune* after the papers merged in 1980. She married Sidney Schoenberger, a friend since her youth, in 1978. He died in 1980.

During her second phase as a New Orleans journalist, Miss Roehl wrote long series for the *States-Item* about Esplanade Avenue and the Garden District, drawing on historical materials and the memories of people who had lived in the districts' grand houses in an era when women didn't aspire to have careers and horse-drawn carriages still rattled along the streets.

One of her most prized assignments was an interview with Mother Teresa when the nun visited New Orleans in 1976. After their conversation, Miss Roehl said she felt the same way she did after interviewing Helen Keller: that she had been in the presence of a saint.

— *November 4, 1997*

Rosa Freeman Keller

A genteel champion of civil rights

Rosa Freeman Keller, the debutante daughter of a wealthy white family who became an outspoken advocate of the rights of women and African Americans, died Monday at her New Orleans home of heart disease. She was 87.

Mrs. Keller, a maid in the 1932 Comus ball when her father was king of Carnival, became a virtual outcast in some circles during the early 1960s because of her work on behalf of peaceful integration of the city's public schools. Lifelong acquaintances stopped speaking to her, and strangers made threatening phone calls to her home.

But her dedication to the betterment of the city's black population was unshakable, and in time, she was showered with awards.

"I used to wonder, why me?" she said of the pressures that intensified so sharply in the 1960s that she nearly considered abandoning the work she began in the aftermath of World War II. "But I had gotten to be a trusted member of the black community. I couldn't let them down."

Later, as businesses were forced to integrate, Mrs. Keller used her connections to help African Americans get jobs. Working with the Urban League, she called on bank and store presidents because "they were my friends," she said in a 1983 interview. "I had access. I could open the doors."

By such actions, "she went beyond being a role model," said Jessie Dent, the widow of former Dillard University President Albert Dent. "She stepped out of the traditional role to do things women wouldn't have dreamed of doing."

Throughout those turbulent years, Mrs. Keller remained unfailingly courteous, letting people know where she stood without becoming strident.

"You don't keep your old friends by flaunting things in their faces, things you know are going to make them uncomfortable," she said. "There are gentler ways."

From the beginning, Rosa Freeman Keller seemed destined for a life of gentleness. She was born in New Orleans on March 31, 1911. Her parents, A. B. and Ella West Freeman, were Georgians who came to New Orleans in 1906 to start the local franchise of a new soft drink.

Because of New Orleans' reputation for the consumption of liquor, wine and coffee, more than one friend was dubious about A. B. Freeman's chances for success.

But Freeman was lucky. His soft drink was Coca-Cola, and he made enough money to buy other franchises and to become a philanthropist and a civic leader.

He was invited to be Rex in 1932, and, on a whim, his daughter Rosa decided to make her debut that season. She was queen of Nereus and the now-defunct Nippon and a maid in several courts, including Comus'.

"The whole damn family had fun together," she said.

Amid the party-going, she met Charles Keller Jr., a West Point graduate. They were married in December 1932.

It was during her husband's overseas military service in World War II that Mrs. Keller began to feel strongly about social injustice.

"Black guys got drafted and sent overseas—in segregated units—and then they came back, and they're supposed to sit in the back of the streetcar? That really upset me," she said. "When you need 'em, you use 'em? They used a lot of women, too, and then, when the men got home, they gave the jobs back to the men. That's wrong. I'm not the world's greatest feminist, but we had to get these things straight."

For Mrs. Keller, that task started in 1945 with work for the Young Women's Christian Association. As a board member, she came in contact for the first time with professional black women—"lovely women, whom I never knew existed," she said. "We had no way of communicating before."

She led the fundraising drive to build the YWCA's Claiborne Avenue branch. It was the first time white people had staged a community-wide campaign for a building whose principal users would be African Americans.

Later, she and her husband were part of a group that built Pontchartrain Park, a Gentilly suburb designed to give black people a chance to own homes.

In 1945–46, Mrs. Keller was active in the mayoral campaign in which deLesseps "Chep" Morrison defeated longtime incumbent Robert Maestri. She was one of a group of broom-toting women who marched to dramatize Morrison's desire to sweep out machine politics.

Morrison's victory "was the first time that women had made a difference in New Orleans politics," she said. "We were quite shocked that our candidate had won. It was a moment of discovery: Women could play a crucial role in setting community goals."

In time, she helped found the Independent Women's Organization, a political organization for women, and served on its board from 1954 to 1967. In the 1980s, Mrs. Keller was a founding member of the Committee of 21, an organization dedicated to getting more women elected to public office.

Political activity is vital, she said, "because the people we elect make all of the difference. If good people don't get out and help people get elected, well, who's going to help them?"

In 1953, Morrison appointed her to the New Orleans Public Library's board of directors. She was its first female member and, eventually, the first woman to lead it.

Shortly after her appointment, the board began discussing construction of a branch in the Broadmoor neighborhood. As was true of all but three small branch libraries at the time, the Broadmoor building was planned for white people only, although the area had a substantial black population.

To integrate the Broadmoor branch, Mrs. Keller worked out a strategy with Albert Dent, then Dillard's president. First, Dent organized a group to petition the library board to let black people use the music section at the whites-only Latter Memorial Library on St. Charles Avenue. Evidence that black and white New Orleanians could share Latter peacefully would be used as a wedge for integrating the Broadmoor branch.

But, as Mrs. Keller recalled, it wasn't easy. "You would have thought I had suggested assassination," she said. "It got so ugly."

At her behest, Morrison addressed the board, and the organization caved in more completely than she had expected, agreeing in 1954 to desegregate every public library in the city.

In 1955, Mrs. Keller was appointed to Dillard University's board of trustees. She served on the board the rest of her life.

Having attended Newcomb College and Hollins College in Virginia without graduating, she received an honorary doctor of humane letters degree from Dillard in 1980. She and her husband were awarded honorary degrees from Xavier University and Loyola University School of Law in 1984, and in 1986, she received an honorary doctorate from Tulane University.

After her son, Charles Keller, died in 1980, she started taking classes at Loyola University, not only to keep learning but also to distract her from painful memories. The experience awakened an interest in education for older people, and eventually she became co-chairwoman of Touro Infirmary's Woldenberg Center for Gerontological Studies.

She also lent her name to what became the Rosa Keller Campus, a program under which all accredited colleges in the New Orleans area offer free courses to older people.

But public-school desegregation was the work for which Mrs. Keller became best known. As the integration controversy raged, she was a founder of Save Our Schools, an organization that was determined to keep the city's schools open as court-ordered desegregation took hold in 1960.

Two years later, using money she had put aside for a fur coat, she paid for the federal lawsuit that integrated Tulane University. The plaintiffs were two Dillard alumnae, Barbara Marie Guillory and Pearlie Hardin Elloie, who wanted to do postgraduate work at the Uptown school.

U.S. District Judge J. Skelly Wright, who had ordered the desegregation of New Orleans' public schools, ruled in their favor. Once they were admitted, the students used the Kellers' Uptown home as "a kind of headquarters, a student union building," Albert Dent said.

Mrs. Keller's work to bridge the racial gap was constant, but it wasn't always so well noticed. In 1953, she organized a field trip to Dillard, a historically black university, so the members of her daughter's Uptown Girl Scout troop could hear Eleanor Roosevelt speak. Six years later, despite a downpour, she marched in an academic procession at the Gentilly campus with fellow Dillard trustees to hear the Rev. Martin Luther King Jr. deliver the baccalaureate address. She later said it was one of the highlights of her life.

In the early 1960s, before black women were allowed to join the League of Women Voters, Sybil Morial founded the Louisiana League of Good Government, an organization Mrs. Keller supported with her enthusiasm and money.

"She had great courage and determination and belief in her convictions," said Morial, the widow of one New Orleans mayor and the mother of another. "She went on and on. She was fearless, and, in her very ladylike Southern way, she got her message across, and people didn't refuse her."

As a result of trying to bring the races together, Mrs. Keller gained a reputation among some New Orleanians as a radical. "I just thought I was being a good Christian," she said.

As for those who snubbed her socially because of her civil rights work, she said, "You don't lose your friends doing things like this. There were people who didn't speak to me for a while, but they weren't real friends."

— April 15, 1998

Elinor Bright Richardson

She was the last survivor of a bygone era

Elinor Bright Richardson, who charmed New Orleans in 1920 as the first queen of Carnival after World War I, died Friday at Ochsner Foundation Hospital. She was 99.

Mrs. Richardson, who viewed that year's Rex parade with Gen. John J. "Black Jack" Pershing, commander of the American Expeditionary Forces in World War I, had been for years the longest-surviving of Rex's consorts.

She also was the last survivor of an era in New Orleans that could have been chronicled by the novelist Edith Wharton. It was a world of chaperones and dance cards, a time when debutantes in white gowns sat primly in boxes in the French Opera House, waiting for society's leaders to come to them.

Mrs. Richardson, one of 57 young women presented in November 1919, was in the final such coterie. A month after her appearance at the opera house in an event that traditionally marked the start of New Orleans' social season, the French Quarter landmark, a center of New Orleans' cultural life, burned to the ground.

Mrs. Richardson, a native New Orleanian who grew up in a St. Charles Avenue home with seven servants, reigned over a celebration in a city starved for Carnival: The war had pre-empted the annual rite in 1918 and 1919.

With three years' worth of debutantes to be presented, there was no shortage of prospective queens, but Elinor Bright had the inside track. Her great-uncle had ruled over Carnival in 1879, and her mother, Ella LeBaron Mehle Bright, had been asked to be queen of Carnival in her mid-teens. She had to turn it down because her mother—Mrs. Richardson's grandmother—thought she was too young.

Elinor Bright's consort in 1920 was John F. Clark, president of the Cotton Exchange. Among the dukes were her brother, Edgar, who would be Rex in 1956, and Edmund E. Richardson, whom she married in 1935.

The day before Fat Tuesday, Pershing addressed 20,000 cheering spectators in Lafayette Square. On Mardi Gras, with a medal from the Rex organization pinned to his military tunic, he joined the queen on the Boston Club balcony overlooking Canal Street to view the parade, a mule-drawn procession of 20 floats depicting "Life's Pilgrimage."

"Pershing was very nice—and stiff," Mrs. Richardson recalled in a 1985 interview. "It struck me he was doing a duty."

The ball that night at the Athenaeum, at St. Charles Avenue and Clio Street, was preceded by a quail-and-champagne supper for the queen, her king and Pershing.

The queen's mid-calf gown, glowing with beaded flowers and vines, came from Europe, as did her crown and scepter. Her green velvet mantle, a pearl-studded creation with jeweled sunbursts and flowers, trailed 20 feet behind her.

"It was like pulling a barge," she said.

When the ball ended at midnight, she headed for the French Quarter to party with her court and Pershing's aides. Among the young soldiers on that outing was George C. Marshall, a future five-star general, principal architect of the Allied victory in World War II, and originator of the Marshall Plan, for which he would receive the Nobel Peace Prize.

Mrs. Richardson, who was president of the Junior League of New Orleans in 1925–26, started a fundraising revue that provided money for the organization's charities.

In later years, she amassed one of the finest collections of Regency silver in private hands. She let the New Orleans Museum of Art show 22 pieces in connection with its 1990 Odyssey Ball.

Her collection started with a 95-piece place setting from her mother. "She entertained a lot," Mrs. Richardson said.

Mrs. Richardson, whose husband died in 1962, was presented to the Rex court in 1970 on the 50th anniversary of her reign. In 1995, 75 years after she wore the crown, Mrs. Richardson, sitting in a wheelchair, was saluted at Rex's 1995 ball with a floral tribute.

"When they gave her the orchid, she took it like a scepter," said Anne Milling, who was at the ball. "They went crazy. It was the perfect touch."

— *August 22, 1998*

Mary Morrison

She was an early, visionary preservationist

Mary Morrison, a Mississippi transplant who spent nearly six decades fighting to maintain the French Quarter's historic character and distinctive charm, died Friday at her home there. She was 88.

Ever since she and her husband, Jacob H. Morrison, moved into New Orleans' oldest neighborhood in 1939, Mrs. Morrison seemed to be in the middle of every preservation struggle there, whether it was protecting buildings from demolition, opposing a riverfront expressway or, more recently, battling Formosan termites.

"I never thought of the French Quarter without Mary," said Ann Masson, a preservation and museum consultant who also was a neighbor and friend.

Mrs. Morrison, a native of Canton, Miss., graduated from Delta State College (now Delta State University) in Cleveland, Miss.

When she and her husband settled on Ursulines Street in a house they bought for $3,000, only a few people thought much about historic preservation. Indeed, many of the French Quarter buildings that constitute the heart of the city's architectural heritage were in sad shape.

The neighborhood was "a slum," she said last year.

But because Mrs. Morrison was an outsider when she settled there, "she saw what many New Orleans people could not see: the great potential of this place—its scale and intimacy and beauty—and the fact that it was something worth preserving," said James Derbes, a preservationist who years later was one of Jacob Morrison's law partners. "That was the driving force throughout her life."

The first fight in which she was involved centered on a men's room that the owners of the Napoleon House wanted to erect in the courtyard of the venerable bar at Chartres and St. Louis streets.

Even though the change was minor and not visible from the street, concerned residents of the Quarter, also known as the Vieux Carré, viewed the proposed alteration as a threat to one of the district's oldest buildings.

The residents took the Napoleon House to court. Eventually, the case went to the state Supreme Court, which held in 1941 that the Vieux Carre Commission, established in 1937, has jurisdiction over any exterior changes in the Quarter.

That decision became a model for preservation around the country because it mandated the protection of the *tout ensemble,* or overall appearance of a community, not just specific buildings, said Sally K. Reeves, an archivist in the Notarial Archives.

From that point on, Mrs. Morrison's course was set.

"I would consider her a preservation stalwart who never tired, never flagged in her commitment," Reeves said. "She never shrank from attending meetings, making statements at the City Council and writing letters to the editor. . . . She had a profound understanding of the quality of life and its importance to New Orleans citizens."

Throughout her years of crusading, "she never lost that enthusiasm and that unwavering dedication to the preservation of those buildings," said Henry Lambert, a real-estate developer and former director of the Vieux Carre Commission.

"She wouldn't compromise those things," he said. "Her interest was pure."

"She was a real lady, and there seem to be fewer of them in the world," Masson said. "She could be forceful and speak her opinion, but she was never strident. She could be your opponent, but not your enemy."

But her life wasn't all preservation crusades. Mrs. Morrison was the former vice president and recording secretary of Le Petit Salon, a women's organization housed in the French Quarter; chairwoman of the board of St. Mark's Community Center; and a member of the Vieux Carre Bible Study Group, which met regularly on Wednesdays for more than 50 years.

Her husband, her frequent partner in her campaigns, joined her in restoring two houses the couple bought on Gov. Nicholls Street.

The author of *Historic Preservation Law,* a seminal book on the subject, he was the brother of deLesseps S. "Chep" Morrison, who defeated Robert Maestri in 1946 to become New Orleans' reform mayor. Jacob Morrison died in 1974.

Mr. and Mrs. Morrison also worked for political reform, starting in the 1940 state elections in which gubernatorial candidate Sam Jones led the drive to sweep out the last remnants of Huey P. Long's machine. They were poll watchers that year, and for years she was an election commissioner.

They were joint recipients of the Louise Dupont Crowninshield Award, the highest honor from the National Trust for Historic Preservation, and the Elizebeth T. Werlein Award from the Vieux Carre Commission.

Mrs. Morrison received a host of other accolades for her preservation work.

"She was a giant," said William E. Borah, a New Orleans lawyer and preservationist. "Mary was unique. "These are nationally historic landmarks, and they must be protected for our quality of life, not only for New Orleans but also for the country. Mary knew it."

— February 27, 1999

John Minor Wisdom

A judge who reshaped the South

John Minor Wisdom, a giant among federal judges during the tumultuous years that saw offical segregation end in the South and civil rights at last extended to black Americans, died Saturday at Ochsner Foundation Hospital. He was two days short of his 94th birthday.

In nearly 42 years on the 5th U.S. Circuit Court of Appeals—technically, he never retired—Judge Wisdom ordered integration at the University of Mississipi and joined decisions that eliminated racial discrimination in jury selection and voter registration in Louisiana.

Between 1965 and 1967, he wrote several decisions that forced foot-dragging school boards to integrate schools more quickly and spelled out the procedures, including busing, they would have to follow.

In one ruling, he described an ideal education system that included "not white schools or Negro schools—just schools" and concluded, "The clock has ticked the last tick for tokenism and delay in the name of 'deliberate speed.'"

Although Judge Wisdom said in a 1983 interview that he felt legislation was a major factor in helping the civil rights movement meet its goals, "I think that I have played a part in it," he said. "I'm not kidding myself. I don't exaggerate the part I've played, but I recognize that I did play an important part. It was a part that had to be undertaken by somebody. I think I've helped."

In recognition of his work, President Bill Clinton awarded him the Presidential Medal of Freedom, the country's highest civilian honor, in November 1993. The Court of Appeals building, where he helped make history, was named for him in 1994.

In August 1996, the American Bar Association gave him its highest honor, the American Bar Association Medal, for "conspicuous service to the cause of American jurisprudence."

"Judge Wisdom made courageous and significant contributions to this nation's progress toward equality among its citizens," ABA President Roberta Cooper Ramo said in announcing the award. "Judge Wisdom was a moral and intellectual leader on a court that made heroic decisions despite strong pressures from regional political leaders of the times, and often risking personal harm. The decisions he wrote still stand as bright beacons from a dark time."

The son of a businessman who fought for the White League against Reconstruction forces in the Battle of Liberty Place on Canal Street in September 1874, John Minor Wisdom was born May 17, 1905, in New Orleans and attended Isidore Newman School.

He graduated from Washington and Lee University in 1925 and went to Harvard University to study English literature. After a year, however, he returned to New Orleans and enrolled in Tulane University Law School.

He graduated first in his class in 1929, was admitted to the bar and later founded the law firm Wisdom and Stone with his classmate Saul Stone. It eventually became Stone, Pigman, Walther, Wittmann, and Hutchinson.

During World War II, Mr. Wisdom was a captain in the Army and later rose to the rank of lieutenant colonel in the Office of Legal Procurement. He was awarded the Legion of Merit by President Harry Truman for his services during the war.

Mr. Wisdom joined Louisiana's tiny Republican Party because, he said, he believed in promoting a two-party system, and he became a Louisiana representative on the Republican National Committee in 1952.

He was an early backer of Dwight D. Eisenhower's presidential aspirations, and in the 1952 nomination battle between the World War II hero and Sen. Robert Taft of Ohio, Wisdom pushed successfully to have Louisiana's pro-Eisenhower delegates seated at that year's Republican convention. That action helped provide the momentum that led to Eisenhower's nomination, and New Orleans tour guides later pointed out Judge Wisdom's Garden District home as the dwelling of the man who helped make Eisenhower president.

In private practice, Mr. Wisdom developed a reputation as an expert on trusts. In a case in which he represented the grocery-store owner John Schwegmann, he successfully argued against retail price-fixing laws before the U.S. Supreme Court. He was largely responsible for the adoption of Louisiana's new trust code.

In 1957, Eisenhower appointed him to the 5th U.S. Circuit Court of Appeals, which then included Louisiana, Mississippi, Texas, Alabama, Florida, and Georgia.

It was a momentous time to be a federal judge. Three years earlier, the U.S. Supreme Court had outlawed public school segregation in the landmark case of *Brown vs. the Board of Education of Topeka, Kan.*, but left to other judges the task of fleshing out its mandate of desegregation "with all deliberate speed."

"I think everybody realized that after *Brown*, there would be many important decisions," Judge Wisdom said in 1983. "I did realize that it would have to start in the South because that was where the problem was worse. It just had to start where segregation was the law."

Segregation, he said, "was just plain wrong. . . . I started off before I was on the court feeling that way. I think I was a little more conscious of social problems than most of my friends. And any exposure to the social problems that exist today, and existed, for that matter, in the '40s and '50s, leads one to the conclusion that something has to be done to help solve this racial problem. The more exposure you get to this problem, the more you realize that the blacks have had a raw deal for 300 years, and that we owe a debt to them. . . .

"I came on the bench, and we started getting case after case which made it very clear that the blacks were not getting a fair shake. . . . They had no blacks on juries; there were no registered black voters. These things, I think, were building up, and I think they built up in me as time went along.

"When I was first appointed to the court, I was much more moderate than I am now. It was a gradual progression in my philosophy. It started before I was on the court but was accelerated once I got on the court and realized what was happening."

Judge Wisdom aligned himself with three other 5th Circuit judges: John Brown of Texas, Elbert Tuttle of Georgia, and Richard Raylor Rives of Alabama, all now dead. They became known as "The Four," a coalition that worked consistently for black rights. They were effective together and separately as members of the three-judge panels that heard many civil-rights cases.

Judge Wisdom's first major decision came in the case of two black New Orleans men convicted of rape and sentenced to death. They contended their constitutional rights had been violated because African Americans had been excluded from the jury.

Judge Wisdom agreed. In addition to staying their execution, he wrote a decision that overturned Orleans Parish's jury-selection system.

In 1962, he wrote the historic order forcing the admission of James Meredith to the University of Mississippi, then both the symbol and bastion of Southern defiance to the growing civil-rights movement.

The order touched off angry resistance from students and state authorities and forced President Kennedy to take control of Mississippi's National Guard. But Meredith got in.

A year later, Judge Wisdom wrote a decision striking down Louisiana's voter-registration law, saying a section of the statute requiring applicants to interpret parts of the Constitution discriminated against black people because it was used to keep them from voting.

"A wall stands in Louisiana between registered voters and unregistered, eligible Negro voters," he wrote. "We hold: This wall, built to bar Negroes from access to the franchise, must come down."

As a result of the changes during those decades, "the Constitution is both color-blind and color-conscious," Judge Wisdom said in a 1987 forum at Tulane. "It is color-blind to prevent discrimination, and it is color-conscious to correct past discrimination."

Long after the early years of the civil-rights movement, Judge Wisdom asserted his theory of a color-conscious Constitution when he said black workers should be allowed into job-training programs even if they had less seniority than their white colleagues. He wrote this as a dissent in a case that Brian Weber of Gramercy, La., brought against Kaiser Aluminum. The Supreme Court upheld his view in a decision reversing the lower court and upholding affirmative-action programs.

"He represented a new breed of white judicial leadership, and he must be looked upon as a brave and courageous member of the bench who helped tear down the walls of segregation and the walls of racial discrimination," said U.S. Rep. John Lewis, D-Ga., a veteran of the civil-rights movement. "He represented . . . the best the South had to offer."

While Judge Wisdom was advancing the cause of civil rights, two of his pet dogs were poisoned, rattlesnakes were tossed into his yard, and he got crank telephone calls late at night. But he kept his telephone number listed and his office door open, and, he said, "I don't think I've ever lost a friend."

He joined the Urban League, but also kept his memberships in the all-white Boston and Louisiana clubs. "I can't change their minds, and they can't change my mind," he said. "They respect me, and I probably help the situation a little by not getting out of those clubs."

In 1977, when he was 72, Judge Wisdom changed his status from active to senior judge, a move that relieved him of administrative duties but let him continue to hear cases and write opinions.

He received honorary degrees from Tulane, Harvard University, Oberlin College, Middlebury College, and San Diego University. He was a former chairman of the board of trustees of Washington and Lee. In 1986, Tulane Law School named him one of its distinguished graduates, and in May 1989, he received the Edward J. Devitt Distinguished Service to Justice Award.

In its centennial issue in 1977, the *States-Item* newspaper said Judge Wisdom had been the most influential New Orleanian in the legal profession during the preceding 100 years.

"I enjoy my work," he said in an interview. "I've been through a period where there was some tension, but I got through it all right, and, looking back on it, I feel that it was important and worthwhile.

In his book *Unlikely Heroes*, Jack Bass said Judge Wisdom was one of "a handful of remarkable men who prevailed by meeting the demands of the time with an innovative and creative judicial response that restructured an unjust social order, helped shape the nation in a second reconstruction and left a permanent imprint on American history."

— *May 16, 1999*

Enrique Alferez

Sculptor who left his legacy throughout New Orleans

Enrique Alferez, a prolific sculptor whose sleek, streamlined works grace parks, buildings and public spaces throughout New Orleans, died Monday of lung cancer at his home. He was 98.

A native of Mexico who discovered New Orleans in the late 1920s, Mr. Alferez remained active in his Irish Channel studio well into his 10th decade, rounding out a life rich and lengthy enough to have included service as a young man with rebels loyal to Pancho Villa, the Mexican revolutionary.

Admiration for Mr. Alferez extended well beyond New Orleans. He executed commissions across the United States, as well as in Canada, South America, Europe, and Asia. But the greatest concentration of his work is in his adopted hometown.

In addition to executing private commissions, he created pieces for 20 public sites in the New Orleans area, including sculptures and benches in City Park's Botanical Garden, wood panels at the St. Bernard Parish Courthouse, the allegorical aluminum grill over Charity Hospital's Tulane Avenue entrance, a fountain at Lakefront Airport, the Molly Marine statue on Canal Street, a statue of the teacher and activist Sophie B. Wright in a Lower Garden District park, and two statues flanking the entrance to the LL&E Tower on Poydras Street.

His wife, Peggy, said Monday that with him "every day was an adventure." She described Mr. Alferez as, above all, a romantic, a man who brought idealism as well as passion to everything he was involved in.

As evidence of his fervor, she recalled his jumping out of a fifth-story window decades ago during a heated argument with an architect, barely grabbing onto the sill to avoid what surely would have been a fatal plunge.

The son of a man who earned his living crafting plaster saints and other religious objects, Mr. Alferez discovered his fascination with sculpture at his father's side, then refined his talent at the Art Institute of Chicago.

A stopover in the French Quarter en route to Mexico in 1929 began a lifelong love affair with New Orleans. Eventually, Mr. Alferez set up a studio in a former church while maintaining a Mexican residence and work space on a hillside outside Morelia.

Not everyone admired Mr. Alferez's creations, many of them executed in a style that melded the art-deco look that flourished internationally before World War II with more naturalistic touches evocative of his native Mexico.

Some of his nude works—the figures in "Fountain of the Four Winds" at Lakefront Airport and "The Family," which depicts naked parents holding an unclothed child—touched off controversies and front-page newspaper stories in which officials clamored for their removal.

The airport fountain remains intact, but "The Family" was pulled off the Municipal Courts Building's facade and sold at auction.

A sculpture of the Virgin Mary in which Mr. Alferez depicted the mother of Christ wearing something shorter than the traditional flowing robe, prompted one outraged spectator to say, "She has legs!"

"Doesn't every woman you know?" Mr. Alferez replied.

"He had a penchant for pulling the leg of officialdom," said Luba Glade, a former art critic and dealer and a longtime friend. "He just loved all that (notoriety); he really loved it. . . . He was sort of an *enfant terrible.*"

The youngest of nine children, of whom six survived, Mr. Alferez was born May 4, 1901, in San Miguel de Mezquital, a small town now known as Miguel Auza in the Mexican state of Zacatecas.

When he was 12, Enrique broke a glass tube at school that he thought was valuable and ran away from home because, he said years later, he didn't want his family to have to pay for his mistake.

During this time, Mexico was racked by revolution, and federal troops surrounded the town of Durango, where the Alferez family was living. Somehow, Enrique and a school friend managed to slip past the federal forces and fall into the hands of rebels.

"They thought we were federal spies, and some of them wanted to shoot us," Mr. Alferez said. "But the leader gave us a choice: Either join up with them or be shot. We joined up! So I became a revolutionary."

The leader of these forces was the legendary Pancho Villa. Because Mr. Alferez could draw, Villa's deputies sent the fledgling artist into enemy territory to make maps.

A self-described coward, Mr. Alferez said he drew them from a safe distance. After 10 increasingly precarious years with the rebels, he deserted in 1923, fleeing across the border to El Paso, Texas, where he got a job as a janitor in a framing shop.

He later went to work as a retoucher for a photographer who gave him an original Rodin bronze.

In a lecture in El Paso by the sculptor Lorado Taft, Mr. Alferez glimpsed his life's work. "I decided that's what I wanted to do," Mr. Alferez said in a 1988 interview.

Taft, who taught at the Art Institute of Chicago, encouraged him to visit if he ever came north. A year later, Mr. Alferez arrived at the school, wearing an old Mexican army cape and carrying two cardboard suitcases and a scholarship from Kiwanis International.

After enrolling at the institute, all he had left was $15, but Taft invited Mr. Alferez to join a group of students who lived and worked in Taft's studio on campus. He stayed three years.

In the studio, Mr. Alferez became aware of the elegant art-deco movement, a streamlined, geometric style that complemented the skyscrapers springing up in America's larger cities. One of art deco's foremost exponents was the innovative designer Norman Bel Geddes, with whom Mr. Alferez found work.

Mr. Alferez's earliest public works in Chicago—fifth-floor reliefs for a Michigan Avenue office building and carved-walnut elevator doors for the Palmolive Building—show his mastery of this style.

But art was not Mr. Alferez's only association with the bold new world of skyscrapers. Each day at noon, he received $5 for climbing to the roof of the Wrigley Building—398 feet above Michigan Avenue—to unfurl the Stars and Stripes.

He drew crowds. "I guess they wanted to see if I would fall," he said in a 1988 interview. "After a while, I would show off—you know, pretend I'd slip and was going to fall. God, I was such a kid!"

In 1929, Mr. Alferez was heading for Yucatan when he ran out of money in New Orleans and decided to stay, quickly establishing a reputation as a colorful and impulsive character.

He carved statues of the Virgin Mary and three saints for the Church of the Holy Name of Mary in Algiers, a community across the river from downtown New Orleans.

Franz Blom, director of Tulane University's Middle American Research Institute, hired him to help make a plaster cast of Mayan ruins in Yucatan for display at the 1933 Century of Progress Exposition in Chicago.

Back in New Orleans, Mr. Alferez got a job teaching at the Arts and Crafts Club and eventually directed the city's sculpture program for the Depression-era Works Progress Administration.

The WPA changed the face of City Park. Workers planted trees and installed walkways, canals and roads, and artists turned it into an outdoor art-deco display.

Massive concrete eagles stand guard along Roosevelt Mall, and Mr. Alferez's reliefs of athletes adorn the gates to Tad Gormley Stadium. The park's greatest concentration of art deco—and of Mr. Alferez's work—is in the Botanical Garden, where satyrs perch atop concrete columns carved to resemble cornstalks. Concrete dogs crouch beneath low-slung benches, and limestone reliefs show women lounging on either side of the central brick plaza, where the Shriever Fountain rises, showing a woman balancing an urn on her right shoulder.

In May 1993, a street in the park, near the New Orleans Museum of Art, was renamed Enrique Alferez Drive.

Mr. Alferez's other major WPA project was "Fountain of the Four Winds," a sculpture at Shushan (now Lakefront) Airport using four nudes—three women and a man—to represent winds from the four principal compass points. These figures are in the middle of the fountain, surrounding a partially submerged globe.

"The whole thing seemed to be going well until some puritanical SOB insisted that I was contaminating the morals of our WPA men because one of the figures was a nude male," Mr. Alferez told Glade in an interview.

The censorious critic—a WPA official—threatened to break up the sculpture with sledgehammers, obliging Mr. Alferez to guard it with a rifle one night as the controversy grew. Finally, Lyle Saxon, a New Orleans author who led the WPA's Writers Project, wrote to Eleanor Roosevelt about the brouhaha, sending her a photograph and asking her to intercede.

The first lady wrote back, saying she saw nothing wrong with the sculpture, and it was saved.

With "The Family," his first public commission after World War II, Mr. Alferez was less lucky.

Amid furor over the nudity, city officials pulled the sculpture down from the Municipal Courts Building at St. Louis and North Rampart streets and, within six months of its 1951 debut, offered "The Family" at auction.

It brought $2,400, $600 more than Mr. Alferez had been paid for a work he considered one of his finest.

The experience was bitter, but Mr. Alferez told Glade he knew what he was getting into when he decided to become a sculptor.

"Nobody told me to do it," he said. "I did it myself. I knew how hard life would be, but I did it anyway."

— September 14, 1999

Betty Werlein Carter

She mixed progress and propriety

Betty Werlein Carter, a well-born New Orleanian who, with her husband, led a scrappy newspaper in the Mississippi Delta to national prominence in the fight for civil rights, died Thursday at her Uptown home of complications of pulmonary hypertension. She was 89.

True to the morés of her class and era, Mrs. Carter subordinated her professional identity to that of her husband and collaborator, the legendary Hodding Carter Jr., editor of the *Delta Democrat-Times*, the newspaper they founded in Greenville, Miss.

Mr. Carter was awarded a Pulitzer Prize in 1946 for editorials advocating racial tolerance, but Mrs. Carter, in addition to her many roles as a civic leader, was acknowledged as "the editor's editor." She not only cleaned up her husband's prose but also smoothed feathers in the community that he sometimes ruffled.

He died in 1972; she continued as president of the paper until its sale in 1980.

"Betty was, to a great extent, the brains and conscience of the *Delta Democrat-Times*," said Curtis Wilkie, a former New Orleans-based reporter for the *Boston Globe* who holds an endowed chair in Southern journalism and politics at the University of Mississippi.

"They formed a pretty good team," said former Mississippi Gov. William Winter, a longtime friend. "They were writing things that did not endear them to a great many people in this part of the country at that time, and so she formed a very strong backup to him in his crusading efforts in Greenville and was as fearless as he was."

Indeed, Mrs. Carter's reminiscences of the struggle for a more enlightened South included occasionally harrowing vignettes, such as the time she posted herself on the central staircase of the family home, a shotgun across her knees, in case the Ku Klux Klan tried to make good on threats against the newspaper family.

Besides working with her husband and rearing her sons—including former State Department spokesman and television personality Hodding Carter III and New Orleans real-estate developer Philip Carter—Mrs. Carter had causes and writing projects of her own. She organized a seminar on education problems, led the Mississippi public-broadcasting board, set up after-school and summer recreation programs, and wrote articles for such magazines as *Smithsonian*, *American Heritage*, and *Ford Times*.

She also wrote a book about mules, a subject that fascinated her. "She identified very strongly with the mule," Philip Carter said. "I think it was unconscious, but maybe she identified because there's no glory attached to being a mule. You do all the work. For much of her life, Mother has been doing an awful lot of work. Some felt she was never fully recognized for the exemplary toil."

Born into the New Orleans family that founded Werlein's for Music, Mrs. Carter possessed a keen intellect, an insatiable curiosity and a finely tuned social conscience.

Yet despite her presence in the vanguard on many issues, Mrs. Carter also seemed a throwback to a gentler, more courteous time: She wrote thank-you notes promptly, she never failed to ask in her throaty purr about friends' children, and she set out place cards for dinner parties.

Once, when she entered a restaurant carrying a camellia from her yard, the proprietor knew just what to do: She rushed to find a finger bowl and fill it with water so the flower could float at Mrs. Carter's table.

"She's the last of the ladies," New Orleans restaurateur Iler Pope said. "She just absolutely was the embodiment of what a Southern lady should be in every way—in the way she conducted her life, in the way she dealt with people, and in the way she kept up with what was going on."

"Betty Carter was a timeless individual," said former Hendrix College President Ann Die, who befriended Mrs. Carter when Die was Newcomb College's dean. "Regardless of the era she would have lived in, she was the sort of person who was always looking for ways to make life better."

Mrs. Carter, the eldest of four children, grew up in a swirl of activity. Her mother, Elizebeth Werlein, was an intellectual and activist and, later, a leading force in the fight to preserve the French Quarter's architecture and ambience.

Werlein invited all manner of guests into her home. Once, Mrs. Carter remembered, she descended the stair to find a group of men working on a constitution for Mexico.

She graduated from the Louise S. McGehee School and Newcomb College. At Newcomb, she was president of the student body and assistant editor of the student newspaper.

While in college, she met Hodding Carter, a reporter for the *New Orleans Item*. "Dad proposed on the strength of a $5 raise," Philip Carter said, and they married shortly after her graduation. They moved to Jackson, Miss., where Mr. Carter had a job covering the Legislature for the Associated Press, but he was fired for insubordination.

They moved to Hammond, La., where he founded the *Daily Courier*. The paper took a decidedly anti-Huey Long position in its editorials, and Hodding Carter was fiercely outspoken in his opposition to the politician known as the Kingfish—so much so that when Mrs. Carter heard that Long had been shot by a man in a white linen suit, she dashed to the closet to make sure her absent husband's white suit was there. It was.

In 1936, the Carters were invited to Greenville by a committee wanting a strong newspaper in the Mississippi Delta city. Using money from that group and the sale of the *Courier*, the couple founded the *Delta Star*, with Mrs. Carter as advertising manager. Two years later, her husband acquired the *Democrat-Times*, and the merger resulted in the *Delta Democrat-Times*.

When the United States entered World War II, the Carters moved to Washington, D.C. He was editor of the Middle East edition of *Stars and Stripes*, the military newspaper, and she was a researcher for the Office of War Information, where she shared a desk with the fledgling historian Arthur M. Schlesinger Jr.

"She sparkled," Schlesinger said. "She lifted everyone's spirits. Everybody adored her."

Working on a national level with academics, writers, and journalists that included Robert E. Sherwood and Archibald MacLeish, "Mother was in her glory," Philip Carter said.

Mrs. Carter also was a researcher on the future of postwar aviation for Bernard Baruch, a philanthropist and longtime confidant of presidents from both political parties.

When the war ended, her husband decided they should return to Greenville.

"Mother felt she had gotten her marching orders to be more of a traditional wife," Philip Carter said. "As with everything in her life, Mother embraced this. At every school we went to, Mom was the PTA president, and she was the president of both (of Greenville's) garden clubs."

At the newspaper, Mrs. Carter was features editor, farm-page editor, women's editor and editor of the land-use section. She was president of the

Junior Auxiliary, state president of Church Women United, a member of her church's vestry, and a board member of the Greenville Day Care Center, the Greenville Symphony, and Greenville Community Concerts.

Mrs. Carter also was a member of the National Committee for UNICEF and the Marshall Scholarship Selection Committee for the Gulf South. She was the first woman elected to the Rhodes Scholarship Selection Committee for the Gulf South.

"She was extremely bright, and she could never sit still and not do something challenging," said the novelist Ellen Douglas, a friend and former Greenville resident.

After her husband won the Pulitzer Prize, Mrs. Carter also became hostess to a steady stream of visitors to Greenville, many of whom were guests at Feliciana, the Carters' home.

"The house was always full of Englishmen, Spaniards, South Africans, Germans and Belgians," Philip Carter said. "Anyone with a foreign accent coming through the state of Mississippi seemed to end up on our doorstep."

Mrs. Carter also was on the advisory boards of the *Mississippi Episcopalian* newspaper, the Center for the Study of Southern Culture, Agenda for Children, and Planned Parenthood of Louisiana.

Newcomb College named her its outstanding alumna in 1980, and Tulane University gave her an honorary doctorate in 1983. She also received honorary degrees from Bowdoin College, her husband's alma mater, and Millsaps College.

During Winter's term as governor, he wanted to set up free public-school kindergartens, so Mrs. Carter led a 1982 rally in Greenville for the legislation, and she worked the crowds with Winter and his wife, Elise.

"It passed," Winter said. "One does not say no to Betty Carter."

— March 3, 2000

Myldred Plauché Landry

A Mardi Gras queen and Pearl Harbor survivor

Myldred Plauché Landry, a member of Carnival royalty who survived the bombing of Pearl Harbor and was a frequent guest in the Truman White House, died Thursday of cancer. She was 92.

Mrs. Landry, who had grown up in a French-speaking household that was suffused with Carnival, acquired a lifelong reputation as a witty, fun-loving eccentric. At her debut party in 1929, where her parents had invited guests "to meet Chickie," the honoree, clad in yellow marabou feathers and a chicken hat, popped out of an egg.

Growing up in an Esplanade Avenue mansion that no longer exists, Mrs. Landry was born to a couple deeply involved in Carnival. Her father, Henry Plauché, was captain of The Atlanteans for 40 years. Mrs. Landry's mother, Leda Hincks Plauché, designed floats and costumes for such old-line organizations as Proteus and Rex. She also made all the gowns for her daughter's debutante season, when Mrs. Landry was queen of Proteus and Atlanteans, and a maid in the courts of Momus and Rex.

"She grew up with an increased appreciation of Carnival, and she adored it," said Henri Schindler, a close friend who also is a float designer and Carnival chronicler.

A graduate of Newcomb College, Mrs. Landry left New Orleans after marrying Robert B. Landry. He joined the Army Air Corps and became a captain who flew fighters and bombers. They were at Pearl Harbor when the Japanese attacked it on Dec. 7, 1941, propelling the United States into the conflict.

After World War II, the Landrys lived in Washington, D.C., because he was President Truman's Air Force aide.

"She was a staunch, longtime Truman admirer," Schindler said, adding that the Landrys and Trumans frequently traveled together.

The marriage ended in divorce.

When Mrs. Landry returned to New Orleans, she worked for the Krewe of Mystery and, later, the Krewe of Athenians.

"She was also an ardent supporter of women's intellectual development, civic awareness and understanding of current events," said Norris Williams, a longtime friend.

Even as Mrs. Landry advanced in years, she still looked forward to touring the Rex den each year with Schindler to see the floats he had designed for the king of Carnival's parade before they hit the streets.

In 1980, she was once again the object of attention at a Carnival event. Wearing a yellow gown, she was escorted around the floor at the Proteus ball to mark the 50th anniversary of her reign.

— *October 13, 2000*

William V. Garibaldi Jr.

A letter carrier with a secret past

For 30 years, residents of Carrollton, Mid-City and Gentilly knew William V. Garibaldi Jr. as the friendly man who delivered their letters and Christmas packages, swapped stories and asked about their families.

But this mild, methodical man, who died Friday at age 84 at Memorial Medical Center, had a part of his life that he never discussed during his daily rounds.

For nearly four years during World War II, Mr. Garibaldi was a spy, one of the few African-Americans in the Army's Counterintelligence Corps.

In the United States, Europe, Asia and Africa, he investigated illegal trading, helped protect President Franklin D. Roosevelt, and, in the spring of 1944, made sure information about D-Day wasn't leaking out.

He became a sergeant and was awarded the Bronze Star.

His service "was the thing he was most proud of," said Brenda G. Hatfield, one of his daughters.

When she was born in 1943, her father was in Casablanca, Morocco, where, he said in a family video, he saw soldiers training for the landing in France that would come on June 6, 1944.

In the months before D-Day, Mr. Garibaldi was posted to Liverpool. In the video, he said his duties included eavesdropping on conversations in pubs to make sure no one was talking about the invasion.

Mr. Garibaldi, one of about a dozen black Americans in the Counterintelligence Corps in England, was briefly assigned to the contingent protecting Roosevelt during one of his overseas trips during the war.

Because it was the first time an African American was part of that elite group, no one knew how to regard him, his daughter said, adding, "They kept him out of the way."

A native New Orleanian who grew up speaking French as well as English, Mr. Garibaldi earned a bachelor's degree with honors in biology and chemistry from Dillard University.

He had wanted to go to medical school, but he was drafted while he was working as a mail carrier, his daughter said.

Despite serving with white soldiers in the Army, he returned to a society that remained segregated. Because he wanted to stay in New Orleans, he picked up his mailbag again, like many other black men, Hatfield said.

"These people had degrees, but there were no other jobs for them," she said. "For us children, they were the working middle class."

After retiring in the early 1970s, he was manager of the Corpus Christi [Catholic Church] Credit Union.

Mr. Garibaldi was a member of Phi Beta Sigma fraternity, the National Association for the Advancement of Colored People and Branch 124 of the National Association of Letter Carriers, which honored him as one of its founding members.

— *June 13, 2001*

Eudora Welty

A Mississippi writer who gained global acclaim

Eudora Welty, whose witty, richly detailed depictions of small-town Mississippi life carried her beyond regional acclaim to international literary honors, died Monday of pneumonia in Jackson, Miss. She was 92.

Miss Welty, who lived and worked most of her life in the Jackson home her parents built in the 1920s, counted a Pulitzer Prize, a National Book Award, and the Presidential Medal of Freedom among laurels bestowed upon her.

"I would put her 'way up at the top of Southern writers, and I think most serious writers would put her in the top class of American writers," said Cleanth Brooks, a renowned literary critic and longtime friend. "I don't see any rivals that would top her. She's one of our best."

Brooks was a founding editor of the *Southern Review*, the Louisiana State University magazine that published one of Miss Welty's earliest short stories in 1937.

In her stories and novels, Miss Welty fashioned complex, fascinating tales from the most ordinary events—a family reunion, for instance, a parent's death, or, in "Why I Live at the P.O.," her best-known short story, a defiant move from the family home to what the character called the "next to smallest post office in the entire state of Mississippi."

"Great writing often deals with fairly simple things," Brooks said. "If you look over the field of literature, it hasn't always been about heroes or the great thunderous note of tragedy. We've had a great deal of splendid literary prose that has dealt well with the simple facts of everyday life."

Like Anton Chekhov, the Russian playwright and short-story writer with whom she was sometimes compared, Miss Welty specialized in the complex connections that bind people, said Peggy Whitman Prenshaw, a professor of English at the University of Southern Mississippi in Hattiesburg.

"This may issue from her experience," Prenshaw said, "because I think women in the South are trained to regard themselves in terms of their connections with other people. It's often more difficult for men to see that life is successfully lived out without winners and losers."

Ironically, the uncanny vividness with which Miss Welty evoked her native state, right down to the fading wallpaper and the smell of cut flowers in a vase, may have limited her audience.

"Most people look at her writing and see South, South, South and take a very superficial look at her work," said Noel Polk, a professor of English at the University of Southern Mississippi and the founding editor of the Eudora Welty Newsletter. "People have only barely begun to see the human condition, the secrets of human relationships that she has written about."

Even though she spent virtually her entire life in Jackson and set her works in Mississippi, Miss Welty shouldn't be pigeonholed as a regional writer, he said. "She talks of place as being a jumping-off point. It has as much to do with the imagination as the topography."

Miss Welty's fame was worldwide, and she was a frequent lecturer on college campuses. She won the Pulitzer Prize in 1973 for *The Optimist's Daughter*, and in 1980, President Jimmy Carter awarded her the Presidential Medal of Freedom, the nation's highest civilian honor.

"I feel that I've been very lucky," she told the novelist Anne Tyler in a 1980 interview.

Miss Welty, who never married, started writing in 1936, after roaming the state as a publicist for the Works Progress Administration. Besides touting the activities of that New Deal agency in stories for county newspapers, she took photographs, some of which were later published.

Then she settled in her parents' home and started writing. Except for trips and unsuccessful attempts to write in New York City and San Francisco, she never left.

"She realized her place was in Jackson," said Michael Kreyling, a professor of English at Vanderbilt University and a longtime Welty authority and friend. "She deviated from the tragic romantic pattern we have for American writers like Hemingway and Fitzgerald. . . . She wrote great stuff in a sort of natural, nondestructive way and turned an ordinary life into great literature. She didn't have to go to Kilimanjaro or drink herself to death in Hollywood to have great ideas."

"I must have always had the character of a child who was sitting there looking—an observer from the outside," Miss Welty once said in an interview. "Being an observer gives me the greatest pleasure."

She was a good listener, too. In *One Writer's Beginnings*, her account of the events of her youth that shaped her as a writer, Miss Welty recalled with delight setting off on Sunday afternoon rides in the family car. Sitting between her mother and one of her mother's talkative friends, young Eudora would say, "Now talk," and the stories would flow.

"Long before I wrote stories, I listened for stories," she said. "Listening for them is something more acute than listening to them. I suppose it's an early form of participation in what goes on. Listening children know stories are there. When their elders sit and begin, children are just waiting and hoping for one to come out, like a mouse from its hole."

Her parents stoked her passion for stories. Her father, an officer in a Jackson insurance company, used much of his salary to order books for Miss Welty and her two younger brothers. Before she could read them herself, Miss Welty said, she constantly pestered her mother to read to her.

"I cannot remember a time when I was not in love with them—with the books themselves, cover and binding and the paper they were printed on, with their smell and their weight and with their possession in my arms, captured and carried off to myself," Miss Welty wrote in *One Writer's Beginnings*.

She started college at Mississippi State College for Women but transferred to the University of Wisconsin in her junior year. Although her parents supported her desire to be a writer, her father thought she also should have a more reliable way to earn a living, so after graduation, she said she headed to the Columbia University School of Business "to study typing and other stuff."

"I wasn't crazy for the idea of a degree from Columbia," she said in an interview with the *Times-Picayune*. "I just wanted to live in New York for a year. I had to pick a major subject, and I picked advertising, which wasn't awfully good because all at once, when the Depression hit, nobody had any money to advertise with. For that matter, nobody had any money to do anything with."

She returned to Jackson and got a job at WJDX-AM, the city's first radio station, which her father had founded. Then she joined the Works Progress Administration, a New Deal program, and traveled to towns she had known only as points on a map.

She saw and photographed the poor, black and white, who had been hit hard by the Depression. She and her box camera went into homes, stores, and, on one memorable occasion that she later wrote about, a country church where she watched a pageant in which worshipers assumed the plumage and personalities of exotic birds.

"I saw my home state at close hand, really for the first time," she said.

And she wrote, using a red portable Royal typewriter her father had given her. Every so often, she traveled on the cheap to New York City to peddle her stories.

She was finally published in 1936, when a small magazine, *Manuscript*, brought out *Death of a Traveling Salesman*. Then came her debut in the *Southern Review* and, in 1938, an appearance in the *Atlantic Monthly*.

Her career was under way. Her first collection of stories, *A Curtain of Green*, was published in 1941 with an introduction by the novelist Katherine Anne Porter.

"Miss Welty has written some of the most memorable short stories to appear in print during the last few years," a 1942 article in the *New York Times Book Review* said. "Each story is distinct, purely individual, born of its subject and a point of view that is so wide and deeply understanding that it is as though there were no brand of one mind upon the stories. Their outstanding similarity is formed of the intensity that went into their writing. They create moods as powerful as the moods developed by good poetry."

She was invited to join the *Times* staff, and she reviewed battlefield reports from North Africa, Europe and the South Pacific. When a *Times* editor suggested that a Southern lady might not be the best judge of military strategy, she adopted a pseudonym, Michael Ravenna, and became widely cited.

"Invitations from radio networks for Mr. Ravenna to appear on their programs had to be politely declined on grounds that he had been called away to the battlefronts," a 1970 *Times* story said.

Miss Welty returned to Jackson after a summer and kept on writing stories that showed a keen eye and a delightful sense of humor. Probably her best known is "Why I Live at the P.O.," a rollicking first-person account of a family quarrel that has become a fixture in short-story anthologies.

"I have been told, both in approval and in accusation, that I seem to love all my characters," she wrote in a preface to a collection of her work.

But not all Miss Welty's characters were lovable, and not all her stories bubbled with sly humor. Anger, she said, was the motivation for "Where Is the Voice Coming From?" which she wrote for the *New Yorker* on the night in June 1963 when the civil-rights leader Medgar Evers was murdered in his Jackson driveway.

Even though she could not have known who killed Evers, Miss Welty wrote the story from the killer's point of view. In writing it, she said, she felt a "necessity . . . for entering into the mind and inside the skin of a character who could hardly have been more alien or repugnant to me."

Miss Welty ventured into a longer form of storytelling with *The Robber Bridegroom*, a 1942 novella. She followed that four years later with the somewhat longer *Delta Wedding* and, in 1954, *The Ponder Heart*.

That was to be her last novel for 16 years, until *Losing Battles* appeared and divided the Welty faithful. This massive, ambitious book has very little plot—most of the novel is rooted in overlapping stories told at a family reunion—and while some scholars such as Reynolds Price of Duke University hailed it as a great achievement, others were disappointed.

Her next novel, *The Optimist's Daughter*, which drew heavily on childhood trips to West Virginia, won the Pulitzer Prize.

She also won the National Institute of Arts and Letters Gold Medal, the National Medal for Literature, the National Medal of Arts, the Howells Medal for Fiction from the American Academy of Arts and Letters, and four O. Henry first prizes for her stories.

In 1988, she was the first recipient of an award that the Fellows of Phi Beta Kappa, an arm of the undergraduate honor society, established to recognize "excellence, creativity and outstanding intellectual achievements that uniquely enhance human understanding."

In November 1991, she received the $10,000 National Book Foundation Medal for Distinguished Contribution to American Letters for works described as "a unique and evocative body of work in which regionalism becomes universal."

She held professorships at Smith and Bryn Mawr colleges, and she received honorary degrees from Smith, the University of Wisconsin, Western College for Women, Millsaps College, and the University of the South.

In November 1993, the University of Burgundy in Dijon, France, not only conferred an honorary doctorate upon her, but also gave her its arts medal and named its center for women's writing "Eudora." It was her second honor from France. The French government knighted her in 1987, proclaiming her a Chevalier de l'Ordre des Arts et des Lettres.

Late in 1998, Miss Welty became the first living author whose works were included in the Library of America series. Richard Ford, the Pulitzer Prize-winning novelist and a longtime friend, was the project's editor.

Around that time, James Olney, co-editor of the *Southern Review*, said, "There has been in our time no more assiduous practitioner of fiction than Eudora Welty."

By that time, Miss Welty had stopped writing but was still a delightful companion, Ford said. In conversations, "her voice became deep, conspiratorial, like she was sharing something with you," he said. "It was a conspiracy of kindred souls. She was conspiring with you about something wonderful."

In April 1999, the annual Oxford Conference on the Book, held at the University of Mississippi, was dedicated to her. Four months later, the Southern Book Critics Circle gave her its Distinguished Achievement Award for her lifetime contributions to Southern culture. And in October 2000, Miss Welty was one of 10 women inducted into the National Women's Hall of Fame.

Despite her honors, Polk said, too many critics regarded Miss Welty as "a nice little old lady writing nice little old stories."

But after the 1984 publication of *One Writer's Beginnings*, which became a best seller, and a series of academic conferences on her work, opinions changed, and a new generation of scholars took an interest.

When such acclaim was brought up, "she would laugh at it," Polk said. "She generally disallowed the topic as not being worth talking about. She just said, 'I like the story, and I write the best way I can.'"

— *July 24, 2001*

Jamie Shannon

"He had magic in his hands"

Jamie Shannon, the exuberant, innovative chef who led Commander's Palace's already fabled kitchen to a string of national awards, died Friday of cancer at the University of Texas M.D. Anderson Cancer Center in Houston. He was 40.

"He had magic in his hands and a fire in his belly and a twinkle in his eye," said Ti Adelaide Martin, a member of the family that owns the Garden District restaurant. "He was the quintessential hospitality person. He wanted to make people happy."

Mr. Shannon, who delighted in finding new ways to cook standard fare such as crawfish, oysters, and game, worked in the Commander's kitchen for 17 years and was executive chef for the past 11.

During that period, Commander's won the James Beard Foundation Award in 1996 as America's outstanding restaurant, as well as the organization's 1993 award for outstanding service.

Mr. Shannon won the foundation's 1999 award as the best chef in the southeastern United States.

The restaurant also topped restaurant polls taken by the Zagat Survey, *Southern Living* magazine, and *Food & Wine* magazine.

Last year, he and Martin collaborated on *Commander's Kitchen*, a cookbook that combined recipes with stories about the restaurant. Unlike cookbooks from other outposts of haute cuisine, the book was approachable enough to let everyday cooks use it, reviewers said.

Mr. Shannon's fame grew last summer when the Turner South cable network aired "Off the Menu at Commander's Palace," which let audiences see him not only in the kitchen but also on his beloved motorcycle and in bayous and the Gulf of Mexico, his trademark ponytail blowing in the breeze as he tracked down seafood and game for the restaurant.

For his friends, the series was bittersweet because by the time it aired, Mr. Shannon was waging his battle with cancer.

But his disease didn't stifle his creativity, Martin said. "I was sitting with him in his hospital room and talking about menus. He always wanted to know what the next thing was."

Although he found fame in south Louisiana, Mr. Shannon had not intended to stay in New Orleans for more than a few months before heading to California, said Lally Brennan, another member of the family that owns Commander's.

"He went to Mr. B's, but there were no openings," she said. "My brother Ralph said Emeril (Lagasse, then Commander's executive chef) needed someone, so he went to work there."

After starting with sauces, Mr. Shannon moved on to salads and hors d'oeuvres before becoming Commander's morning and brunch cook. He moved up the ranks to become sous-chef, executive sous-chef and, upon Lagasse's departure to open the restaurant bearing his first name, executive chef.

At that point, he was not quite 30. But he had been training for such a role for much of his life.

Born in Sea Isle, N.J., James P. Shannon was the great-grandson of European immigrants who operated a restaurant in Philadelphia. He spent childhood summers on their farm and developed an appreciation for food that came from the land. Local fishers taught him about preparing the catch.

Mr. Shannon's first food-related jobs were in a local cafeteria, where as a teen-ager he worked his way up from busboy to cook, and a boardwalk restaurant in Wildwood, N.J.

By that time, he had decided to make cooking his life's work, and he received a scholarship to the Culinary Institute of America in Hyde Park, N.Y., one of the country's foremost training grounds for chefs.

He decided to specialize in American cuisine, which would undergo a revolution in the late 1970s and early 1980s, led by innovative chefs such as Paul Prudhomme of New Orleans and Alice Waters of Berkeley, Calif.

His first postgraduate job was at Ivana restaurant in the Trump Towers Hotel and Casino in Atlantic City, N.J. But it specialized in European-inspired nouvelle cuisine, not the American type of cooking that Mr. Shannon liked. So he decided to move to New Orleans.

Almost from the moment he arrived at Commander's, his talent and ambition were evident, said Ella Brennan, the restaurant's matriarch. "He had the passion for whatever he was doing and the excitement of it," she said. "He was never bored. He went to work every day with 87,000 things he wanted to do."

— *November 24, 2001*

James Roberts

He embalmed Jayne Mansfield

James Roberts, who helped prepare Jayne Mansfield and some of New Orleans' most notable citizens for burial, died Saturday of heart disease at Bultman Funeral Home, where he had worked and lived for 51 years. He was 82.

Mr. Roberts lived in one of the funeral home's four apartments, sharing space on the second floor with the casket showrooms. "He was as proud of that building as if it were his own," funeral director Billy Henry said.

Known as the mortuary's unofficial historian, Mr. Roberts delighted in giving tours of the building at St. Charles and Louisiana avenues. His formal title was funeral assistant, a description that covered such behind-the-scenes chores as picking up bodies at hospitals and private homes, putting them in caskets and arranging makeup and hair.

During services, Mr. Roberts, a tall man with dark hair, stood in the lobby, speaking in low, comforting tones as he greeted mourners and directed them to the proper parlor or chapel.

"He was opening the doors of his home," Henry said.

A native of Hope, Ark., who had served in the Army in World War II and was part of the postwar occupying force in Japan, Mr. Roberts wasn't sure what he was going to do after he was discharged, said Foster Guillory, Bultman's manager.

When Mr. Roberts was touring New Orleans before going back to Arkansas, Fred Bultman, the funeral home's owner, happened to meet him, struck up a conversation and offered him a job and a place to live, Guillory said.

Even though living in a funeral home might sound odd, it made sense when Mr. Roberts entered the business because pagers didn't exist and not everyone had a telephone, Guillory said.

"You either lived in the building or close to it," he said. "Jim liked living where he was because all he had to do was walk across the house, grab a cot, go downstairs, get in a hearse, remove the body, and go back home."

Mr. Roberts, who retired in the mid-1990s, helped arrange final rites for some of New Orleans' most notable citizens. But his best-known client was Jayne Mansfield, who was brought to the Garden District mortuary early one July morning in 1967 after being killed in a car crash on U.S. Highway 90 en route to New Orleans.

Because of his job, Mr. Roberts was able to refute the rumor that Mansfield had been decapitated. "She was fully intact," he said in an interview. "I know. I embalmed her."

The rumor apparently started when someone saw the movie star's wig atop a stand on the dashboard.

Besides his funeral-related work, Mr. Roberts was often the chauffeur and escort for Muriel Bultman Francis, an arts patron who was a member of the family that used to own the business.

Friends recalled Mr. Roberts' acts of kindness, such as driving a Bultman car through Carnival crowds to be sure that nurses reached Touro Infirmary on time.

Carnival was the source of a story that made Mr. Roberts decide he was in the right place, Guillory said.

One Mardi Gras, the funeral home got a call that someone had been run over by a float at Washington Avenue, several blocks from the funeral home.

"They parked at Prytania and walked over to St. Charles Avenue with a cot," Guillory said. "They had to push people back to get to the body because people were still jumping for beads. Jim said that if people were this crazy, he knew he was home."

— *December 20, 2001*

Ruth Fertel

She reigned over a global empire of steak

R uth Fertel, who mortgaged her home to buy a restaurant that became the genesis of an international chain grossing more than $330 million a year, died Tuesday of cancer at Ochsner Foundation Hospital. She was 75.

By the time of her death, chefs in 82 Ruth's Chris Steak House restaurants across America and in Canada, Mexico, Puerto Rico, Taiwan, and Hong Kong were serving up about 16,000 steaks every day. The chain with the name that its founder described as "a tongue twister and a half" has consistently won high marks in reader polls conducted by such magazines as *Bon Appétit* and *Restaurants and Institutions*.

In January 1999, Ms. Fertel sold a majority interest in the chain to a Chicago investment firm.

In New Orleans, the flagship Ruth's Chris, at North Broad and Orleans avenues, achieved mythic status, both as a place to get prime beef and as a required election-eve stop for politicians with a yen to table-hop, preen and play prophet.

After elections, it was the spot where losers paid off their bets. "I have learned everything about politics through my years of dining at Ruth's Chris," said U.S. Sen. Mary Landrieu, D-La. "In New Orleans, Ruth's Chris has become not only a place of business but also a way of life."

Success brought honors that covered many walls, including the Restaurant Business High Performance Leadership Award, *Restaurants and Institutions* Magazine's Executive of the Year Award, the Horatio Alger Award, and the Ella Brennan Savoir Faire Award from the American Culinary Federation's New Orleans chapter.

Yet despite her trademark red blazer and her apparent pleasure in greeting patrons and serving up prime beef, lyonnaise potatoes and creamed spinach, Ms. Fertel was a shy woman who seemed bemused by all the attention.

"There's really no great mystery to what we do," she once said. "We have a great product and great people."

She made that statement in an interview about entrepreneurship for *A Business of Their Own*, Gregory K. Ericksen's book about 12 successful businesswomen.

Because of her international success, Ms. Fertel is often cited as a role model for aspiring businesswomen. But when she launched her business in 1965, such models were scarce.

That year, Ms. Fertel was a divorced mother of two teen-age sons who was making $400 a month as a laboratory technician at Tulane University. With her sons nearing college age, Ms. Fertel knew she would need more money and started scouring the classified advertisements in the *Times-Picayune*, looking for opportunities.

Chris Steak House was on the block, and Chris Matulich was asking $18,000 for the restaurant at North Broad Street and Ursulines Avenue. Using her house as collateral, Ms. Fertel borrowed the $18,000, plus $4,000 for food and equipment.

On her first day she sold 35 steaks for about $5 apiece. Because she was the only person on the premises who knew anything about butchering, Ms. Fertel, who stood 5 feet, 2 inches tall and weighed 110 pounds, had to cut the 30-pound loins herself with a handsaw.

In those early months she also did almost every other chore as well, including keeping the books, taking reservations, showing customers to tables, and substituting for the dishwasher and chef on their days off.

Three months after she opened, Hurricane Betsy slammed into New Orleans, cutting off electricity to hundreds of thousands of people—and threatening to spoil hundreds of pounds of refrigerated meat.

So she cooked everything she had, Ericksen said, and asked her brother to distribute it to people in need, many of whom later turned up as grateful customers.

"We went out of our way to please customers," Ms. Fertel told Ericksen. "We spoiled them. One of our regular Sunday customers was operated on for his teeth and couldn't bite into a steak. So I chopped his steak in the grinder, formed it into the same shape as before and served it to him. He was thrilled."

As her business grew, Ms. Fertel bought a building four blocks away and rented it out as a profitable party venue. In 1975, after fire struck the original restaurant, she moved the whole operation to North Broad and Orleans.

[It was forced to close after Hurricane Katrina-related floodwaters over-whelmed it in August 2005.]

At the new location, Ms. Fertel had to come up with a new business name because the terms of the sale under which she bought her original restaurant forbade her to use Chris Steak House for any other eatery.

Not wishing to lose the identity she was developing, Ms. Fertel simply added her first name.

The name may have been quirky, but it was memorable. One writer for *Fortune* magazine quipped that it should be used as a sobriety test because, he said, anyone who could say, "Ruth's Chris Steak House," three times couldn't possibly be drunk.

In 1976, when a loyal customer moved to Baton Rouge, he was so loyal that he regularly drove 80 miles each way for a steak. Tired of the commute, he pleaded with Ms. Fertel to let him open a restaurant in Baton Rouge.

It was a success from the beginning, Ms. Fertel said, and the start of a chain that, at her death, operated in 27 states and the District of Columbia, as well as Canada, Mexico, Puerto Rico, and Asia.

While she was making money, Ms. Fertel was helping others. In addition to more conventional kinds of philanthropy, she remembered her own hard times and made a point of hiring single mothers as waitresses.

When a friend decided to become a restaurateur, Ms. Fertel co-signed and guaranteed the business loan. She was "extending a helping hand that leaves no fingerprints," a friend said.

At her death, she was involved in underwriting and planning for the Ruth U. Fertel Culinary Arts Building at Nicholls State University in Thibodaux, La.

Although she called herself lucky, Ms. Fertel worked hard from the be-ginning, telling Ericksen she was "always trying to do as well as the boys did."

Born Ruth Udstad, she grew up in the Plaquemines Parish community of Happy Jack, finished high school at 15 and graduated from Louisiana State University at 19 with a double major in chemistry and physics.

Ms. Fertel tried graduate school and teaching but didn't like either one. After her divorce, she found she had a flair for making drapes, spreading the fabric on her living-room floor and working on her hands and knees. She gave that up when her knees gave out, then landed a job she liked in Tulane's cardiovascular-research lab.

Realizing she had reached a dead end and needed more money for her sons, she took a chance on the restaurant.

"How she was able to take that little idea she had and go all the way with it was absolutely amazing," said Ella Brennan, a member of the family that runs Commander's Palace and other New Orleans restaurants. "This lady, to me, was extraordinary. She kept plowing along, and she built this empire. She did it very well, with style and grace."

"She might have had a much easier time of it all had she done something less daunting, but what fun would that be?" *Esquire* magazine food critic John Mariani said. "Ruth Fertel is an American original whose first aim has always been to please. And if she happened to make a fortune doing it, well, that's just fine with everybody."

She was buried in a Metairie Cemetery tomb that she and her friend Lana Duke had bought in 1999. To celebrate that acquisition, they held a party in the graveyard.

— April 17, 2002

Charles J. Hatfield

He inadvertently helped create a law school

Charles J. Hatfield, who inadvertently helped create Southern University Law Center in Baton Rouge when he sued in 1946 to integrate Louisiana State University's law school, died Friday of complications from pancreatic cancer at Memorial Medical Center's Mercy campus in New Orleans. He was 87.

In response to Mr. Hatfield's litigation, the state appropriated $40,000 to establish a law school at historically black Southern University in Baton Rouge, making it the first in the state for African Americans.

His attorneys, including A. P. Tureaud of New Orleans and Thurgood Marshall of the NAACP, had earned their degrees at historically black Howard University in Washington, D.C.

But Mr. Hatfield, a Xavier University graduate and World War II veteran, wound up not studying law at all.

Before Southern's center opened in 1947, he moved to Atlanta because Tureaud feared for his client's safety. He earned a master's degree in sociology at Atlanta University (now Clark Atlanta University) in 1948 and returned to New Orleans, his hometown, to acquire a master's degree in education at Xavier in 1950.

Mr. Hatfield, who spent his career teaching in two New Orleans high schools, was a founding member of United Teachers of New Orleans, the teachers' union. Southern honored him twice: on the law center's 50th anniversary in 1997 and at its commencement last month, when it gave him its first-ever honorary law degree.

The university hailed him "for exhibiting courage, foresight and determination in securing for African Americans the right to study law in the state of Louisiana."

Mr. Hatfield was humble about such praise. "Although I never anticipated great acclaim for the things I have done to further the cause of our people, it does make one feel warm inside to be reminded of some benefits mankind has derived," he said in an interview in The Louisiana Education Association Journal.

Mr. Hatfield sued LSU because its law dean, Paul M. Hebert, told him in a letter that "Louisiana State University does not accept colored students."

Similar petitions were filed in 1946 in Oklahoma, Texas, and South Carolina. Mr. Hatfield's suit was unique because he filed on his own without being recruited to do so, said Evelyn Wilson, a professor at Southern University Law Center who is writing a history of Mr. Hatfield and his family.

Defendants were Hebert, LSU President William Bass Hatcher, and LSU's Board of Supervisors. Before they could respond to Mr. Hatfield's suit, the state Board of Education in December 1946 started the process of establishing a law school at Southern that would be open for the 1947–48 term. A month later, the Board of Liquidation of State Debt appropriated $40,000 for that purpose.

Even though Mr. Hatfield never enrolled there, his litigation was hardly in vain, Wilson said.

"Because of the suit, Southern University has a law center," she said. "If nobody had brought any litigation, there probably wouldn't have been a law center."

Mr. Hatfield, who had worked as a postal clerk, taught Spanish, English and social studies at Joseph S. Clark and George Washington Carver high schools. From 1954 to 1972, Mr. Hatfield was active in the black teachers' union and held several offices, including secretary-treasurer, vice president and lobbyist. In 1966, he helped organize the city's first teachers' strike.

When United Teachers of New Orleans was formed in 1972 with the merger of the black and white teachers' unions, Mr. Hatfield was a charter member, and he helped create its credit union. When he retired in 1979, he received UTNO's Pioneer Award in recognition of his union work.

"Charles was a strong union person," said Nat Lacour, a former UTNO president. "We could count on him to be straightforward. He was very interested in the union's work to improve salaries and working conditions. He was very strong in his view about teachers' having a greater voice in decision-making in the school district and their schools."

"Charles was my strong right arm," Lacour said.

— *June 15, 2002*

Nehemiah Atkinson

Playing and coaching tennis kept him young

Nehemiah Atkinson, a passionately devoted tennis player and coach who, in his 80s, ranked as the world's top men's singles player in his age group, died Sunday of cancer at Kenner Regional Medical Center. He was 84.

A black man in a sport dominated by white players, Mr. Atkinson coached generations of tennis players and set up a scholarship fund to help send them to college.

Career highlights included winning in 1999 both the 80s National Hardcourt Championship in San Diego and a doubles title in the World International Senior Tennis Championship in Barcelona.

In 2001, he defeated longtime rival Bob Sherman in Australia to win the World Men's 80s Grasscourt Championship.

"Tennis keeps you young," Mr. Atkinson said in a *Times-Picayune* interview last year. "It stimulates your heart, keeps your body in shape and your eyes sharp."

"The most remarkable thing about him is that he's not remarkable," said Dr. Paul DeCamp, a frequent doubles partner. "He just takes life the way it is."

Former New Orleans City Councilman Jim Singleton, a longtime friend and tennis partner, was amazed by Mr. Atkinson's stamina.

"We'd go out there and play tennis, and you'd swear he was barely 50," Singleton said.

"He was a determined competitor—with a smile," said David Schumacher, the coach of Tulane University's women's tennis team and an occasional doubles partner.

In recognition of Mr. Atkinson's achievements, he became the first African American inducted into the Southern Tennis Hall of Fame, and he received the 1977 Robert F. Kennedy Memorial Ripple of Hope Award.

Despite his zeal for teaching, Mr. Atkinson, who first hit a tennis ball when he was 9 years old, never had a lesson.

"God blessed me with everything I needed," he said in the interview.

After serving in the Army during World War II, Mr. Atkinson worked within the boundaries of segregated society, organizing a club to teach the game to black children and setting up tournaments.

In 1947, he helped found the New Orleans Hard Court Tennis Club, the first such group for local black players, and he organized tournaments for them at Xavier University.

One of 10 children of a New Orleans preacher, Mr. Atkinson grew up blocks from the South Saratoga Street home of the New Orleans Lawn Tennis Club.

In 1974, after the club moved to Jefferson Avenue, the site became the Stern Tennis Center, part of the New Orleans Recreation Department, and Mr. Atkinson was its manager until he retired in 1995.

"I'm not bitter," he said in a 1979 interview at the Stern Center in which he recalled the days when segregation limited African-American access to many of the top tennis clubs. "There's no need to be bitter. That was the law. It's kind of funny: Now those who had once shut me out, I invite here to play."

Mr. Atkinson later was a member of the New Orleans Lawn Tennis Club. Until he became seriously ill, he continued to play regularly at the Stern Center as well, said Howard Kuntz, a friend and tennis partner for 20 years.

"If it wasn't right, he'd get out there and sweep up the court and mow the grass," Kuntz said. "I'd tell him, 'There are people to do that,' but he'd do it himself. He wanted to keep those courts in good shape."

— *February 14, 2003*

Rodney Fertel

He brought gorillas into local politics

Rodney Fertel, who became a local political legend by promising to buy a gorilla for Audubon Zoo if elected mayor of New Orleans, died Tuesday at Kindred Hospital. He was 81.

Mr. Fertel received only 310 votes in the 1969 primary, but he kept his promise, traveling to Singapore, where he bought two gorillas.

"For any city to have culture, it has to have a good zoo," he said in an interview. "My motives? They're nothing. Just to better things."

The heir to a New Orleans real estate fortune, Mr. Fertel first became fascinated by the primates in 1965, on a trip to Europe that included a visit to the zoo in Antwerp, Belgium.

"He just spent hours in front of the gorilla habitat," said his son Randy Fertel, who accompanied him.

"Gorillas have their own language," Rodney Fertel said in a 1976 interview. "If we could understand what they're saying, we might solve all the problems of the Earth."

The man who introduced gorillas to local politics was born Rodney Fertel Weinberg in Denver in 1921. He moved to New Orleans as a child and graduated from Alcée Fortier High School, where he excelled at basketball, swimming and football. He attended Louisiana State University for a year.

When he was 21, he inherited millions from his grandmother, Julia Fertel, who had invested heavily in local real estate. To honor her, he dropped his last name, Randy Fertel said.

With his money, Mr. Fertel never had to hold a job, his son said, so he was able to pursue activities including gambling, sports and racing thoroughbreds, one of which he named Fertel's Gorilla.

He met his future wife, Ruth Udstad, when she was an LSU student and a regular rider at a Baton Rouge stable Mr. Fertel owned.

Married in 1947, they divorced in 1958. Seven years later, she opened a restaurant—the first of what would become the celebrated international chain known as Ruth's Chris Steak House. She died last year.

While his wife was busy, Mr. Fertel had to look for ways to fill his days, his son said. He hung out with racetrack personnel, worked out, ran unsuccessfully for mayor and Congress, and traveled, circling the globe five times, sometimes using oat bags from the Fair Grounds as luggage.

On one trip, he and his son spent time in Barcelona, Spain, with the surrealist artist Salvador Dali.

"Dali's capes and wild eyes and outrageous mustache were all it took," Randy Fertel wrote of their meeting. "Dad had found a soul mate."

In an interview, Mr. Fertel said he had no regrets about the life he had chosen.

"I'm proud of being called the Gorilla Man," he said. "I did what I said I was going to do. I hate to think what they would call me if I didn't do what I said."

— *May 21, 2003*

Iris Kelso

A pioneering political reporter who was "one of the boys"

Iris Kelso, a reporter and columnist whose honeyed drawl and impeccable manners masked her steely determination to get the story, died Sunday of pneumonia at Touro Infirmary. She was 76.

Ms. Kelso, who started covering government when virtually everyone in politics and the press was male, chronicled New Orleans and Louisiana politics for nearly half a century in print and broadcast journalism. She reported on every New Orleans mayor from deLesseps S. "Chep" Morrison to Marc Morial, and every Louisiana governor from Earl Long to Mike Foster.

"Iris was one of the boys," said former Lt. Gov. James Fitzmorris, whom Ms. Kelso covered when he was in city and state government. "She'd come in and make herself very much at home. She accepted the fact that she was a woman, but she was a reporter just like everybody else, and she was going to be the best reporter that she could be."

Ms. Kelso retired from the *Times-Picayune* at the end of 1996. While readers relied on her twice-weekly column for political insights, they were charmed by columns in which she recounted the gatherings of her large family at Christmas and, every summer, at the Neshoba County Fair in her hometown of Philadelphia, Miss.

Besides letting kinfolk—and, by extension, her readers—catch up on family events and gossip, these occasions provided gentle reminders that there is more to life than winning elective office and maneuvering a bill through the Legislature.

The feeling of being solidly grounded in her family "shaped her style," said Denise Hull, a niece. "It let her know the value of family and roots. Every time I run into someone, I'm asked, 'How's Iris?' They say they miss her work, but what they really miss are her family stories."

Born Iris Turner in December 1926, she grew up engulfed by relatives. Because her mother died when she was 4, an assortment of grandparents, aunts and other relatives pitched in to help Homer Turner rear his daughter. An aunt who lived with young Iris and her father was the mother of Turner Catledge, who grew up to be the *New York Times*' executive editor.

Politics was an important part of her upbringing. Her father was politically active and became an ally of Mississippi Gov. Hugh White. A grandfather, a reform-minded Democrat, was a delegate to several national Democratic conventions in the 1920s and 1930s.

Both men were regarded as opinion leaders, and they took that responsibility seriously, Ms. Kelso said in an interview for the Washington Press Club Foundation's oral history project.

"One time my father changed his mind in an election the night before the election," she said, "and he had to get on the road and go tell everybody he had changed his mind."

After two years at Ward-Belmont Junior College in Nashville, Tenn., where she majored in horseback riding, Ms. Kelso earned an undergraduate degree in 1948 at Randolph-Macon Woman's College in Lynchburg, Va.

The college got her a job at the *Hattiesburg* (Miss.) *American*, an afternoon paper, where she was a general-assignment reporter. It was an ideal match, even though she earned less than $50 a week.

"It was a wonderful job because I covered everything," she said. "I covered courts and things like that. I was so manic.... I couldn't stand for a siren to go off without my knowing where was the fire and how could I get there. It was like living on the edge at all times."

Among the people she interviewed was Dr. Alton Ochsner, who had been the first person to link cigarette smoking to cancer. Ms. Kelso, a lifelong smoker, was so unnerved by the prospect of meeting such a luminary that she automatically did the first thing that came to mind: She fired up a cigarette.

Before the fledgling journalist could say a word, "he started on me," Ms. Kelso said. "He gave me the whole roll-out. I had no idea that smoking was even dangerous, and I was so upset because he was such an eminent man, and I didn't take any notes, didn't ask any questions."

Her boss, Andy Harmon, was also a mentor, giving her reams of wire-service copy to read and evaluate and discuss with him. In 1951, feeling his protégée was ready to move on, Harmon used his connection at the *New Orleans States*, one of the city's two afternoon newspapers, to get her a job.

Although she started as a general-assignment reporter, Ms. Kelso was frequently assigned to write feature stories about crime victims and people on trial, as well as the usual run of crimes and fires.

"She was a natural reporter," said Walter G. Cowan, her boss at the *States*. "It was obvious to me right off that she had the ability to talk to people and retain their confidence, even though she had to ask embarrassing questions. It's the kind of thing that rattles new reporters, but she always kept her composure."

When she described her early New Orleans years in the Press Club Foundation interview, Ms. Kelso evoked a rough-and-tumble world out of "The Front Page," where hard-driving, profane, cigar-chomping editors hid liquor in their desks, hollered at reporters, barked into telephones, and yanked copy out of typewriters as the clock ticked toward deadline.

It was an adrenaline rush she never got over. "I love afternoon papers," she said. "I love to cover (a story) as it happens, and I love to run to a phone. I became a very good dictator. I could dictate a story like crazy."

In 1954, after she had been covering schools, Cowan assigned her to City Hall, launching her career as a political reporter.

Although politics was to become the focus for the rest of her career, that particular assignment terrified her, Cowan said. "She walked over to me and said, 'I can't cover City Hall. I don't know anything about city politics,'" Cowan said. "I said, 'Iris, if I thought you couldn't do it, I never would have asked you.' That was the confidence I had in her."

Though she was later hailed as a pioneering female journalist, Ms. Kelso was quick to shrug off such praise, pointing out that many women had been taken seriously as reporters during World War II, when their male counterparts were in the armed forces.

Moreover, she said, New Orleans papers had already assigned women to City Hall, adding, "I benefited from that."

In 1959, Ms. Kelso was sent to Baton Rouge to cover the Legislature. But the big story was Gov. Earl K. Long's mental breakdown and his fight with people who tried to hospitalize him for paranoid schizophrenia, and she was assigned to it.

On one occasion, she interviewed Long when he was wearing long underwear. Even though the story led to an abundance of good stories to remind the rest of the world how unconventional Louisiana politics can be, Ms. Kelso saw the personal tragedy, too.

"I was so touched by the sight of this old crazy man and the tragedy of what was happening to him," she said. "It was just a very emotional thing for me."

In 1960 she married Robert Kelso, a rewrite man for the *States-Item*. He died in 1972.

By the middle of the 1960s, Ms. Kelso said she was tired of being an observer. "I wanted to participate in something, just to do something that mattered," she said in the interview.

So she joined Total Community Action, an anti-poverty initiative. She was responsible for the Head Start program, and she helped set up a medical program that was singled out as one of the best in the country.

"It was the hardest job I ever had, before or since," she said, "but also the most rewarding."

Later on, in the 1980s, Kelso continued her efforts on behalf of those in need as a founding member of Grace House of New Orleans, a residential drug and alcohol treatment program for women.

After two years with Total Community Action, Kelso returned to journalism, but in another medium: television.

The decision-makers at WDSU-TV wanted her to cover politics, even though Ms. Kelso had no experience in broadcasting.

"What she gave us was that instant recognition," said Jerry Romig, the station's program director then. "The moment she came on board, you could sense right away that we gained that recognition because people who had read the paper knew Iris Kelso as a fair, wise journalist. She had that reputation, and it carried over."

During her 11 years at New Orleans' NBC affiliate, Ms. Kelso covered the administration of Mayor Moon Landrieu and the election of Dutch Morial as the city's first black mayor. She won a Peabody Award for "City in Crisis," a series on New Orleans' finances.

Ms. Kelso returned to print journalism in 1978 as a columnist for Figaro, an alternative weekly, although she continued a weekly political commentary, "Saturday Politics," on WDSU.

A year later, she joined the *Times-Picayune* as a political columnist. "She was for good government," Landrieu said, "but she was not such a purist with blinders on that she didn't understand the pulls and the pushes and the tugs in the business.... Of most importance to politicians was that she had their confidence. What was said to her off the record was held in confidence. That was terribly important and made her effective in the sense that she always had access."

For Ms. Kelso, it was a chance to investigate human nature. "I have always been more interested in what politics tells about people than in politics itself," she wrote. "Politics is a profession that tests men and women in ways few of us ever face. It takes them to the heights and drops them just as suddenly. In the dizzying course they follow, people in politics sometimes let you know just who they are."

She shared such moments with her readers, telling them about spending the night in the Governor's Mansion, listening to Moon Landrieu discuss his mother's aspirations for her son, and commiserating with former Gov. John J. McKeithen when he talked of taking out a loan to build a house after a fire destroyed his home.

Interspersed with her political observations were columns about her neighborhood and her family, which, she said in an interview, were her most popular.

"Family" was "a word given almost a religious importance in our home," Ms. Kelso wrote after one Christmas reunion. "We have been together through all the joys of life and many of the sorrows. We have always been there for each other."

Besides spending more time with her family in retirement, Ms. Kelso was able to devote more time to her garden. A daylily has been named for her.

In 1997, she was inducted into the Louisiana Center for Women and Government's Hall of Fame.

— *November 3, 2003*

Bernice Norman

A philanthropist who loved designer purses

Bernice Norman, a philanthropist who circled the world dozens of times and amassed a sizable collection of sparkling, high-priced designer handbags, died Wednesday at her New Orleans home. She was 88.

A Pensacola, Fla., native who lived in New Orleans more than 60 years, Mrs. Norman "never met a charitable event that she didn't support," said Dot Shushan, a longtime friend.

Although Mrs. Norman was a major donor to such organizations as the New Orleans Museum of Art, the New Orleans Philharmonic Symphony, Touro Synagogue, and Touro Infirmary, she also sent smaller gifts to causes that appealed to her after she read their mass mailings, Shushan said, adding, "She supported them all."

Mrs. Norman was a passionate shopper who loved fine clothes and the bright, fanciful handbags by designer Judith Leiber that come in all shapes and sizes and sell for several thousand dollars apiece.

She bought her first Leiber purse about 30 years ago because a saleswoman told her it would go well with a new dress, Leiber said Thursday.

Her collection grew to about 100 bags, said her son, William D. Norman Jr. The purses, some of which resemble puppies, kittens and fruit slices, have gained status as collectibles.

"Judith Leiber bags are the Fabergé eggs of handbags," New Orleans Museum of Art Director E. John Bullard said. In fact, he said, one of Mrs. Norman's Leiber creations resembles a Fabergé egg.

Mrs. Norman donated about 80 of her bags to the art museum, which auctioned them in 1993 to raise money. They brought in nearly $121,000, said Kelly Epler, managing director of New Orleans Auction Galleries Inc. The top bid of $6,325 went for a topaz-colored bag.

Competition was intense at the auction, where the bidders even included Leiber, who showed up to buy some of her designs for her Long Island museum.

Whenever John Abajian, a consignment agent, displayed a purse, he said, "All the women's hands were in the air, grasping, as if I were ready to throw beads from a Mardi Gras float."

Mrs. Norman and her husband, Dr. William D. Norman, were globe-trotters. After his death in a 1975 plane crash, she continued on around-the-world cruises, frequently for months at a time.

No one knew Thursday exactly how many times she had circled the planet, although estimates ranged between 30 and 40.

When someone once asked why she kept making such trips, Mrs. Norman was heard to reply, "Where else would you suggest I go?"

— April 15, 2005

Homer Dupuy

A doctor devoted to all things French

Dr. Homer Dupuy, an internal-medicine specialist and former king of Carnival who carried on a lifelong love affair with all things French, died Saturday at his home. He was 92.

A native New Orleanian who was Rex in 1963, Dr. Dupuy was part of a family whose local roots date back to the 1700s, when Louisiana was a French colony.

Because he had grown up with a strong sense of history and heritage, Dr. Dupuy was always an active participant in just about anything involving the area's Gallic culture, said his daughter Suzanne Dupuy Phelps. He founded and later led France-Amérique de la Louisiane Inc., an organization that boosts French-American ties, and he was chairman of the reception committee when French President Charles de Gaulle and his wife, Yvonne, visited New Orleans in 1960.

A year later, Dr. Dupuy was the head of the committee that erected a fountain in Jackson Square to commemorate that event. Money for that fountain was left over from a fundraising drive Dr. Dupuy had led to acquire a golden equestrian statue of Joan of Arc. After spending several years between the Rivergate and the World Trade Center, the statue is at the junction of Decatur and North Peters streets near the French Market—just a few blocks away from the Bienville Monument honoring New Orleans' founder.

Dr. Dupuy was a member of the commission to erect that sculpture, too. He led the 1968 celebration of the 250th anniversary of New Orleans' founding, inaugurated New Orleans' Bastille Day celebration and helped launch the Council for the Development of French in Louisiana, better known as CODOFIL, the program that brings French teachers to Louisiana to imbue students with their language and culture.

And in 1954, he happened to treat a French graduate student who was stricken with pneumonia while researching a thesis on the Port of New Orleans. The student, whom Dr. Dupuy described in an interview as "a nice young Frenchman," was Jacques Chirac, who was elected France's president in 1995.

When a trade delegation from New Orleans went to Paris in 2002, one member gave the French president a letter from Dr. Dupuy, touching off a warm reminiscence about their time together.

For his work on behalf of Franco-American relations, France named Dr. Dupuy a chevalier, then an officier of the Legion of Honor.

In 1997, the French-American Chamber of Commerce gave him its lifetime achievement award.

"He was one of the old, true Frenchmen," said W. Boatner Reily III, a longtime friend. "He was the heart and spirit of what New Orleans should be."

The son of a physician, Dr. Dupuy graduated from Jesuit High School and Loyola University and earned a medical degree at Louisiana State University. He continued his training at Charity Hospital and the Mayo Clinic and developed a subspecialty in cardiology.

When Dr. Dupuy entered a group practice near Touro Infirmary, he made house calls, which he would continue until he retired in 1971. Among his patients were cloistered nuns, including the Little Sisters of the Poor and the Order of the Sacred Heart.

"He came home for 6:30 dinner, then left to go pay house calls," his daughter said. "We took it as normal. That was part of what he was—a devoted doctor who got a great deal of happiness from that career, knowing he was helping."

He even stepped in for other doctors when they were out of town. At one such call during his bachelor days, the patient's granddaughter, Charlotte Hillyer, answered the door.

"One look was all it took," Dr. Dupuy said in an interview, adding that he kept trying to think of things to check so he wouldn't have to leave this fascinating young woman.

"I don't think any patient had a longer examination without being looked over," he said, chuckling.

They married in 1943. She died in 1998.

During World War II, Dr. Dupuy was a cardiologist in the LSU Army Medical Unit, which served in Italy and North Africa. One day, he was told nothing more than to pack up everything he would need for a consultation on an unnamed dignitary.

The VIP turned out to be Gen. Matthew Ridgway, who had collapsed while reviewing troops in Italy. "We came to the conclusion that it was syncope, a brief loss of consciousness caused by a temporary insufficient flow of blood to the brain," he said.

Although the incident seemed minor, Dr. Dupuy and his colleagues realized that Ridgway's career could be over if superiors learned of the incident and thought he was susceptible to such episodes.

"I took all of his papers," Dr. Dupuy said. "He was an extraordinary man, and I hated to see him out of the service."

His military career flourished. During the Korean War, Ridgway succeeded Gen. Douglas MacArthur in 1951 when President Truman fired him as commander of the Allied forces. Two years later, Ridgway was named Army chief of staff.

"If his records had gone through channels, I think he'd have been canned," Dr. Dupuy said.

Dr. Dupuy, who had been a major, was promoted to lieutenant colonel in the summer of 1945 and named chief of medicine in hospitals in the Pacific Theater. The transfer became moot a few days later, he said, after the United States dropped atomic bombs on Hiroshima and Nagasaki, bringing the war to a swift conclusion.

He returned to New Orleans—to his family, his practice and his civic activities. In 1963, he was named Rex, becoming the first—and, so far, only— man to be a duke, a page and king. At his death, he was oldest former monarch.

Riding at the head of the Rex parade was "a great, great thrill," Dr. Dupuy said. "What impressed me was the people I had known who were reserved, some were depressed in their ordinary lives. Then came their reaction, their enthusiasm, their applause. It was really thrilling."

But, he said, "I think they were applauding the Rex organization rather than Rex himself."

— December 11, 2005

Elizabeth Anderson

An acclaimed chef who was devoted to her work

E lizabeth Anderson, a chef and caterer who won acclaim for dishes such
as shrimp remoulade and a crab concoction bearing her name that she
dished up for more than 30 years in New Orleans' finest homes and most
exclusive clubs, died Sunday in Seattle. She was 89.

A New Orleanian for 73 years, Mrs. Anderson had evacuated to Seattle,
where two of her children live, before Hurricane Katrina hit in August 2005,
said Jessie Dejoie, a daughter.

"She loved what she did," said Fran Villere, a friend who hired her frequently. "You knew that whatever she did was from the heart."

Mrs. Anderson, who was born in Plaquemine, La., "was bred on hard
work, and she seemed to thrive on it," Dejoie said. "My mother cut cane in
the country for 50 cents a day."

Because she found rural life unfulfilling, Dejoie said her mother quit
school when she was 16 and moved to New Orleans, where she started
cooking for families.

In 1959, Mrs. Anderson opened Elizabeth's Restaurant in the Carrollton
section. She moved on to be head chef at the Orléans Club, an exclusive
women's organization with a clubhouse on St. Charles Avenue, and then at
the Pendennis Club, a men's group in the Central Business District.

Mrs. Anderson, who also moonlighted intermittently during those years,
retired in the early 1980s to care for her husband after he suffered a stroke.

"But people continued to call to ask her to do things from home," Dejoie
said. "It just blossomed into a catering company: Elizabeth Anderson Catering."

"She was a damn good cook, and she must have been a damn good busi-
nesswoman to get that business started," said Clive Hardy, who hired Mrs.

Anderson to cater events at the Round Table Club overlooking Audubon Park.

"She was very gracious," he said. "She was very capable, and she knew how to organize help and to get the most out of them."

Along the way, Mrs. Anderson developed signature dishes, including chicken Mornay, a casserole with cream sauce and fresh mushrooms; seafood gumbo; baked bananas; grillades and grits topped with gravy that had simmered for hours; and a dish Mrs. Anderson called crabmeat Elizabeth, consisting of crabmeat, fresh mushrooms, and a special sauce. She served shrimp remoulade with artichoke leaves.

"As soon as people walked into an event and saw the leaves, they knew it was my mom," Dejoie said.

Dejoie took over the business when her mother retired for good in 1992.

In the last years Mrs. Anderson was in the business, Dejoie said, customers included brides whose mothers' and grandmothers' wedding receptions had been catered by Mrs. Anderson.

"She liked hard work and knowing that it was appreciated," Dejoie said.

— April 22, 2006

Sunny Norman

She reigned over the art scene in her stocking feet

Sunny Norman, an art collector and philanthropist who gave lavishly to the visual and performing arts in New Orleans for nearly half a century, died Friday in Haverford, Pa. She was 94.

Mrs. Norman had been evacuated to Pennsylvania before Hurricane Katrina hit New Orleans.

Her real name was Mildred Gould Norman, but she never used her first name, preferring to answer to a nickname she acquired in childhood.

She was the widow of P. Roussel Norman, who headed his family's Morgan City, La., lumber business and loved to create and collect art. Both Normans developed their tastes as collectors and became fixtures on the New Orleans art scene after moving to the city from Morgan City in 1957.

After her husband's death in 1975, Mrs. Norman continued acquiring all kinds of art, serving on local and national arts boards, and encouraging young artists. She once showed her devotion to young talent by replacing her home collection with a University of New Orleans exhibit she had enjoyed at the Lakefront campus. It was a shrewd marketing ploy because the paintings were seen by many more people than had seen the display at UNO, including local collectors.

Her adopted hometown rewarded Mrs. Norman richly, although she insisted that she did nothing more than bring people together—artists with gallery owners and agents, for instance. Among the honors she received were the *Times-Picayune* Loving Cup, the Mayor's Award for Distinctive Achievement in the Arts, the Torch of Liberty Award from the Anti-Defamation League, and the Hannah G. Solomon Award from the National Council of Jewish Women.

After the deaths of Edith Stern and Muriel Bultman Francis in the 1980s, Mrs. Norman became the sole survivor of what had been a triumvirate of wealthy, intelligent women who ruled the city's arts scene and cared deeply about it, said William A. Fagaly, curator of African art at the New Orleans Museum of Art.

"There's nobody to replace those people," he said. "The gusto and the commitment and the drive! They had a vision. They knew what was best for this city, and they did it."

But there was a notable difference. While Stern and Francis were frail, Mrs. Norman was lively, ready to face every situation with good humor. Well into her 83rd year, Mrs. Norman exuberantly worked the crowd at an AIDS benefit, proclaiming that, after stomach and hip-replacement surgery, "I'm the bionic woman!

Mrs. Norman, always a striking figure in vividly colored clothing and arresting jewelry, constantly sought out new talent. Among New Orleans artists she supported early in their careers were Mignon Faget, who went on to found a thriving jewelry business; Maurice Alvarado, a sculptor in glass; and John Scott, the Xavier University painter and sculptor who received a "genius grant" from the MacArthur Foundation in 1992.

She turned up regularly for openings, where she inspected art—and bought it—with the seasoned eye of a connoisseur.

At these gatherings, as well as inevitable fancy-dress parties, friends could always tell when Mrs. Norman was feeling at home: She tended to slip off her shoes as the evening wore on and pad about in her stocking feet. She did this wherever she went, even at a gala in the elegant Hall of Mirrors at Versailles.

The Normans collected paintings, pottery, sculpture, photography and furniture from all over the world. Among their holdings was a 1963 Larry Rivers portrait of Mrs. Norman that has been on view at the New Orleans Museum of Art. It is no ordinary portrait: The face is deliberately incomplete, and parts of her head—lip, hair, and eye, for instance—are labeled in French.

As Mrs. Norman moved through the art world, she met leading artists such as Rivers and prominent collectors such as the Rockefeller family. And she was a member of powerful committees at such renowned institutions as the Fogg Art Museum at Harvard, the National Gallery of Art in Washington, and the Museum of Modern Art in New York City.

She did not flaunt such associations, remarking simply: "People who are interested in art are a lot more fun."

As a result of the network she cultivated, "she could pick up the phone and call anybody," said Sharon Litwin, a close friend who was an assistant director of the New Orleans Museum of Art.

That was exactly what Mrs. Norman did when the New Orleans Museum of Art had been getting nowhere in its attempts to get the Fogg Museum to lend a picture by Edgar Degas for an exhibit of Degas' works in New Orleans. A telephone call from Mrs. Norman clinched the loan, said E. John Bullard, the museum's director then.

Born in Port Arthur, Texas, Mrs. Norman received her nickname at summer camp when she was 11 years old. "It seems that I had a wonderful disposition then," she said in a 1993 interview. "The kids called me 'Sunshine,' which was shortened, thank God, to 'Sunny.' It's a big responsibility, that name."

She graduated from Mills College in Oakland, Calif., with a degree in psychology. She moved to Morgan City in 1937, when she married Peter Roussel Norman, who had taken over the family lumber business after studying engineering at Cornell University.

While he designed a park and golf club and helped with flood control, Mrs. Norman became active in the city's cultural life. She formed a Community Concert Association and hired a professional recreation director to start a free summer program for children. The Normans' interest in art started when Mrs. Norman used the last $50 of her wedding money to buy her first paintings—five Charles Reinike watercolors—to decorate their home.

The works intrigued them, so the couple invited Reinike to Morgan City to give art lessons to them and a few friends.

Mrs. Norman's husband loved the classes and eventually turned to painting as a hobby, but she dropped out after one session.

Nevertheless, she was hooked on art. Both of them started reading up on the subject and, eventually, began to haunt galleries in New Orleans and New York City. He had a simple philosophy for learning about art: "Keep looking."

When they started collecting, Mrs. Norman said, they complemented each other: He relied on his eye; she relied on her gut.

"We looked at things separately," she said in a 1987 Arts Quarterly interview. "Roussel never could get over how I knew something was a good picture because I never saw what he saw. But only in two or three instances did we not agree."

Even though they owned pieces by such celebrated and high-priced artists as Paul Gauguin, Pablo Picasso, Mary Cassatt, and Georgia O'Keeffe, they never regarded their purchases as investments. They never thought they were building a collection, and, she said, didn't philosophize about art.

Art should be fun, Mrs. Norman said. It was a belief expressed in her gift of "Lipizzaner," an abstract horse for children to climb on in front of the New Orleans Museum of Art. When the museum expanded in the early 1990s, she and her sister-in-law, Bernice Norman, financed a gallery in the new wing named for their husbands, who were brothers.

Although art was her special love, Mrs. Norman supported many charitable causes, including public schools, Xavier and Dillard universities, and the American Cancer Society.

"She hardly turned anybody down," Litwin said.

Frequently, Fagaly said, the museum turned to her when it needed money for a particular undertaking. She would give the money, but often insisted on anonymity.

Such generosity was so frequent, Litwin said, that everyone knew who was behind gifts labeled "anonymous." "We call her 'Mrs. Anonymous' at the museum," Fagaly said.

— *January 29, 2006*

Haydel White Sr.

He was a Tuskegee Airman

Haydel Joseph White Sr., a member of the groundbreaking Tuskegee Airmen during World War II, died Saturday, his 85th birthday, at West Jefferson Medical Center of complications from a stroke.

Mr. White, who was born in Wallace, La., and grew up in New Orleans, earned a business degree from Xavier University.

He enlisted in the Army Air Corps shortly after the United States entered World War II and was assigned to Tuskegee Army Air Field in Alabama, where the first African-American airmen were trained.

Mr. White became a captain and spent most of the war there, said his daughter, Wendy Adcock. His bomber squadron was scheduled to fly out to Europe, but the war there ended before the men could depart.

Even though the Tuskegee Airmen were members of an elite corps on their base, they were subject to Jim Crow laws whenever they traveled. On trains, they were relegated to boxcars, Adcock said.

In March 1945, Mr. White participated in what became known as the Freeman Field Mutiny in Indiana. In that incident, 162 black officers defied their commanders and entered the whites-only officers' club instead of going to the facility that had been set aside for them—a rundown building that had housed the club for noncommissioned officers.

They were arrested, but charges were dropped against Mr. White and nearly all of the other officers. He received an honorable discharge in 1946.

After the war, Mr. White worked for the Schenley Corp. and Pepsi-Cola, which sent him to Nigeria, where he opened the country's first Pepsi plant, Adcock said.

When Mr. White returned to New Orleans, he became a longshoreman and was one of the first to integrate the Clerks and Checkers Union. He retired in the early 1980s.

— September 8, 2006

Edward "Bud Rip" Ripoll

A saloonkeeper and fixture of downtown New Orleans

Edward "Bud Rip" Ripoll Jr., an ebullient son of the 9th Ward whose bar bearing his nickname became a cornerstone of life in downtown New Orleans, died Sunday at NorthShore Regional Medical Center. He was 82.

Mr. Ripoll, who frequently sang behind the bar he tended 12 hours a day, was everybody's pal, friends and relatives said.

He played host to politicians seeking office—their framed pictures lined the walls—and he even served a term in the state House of Representatives. He welcomed people who wanted to hoist a few as they bewailed the Saints' misfortunes on the gridiron, and he even bought a round for the women who had been picketing the bar at Burgundy and Piety streets.

That protest occurred more than 30 years ago because Mr. Ripoll didn't admit women, saying he wanted to spare them from offensive language.

But he was, above all, a good host, so he invited them inside. When one asked to use the restroom, he said, "If you can do it in a urinal, be my guest," said Leslie Falgout, Mr. Ripoll's son-in-law.

Mr. Ripoll acquired his nickname in childhood from a relative everyone called Uncle Pauper, said Bonnie Ripoll-Falgout, Mr. Ripoll's daughter. "He told my daddy years ago, 'Bud Rip, will you ever amount to anything?'" Ripoll-Falgout said. "Obviously, he did."

A graduate of Francis T. Nicholls High School who was a Marine during World War II, Mr. Ripoll was a longshoreman and steel worker before signing on at Huerstel's, another 9th Ward institution.

He stayed there until 1960, when his mother-in-law lent him the money to buy the bar "because she'd know which barroom he was in," Ripoll-Falgout said.

But friends and family members said there was more to Mr. Ripoll than pouring drinks and hobnobbing with politicians.

He was a charter member of the Downtown Irish Club, which stages an annual St. Patrick's parade that winds through the 9th Ward, and he sponsored an American Legion baseball team. To pay for repairs to St. Vincent de Paul Catholic Church, Mr. Ripoll organized a golf tournament that became a yearly ritual. Once the church work was done, money from the tournament went to families of police officers killed in the line of duty during the preceding year, Ripoll-Falgout said.

And every December, he collected money from local bars to pay for Christmas baskets of food for needy 9th Ward residents. "There were cans of food and a turkey in each one," Ripoll-Falgout said. "But he sent around friends first to make sure the people were really needy."

He also had a series of unsuccessful political races, one for the 1st City Court clerkship and three times for the state Legislature.

On his fourth attempt, in 1983, Mr. Ripoll, a conservative Republican, won. His explanation was simple: In previous races, he was listed on the ballot as Edward Conrad Ripoll Jr., but before his 1983 campaign, he had his name legally changed to Edward "Bud Rip" Ripoll Jr.

Even though Mr. Ripoll was the only member of his political party to accompany Gov. Edwin Edwards on his gala $10,000-per-person 1984 trip to France to retire his gubernatorial campaign debts, one of Mr. Ripoll's first votes was against a tax bill Edwards favored.

When the governor asked why he voted that way, he replied: "It took me 16 years to become a representative. I'm not going to vote for the first tax bill that comes up."

Some of his more creative legislation fared poorly. One bill would have imposed a tax on the paper used to roll marijuana cigarettes. Even though marijuana was illegal and, therefore, untaxable, "my daddy decided we can at least get money off the paper," Ripoll-Falgout said. "It didn't pass."

Another bill was the flip side of laws banning bars within 300 feet of a house of worship. Mr. Ripoll's bill would have prohibited the leasing or construction of a church or synagogue within 300 feet of a tavern.

Even though Mr. Ripoll said the measure was designed to eliminate "a fly-by-night church" in his district, opposition was swift and fierce, and Mr. Ripoll asked that it be deferred. "I don't want people to think I'm in favor of gambling and beer and against God," he said.

That was in 1987. Later that year, he lost his bid for re-election, and he went back to tending bar.

He and his family moved to Arabi in adjoining St. Bernard Parish in 1994, and he sold Bud Rip's in 1996 to Linda and Kenneth "Turtle" Kennair. The bar's name stayed.

Mr. Ripoll and his family fled St. Bernard Parish before Hurricane Katrina and its catastrophic flooding hit in August 2005, and they wound up across Lake Pontchartrain in St. Tammany Parish.

By that time, he was in declining health from a variety of illnesses, but he marched in this year's Downtown Irish Club parade, "much to my chagrin," his daughter said.

"He had a walker," she said, "and there were police all around him to make sure he didn't fall. He walked four blocks to Markey's Bar, and he walked back, too. Now I'm thrilled that he did it. At the time, I was a nervous wreck."

Shortly after her father died, Ripoll-Falgout returned to Bud Rip's. At the corner spot where Mr. Ripoll always liked to sit, she found an open bottle of beer on a napkin.

"The little barmaid would not let anybody sit there," Ripoll-Falgout said. "I said, 'Who's sitting there?' and she said, 'You know who's sitting there.' I knew before she said it. I was so touched."

The beer, incidentally, was a Budweiser. "What else is Bud Rip going to drink?" she said.

Mr. Ripoll's ashes were put in a brass urn inscribed with his nickname, the years of his birth and death, and these words: "This Bud's for You."

— September 22, 2006

Albert Aschaffenburg

He was a suave hotelier to the stars

Albert Aschaffenburg, who ran the Pontchartrain Hotel when it was an elegant home away from home for the likes of Mary Martin, Richard Burton, and Carol Channing, died Tuesday at Ochsner Medical Center. He was 87.

A lifelong New Orleanian whose father, E. Lysle Aschaffenburg, opened the Pontchartrain in 1927, Albert Aschaffenburg became president in 1968 of the corporation that ran the St. Charles Avenue hotel. He held that position until the hotel was sold in 1987.

The Aschaffenburg family positioned the hotel as a luxurious realm where guests would be pampered and elegant food would be served up in the award-winning Caribbean Room. Among its famous dishes was the mile-high pie, a dessert that got its name from a daunting tower of meringue.

"He certainly knew how to take care of people when they were in his hotel," said Marilyn Barnett, a longtime friend. "In those days, the words used all the time were 'personal service' and 'gratifying service,' and the Pontchartrain gave it."

"He was a representative of the old school of innkeeping, when the guest was the most important thing," said Ronald Pincus, the Hotel Monteleone's vice president and chief operating officer. "He was a gentleman in the truest sense of the word, which is a rarity in this day and age."

With his rich, resonant voice and his suave, stately bearing, Mr. Aschaffenburg exuded the feeling that the hotel conveyed, friends said.

"He had a flair for theatrics," said Bill Langkopp, executive vice president of the Greater New Orleans Hotel and Lodging Association. "If Mr. Albert hadn't been a grand hotelier, he would have been a grand Broadway star."

He put that talent to use, not only when he acted in local theatrical productions but also in the mid-1990s, when he reinvented himself as a part-
time speech teacher at the University of New Orleans.

"That was an incredibly perfect segue," Langkopp said.

Mr. Aschaffenburg was no stranger to the subject because he had earned
a degree from Cornell University in speech communication, said Kevin
Graves, associate dean of UNO's College of Liberal Arts.

Besides, Graves said, "there was a tremendous melody about his voice
that was captivating. . . . What better way to teach students than with the
style of one's own voice?"

Even though Mr. Aschaffenburg was approaching 60 and had never
taught, he was a natural in the classroom.

"He just took to teaching like a duck takes to water," said Graves, who
was chairman of the department in which Mr. Aschaffenburg worked.

Mr. Aschaffenburg taught until last year. Throughout that time, no student ever complained about him, Graves said.

"He had amazing people skills that were, no doubt, the result of his years
in the hotel business that translated to the classroom in an amazing fashion,"
Graves said. "He was beginning his teaching career at a time when many
had long since retired, but he did so with the energy of a 25- or 30-year-old
and would just blow me away."

He served in the Army Air Corps in World War II. He remained in the
Air Force Reserve after the war, retiring as a lieutenant colonel. Mr. Aschaffenburg was fond of corgis and tennis and was a former president of
the Louisiana Hotel-Motel Association.

— June 28, 2007

Harry Tervalon

A waffle-wielding waiter and lifelong Yankees fan

Harry Tervalon, who served up a nonstop patter of corny jokes and commentary about the New York Yankees along with omelets, waffles and pecan pies during a half-century as a waiter at the Camellia Grill, died Thursday of cancer at his New Orleans home. He was 87.

Mr. Tervalon, who was working behind the counter when the white-columned Carrollton Avenue landmark opened in December 1946, retired in 1996, but he kept returning every week to greet customers and hold court, said his son, Harry Tervalon Jr.

When the diner reopened in April 2007 after Hurricane Katrina-related damage was repaired, Mr. Tervalon was on hand for the ribbon-cutting, and he was a regular visitor for the next two months, said Rania Khodr, the owner's wife.

"He was a very sweet guy," she said. "We sat on the porch, and he was signing posters. Ladies would say they drove two hours just to have a picture made with him or have a poster that he signed."

A black mourning ribbon hung on the Camellia Grill's door Friday.

For generations of customers, Mr. Tervalon, also known as "Harry the Waiter," was the embodiment of the Camellia Grill, where people regularly line up to sit on 29 stools and tidy up with white linen napkins.

Mr. Tervalon remembered everyone's name and what regular customers liked, even down to the particular mixture of sugar and cream they wanted in their coffee, the younger Tervalon said.

People remembered him, all over town.

"My father could not walk a block without being stopped," Tervalon said. "In stores, people greeted him.

"Talk about a guy who didn't have a formal education and wasn't a power broker. Doors opened to him all over the city."

Mayors and City Council members were among his regular customers, as were former Gov. Edwin Edwards and the rackets figure Carlos Marcello.

"Once, my father was outside talking to Carlos Marcello, and Carlos kissed him," Tervalon said. "When my father came back inside, he said, 'I hope that wasn't the kiss of death.'"

Another customer who became a chum was Billy Martin, the mercurial manager of Mr. Tervalon's beloved Yankees.

Mr. Tervalon's infatuation with the Yankees began in 1927, when he was a child in the Treme neighborhood and Babe Ruth and Lou Gehrig were part of the formidable Yankee lineup known as Murderers' Row.

One of Mr. Tervalon's most cherished childhood memories was a 1939 talk with Gehrig in the dugout at Pelican Stadium. Less than two years later, Gehrig would die of the degenerative disease that bears his name.

Mr. Tervalon avidly followed the Yankees' fortunes, and he became a font of information and opinions about the team—year by year, game by game and even player by player.

For Father's Day in 1977, his wife gave him a pair of original seats from Yankee Stadium that had been salvaged when the stadium was renovated a few years earlier. Mr. Tervalon named them Ruth and Gehrig and called them "the greatest gift I've ever gotten."

They were washed away in the flood that accompanied Hurricane Katrina, his son said.

Mr. Tervalon's devotion to the Yankees continued undiminished. During baseball season, friends knew that there was only one thing on his mind.

At the Camellia Grill reopening, when a friend talked about what a great day it was for New Orleans, this was Mr. Tervalon's reply: "Can you believe (Alex Rodriguez) hit two home runs last night and the Yankees still lost?"

— *August 25, 2007*

Iler Pope

A restaurateur who served up Southern lore

Iler Pope, a New Orleans restaurateur who regaled customers with tales of her Mississippi childhood while they dined on specialties such as chicken and dumplings, jalapeño corn bread, and banana pudding, died Thursday in her sleep in her Baton Rouge home. She was 68.

Ms. Pope, who had been treated for chronic obstructive pulmonary disease, had lived in Baton Rouge since 2004.

She was a fixture on the New Orleans restaurant scene for a quarter-century, starting with Dante-by-the-River in the Riverbend neighborhood in 1977 and, across the street, Dante Street Deli.

Ms. Pope sold them in 1986 and moved to Mississippi. In 1991, she returned to New Orleans to operate Cafe Atchafalaya on Louisiana Avenue, offering what she called "rather Southern" items in which she blended aspects of Southern and Creole cooking.

The menu included chicken livers with pepper jelly, turnip casserole, gumbo, corn fritters, butterbeans, and cobbler with homemade buttermilk ice cream.

She operated it until 2004. In a 1992 review, Gene Bourg, the *Times-Picayune*'s restaurant critic, said it provided "a reminder of the kinship between New Orleans' everyday traditional cooking and that of the rest of the Deep South."

Ms. Pope was fussy about food. When she started offering fried green tomatoes, before the 1990 movie of that name made them popular, Ms. Pope complained at length about the difficulty of getting just the right kind of green tomato.

She loved to discuss the relative merits of different kinds of greens, and she was proud of the variations she could make on basic Southern cuisine, said Ti Adelaide Martin, a longtime friend who is one of the owners of Commander's Palace restaurant.

"She talked of food like it was a member of her family," Martin said.

Customers doted on her. One couple drove over regularly from Mobile, Ala., for her lamb chops, and one customer faithfully brought bushel baskets of figs to her every year so she could make fig ice cream.

Although she was a tough boss, her staffs loved her—and valued their time in her restaurants.

"She was vital to my growth as a restaurateur," said Richard Hughes, owner of the Pelican Club, who worked at Dante-by-the-River. "She let me take as much responsibility as I could.

By the time he opened his own establishment, after years of watching Ms. Pope, "I realized I knew a lot," Hughes said.

Although Ms. Pope regularly wore jeans and possessed a vocabulary that could peel paint off a wall, she was, unmistakably, a Southern lady.

She spoke in a thick, honeyed drawl made husky by decades of cigarette smoking, and she turned up her nose at any woman who dared to wear white shoes before Memorial Day or after Labor Day.

Although Ms. Pope traded on informality, greeting regulars with hugs, women of a certain age were always addressed with a "Miss" before their first names. Once when a customer entered bearing a camellia from her garden, Ms. Pope knew exactly what to do: She fetched a finger bowl and filled it with water so the blossom could float at the table.

Born Iler Ann Bounds in the Mississippi Delta, Ms. Pope grew up in an environment that sounded like a creation of Eudora Welty. Her family was proudly self-sufficient, so much so that when she went to the grocery store at a tender age, she returned home wide-eyed with this announcement: "Mama! You can buy mayonnaise!"

When she was 10 years old, Ms. Pope regularly drove her grandmother, a matron known as Miss Nett, around her hometown of Drew and even to Memphis, Tenn., even though she was barely tall enough to see over the steering wheel.

Miss Nett was a redoubtable woman, with an answer for every question. Once, Ms. Pope said, this was Miss Nett's reply when she was asked for her telephone number: "I don't know. I never call myself."

Her mother was a restaurant cook, and Ms. Pope cooked briefly in her youth. But by the time she got married, she said, she had gotten so rusty that her mother hired a woman to teach her. It took two years.

After cooking for her family for years, Ms. Pope decided she could make a living by cooking for others.

"Monumental ego" fueled her entry into the restaurant field, she said in a 2001 interview. "You think you can do it better than anyone else, so you decide to open a restaurant and prove it."

— *December 1, 2007*

Warren McDaniels

Patriarch of the family of firefighters

Warren McDaniels, a high school dropout who took advantage of what he called "a second chance at life" and rose to become New Orleans' first black fire superintendent, died Sunday of cancer at River Region Hospice. He was 63.

"We consider ourselves family, and he was the patriarch of the family," said Charles Parent, Mr. McDaniels' successor.

Parent, who said he regarded his predecessor as a mentor, credited Mr. McDaniels with modernizing the department with achievements that included instituting the first-responder program, in which firefighters are trained to provide medical care because, Parent said, they are often the first to arrive at a disaster.

Mayor Sidney Barthelemy appointed Mr. McDaniels to lead the Fire Department in April 1993. He closed out a 33-year career with the department when he retired at the end of 2002.

Unlike many firefighters who grew up dreaming of battling blazes, Mr. McDaniels said he harbored no such ambitions because when he was growing up in the Lower 9th Ward, there were no black firefighters.

"I worked delivering sandwiches across from one of the firehouses," he said in a 1999 interview. "I wasn't even allowed inside. I never aspired to be a firefighter because I couldn't."

Mr. McDaniels, whose grandmother reared him, dropped out of George Washington Carver High School after his sophomore year. He worked odd jobs and served three years in the Navy.

Eight years after leaving school, Mr. McDaniels enrolled in an adult-education program to learn how to drive 18-wheelers. That program gave him the chance to take a test for the General Equivalency Diploma, which, in turn, let him take the test to join the Fire Department.

180

Because of where that test led him, Mr. McDaniels later called the GED "a second chance at life."

In 1999, he was one of 14 recipients of the Cornelius P. Turner Award from the National Association of Educators. The honor is given annually to GED graduates who have made outstanding achievements in education and community service.

Encouraged by George Oliver Mondy Jr., a friend and mentor who was New Orleans' first black firefighter, Mr. McDaniels joined the department in 1969. He earned an associate's degree in fire prevention from Delgado Community College and graduated from the National Fire Academy in Emmitsburg, Md.

Although he joined as a firefighter, Mr. McDaniels moved up during the next 24 years to operator, captain, training captain, deputy superintendent for administration, assistant superintendent and, finally, superintendent.

Others noticed his achievements. In 1992, a year before Mr. McDaniels was named superintendent, he was one of six fire officers nationwide to get a fellowship to study at Harvard's John F. Kennedy School of Government.

"The chief has paid his dues," said Gene Blaum, who worked with him twice: when Blaum was manager of the New Orleans Cultural Center and when both men were on the board of the New Orleans Jazz and Heritage Foundation.

In April 2002, Mr. McDaniels was named metropolitan fire chief of the year by the Metropolitan Fire Chiefs, an organization that includes fire chiefs from the United States, Canada, Europe, Australia, New Zealand, Asia, and the United Kingdom.

In an interview when he retired, Mr. McDaniels said it wasn't the big fires he remembered most, but a series of fires in garbage containers that he and his colleagues put out.

One night, after extinguishing one such blaze, Mr. McDaniels said a woman carrying a baby approached him and his colleagues to thank them and added, "My baby has asthma, and the smoke was choking her."

"That, to me, epitomizes what service is all about," he said. "Service is so much more important than personal success, and people are so much more important than possessions."

— February 26, 2008

Al Copeland

He built his empire with spicy fried chicken

A l Copeland, a hard-charging, high-living entrepreneur who built an empire on spicy fried chicken and fluffy white biscuits, died Sunday in Munich, Germany, of complications from cancer treatment. He was 64.

He had gone to Munich for treatment of his illness, which had been diagnosed in November, said Kit Wohl, his spokeswoman.

Born in poverty, Mr. Copeland burst onto the scene in 1972, when he opened his first Popeyes fried-chicken stand. The Arabi, La., restaurant was the start of a franchise that, under his leadership, had 700 outlets, in the United States, Puerto Rico, Panama, and Kuwait.

The money he earned led to public displays of opulence such as speedboats kept in a glass-walled showroom along Interstate 10 when he wasn't racing them, a Lamborghini sports car parked outside his corporate headquarters, and massive Christmas displays that required sheriff's deputies to direct the traffic outside his suburban home in Metairie.

There also were over-the-top weddings with such touches as fireworks and a model of Cinderella's pumpkin coach.

These marriages ended in equally spectacular divorces. The divorce proceedings from his third wife wound up bringing down the original judge hearing the case as part of a massive federal investigation of courthouse corruption.

During Carnival, Mr. Copeland not only sponsored parade floats in suburban Jefferson Parish but also rode, said Peter Ricchiuti, a Tulane University finance professor who saw Mr. Copeland in one such procession.

Ricchiuti said he overheard this exchange between two other spectators: One man dismissed the spectacle as an indication of new money, but the other man replied, "If I had money, that's what I'd do."

Not even bankruptcy, the result of buying Church's Fried Chicken Inc., stopped him. Although Mr. Copeland lost ownership of his chicken outlets, he retained control of the company making the distinctive spice mixture, and he went on to open restaurants bearing his surname, as well as establishments featuring California cuisine, wrap sandwiches, cheesecake, and Asian fare.

One such restaurant, Straya on St. Charles Avenue, triggered a noisy public feud in 1997 with the novelist Anne Rice. She used her voice-mail message and a series of full-page advertisements in the *Times-Picayune* to attack the restaurant's decor, which included tasseled black curtains and a pair of sleek black-leopard sculptures flanking the entrance to the rest-room area.

"The humblest flop house on this strip of St. Charles Avenue has more dignity than Mr. Copeland's structure," she said in her opening salvo.

One reason she felt so passionately about the building at 2001 St. Charles Avenue was that she said that the Vampire Lestat, her dominant character, left her there, before Straya opened, after seeing his reflection in the window of what had been a Mercedes-Benz dealership.

Rice also said she had planned to open a restaurant, Café Lestat, in a Magazine Street building she owned, but that never materialized.

Mr. Copeland's response, also in a full-page ad in the *Times-Picayune*, was good-humored, offering to treat her to dinner and to help her find Lestat. He even spoke of launching a month-long "Find Lestat" promotion and dressing his staff like vampires.

But he also filed suit, claiming that she had defamed him and that she violated fair-trade laws because "her comments were made in the context of her being a business competitor," Mr. Copeland's lawyer said.

Civil District Judge Robin Giarrusso threw out the suit. Mr. Copeland, accepting defeat, invited Rice to dinner. Rice, who did not accept his offer, moved to California in 2004, settling in Rancho Mirage after brief stints in San Diego and La Jolla.

Straya, a phonetic spelling of "strella," the Spanish word for star, became a Cheesecake Bistro.

This wasn't Mr. Copeland's only high-profile skirmish. In December 2001, he got into a fist fight with Robert Guidry, a former casino owner, and his sons in Morton's The Steakhouse, an upscale restaurant.

The two multimillionaires had been rivals for a riverboat-casino license in 1993. Mr. Copeland lost, and he blamed Guidry. Guidry, who had built much of his fortune on tugboats, contended Mr. Copeland had relied on connections to delay his hearing for the license.

Guidry eventually won the license with the help of then-Gov. Edwin Edwards, but only after paying an Edwards aide $100,000 a month, amounting to more than $1 million.

Guidry, who pleaded guilty to an extortion conspiracy and was a key prosecution witness against Edwards, was sentenced in January 2001 to three years' probation and ordered to pay $3.5 million in a fine and restitution.

Each man accused the other of starting the brawl, in which Mr. Copeland suffered a blow to his left cheek. Guidry and two of his sons spent the night in jail. No charges were filed, and customers requested the Copeland and Guidry tables for months after the fight.

With Mr. Copeland that night was Jennifer Devall Copeland, his fourth wife. They had gone to the restaurant to celebrate their first anniversary.

According to papers filed in 2007, when she and Mr. Copeland were divorced, his net worth in 2004 was about $319 million and his annual income was about $13 million.

The weekend before Thanksgiving 2007, Mr. Copeland learned he had cancer of the salivary glands, a rare form of the disease that strikes no more than three people per 100,000 annually in the United States, according to the American Cancer Society.

Despite his illness and subsequent hospitalization, the Christmas display outside his house in an upscale Metairie neighborhood went on as scheduled, featuring thousands of lights, animated figures, and house-size representations of a teddy bear and Raggedy Ann.

Mr. Copeland was "a classic entrepreneur," Ricchiuti said. "He had disappointments, things that didn't work out, but that didn't stop him. You can't teach that in a business school. It's something inside you. Maybe it comes from a tremendous desire to succeed against all odds."

Copeland, whose family lived for a while in the St. Thomas public-housing complex, never finished high school.

He told friends that the competitive spark hit him when he was working the beverage counter at a local supermarket. A co-worker never stopped drumming up business. When Mr. Copeland asked why, the young man replied, "I'm out to prove I'm better than everybody," said Wohl, who also is a local author and artist.

When he was 18, Mr. Copeland sold his car to get capital to buy a doughnut shop from his brother Gilbert, and he turned the shop into a moneymaker.

Then he watched what happened when a Kentucky Fried Chicken outlet opened nearby. Inspired by the amount of business the store did, Mr.

Copeland decided to start frying chicken. After two years of testing recipes on friends and family, he opened Chicken on the Run in Arabi in 1971. Its slogan was "So fast you get your chicken before you get your change," and Mr. Copeland stood on the median handing out fliers.

But the fledgling business struggled—perhaps, Wohl said, because Mr. Copeland was flavoring it with a mild recipe after friends had told him that the spicy version he had prepared just wouldn't sell.

Realizing that bland fried chicken was going nowhere, Mr. Copeland started using the spicy recipe.

To show that he was operating a new enterprise, he decided to change its name. According to corporate lore, he was stumped until he saw *The French Connection*, in which Gene Hackman won an Oscar for his portrayal of Jimmy "Popeye" Doyle, a brusque, no-nonsense New York City police officer.

At that point, Mr. Copeland knew the business had a name: Popeyes Mighty Good Fried Chicken.

There is no apostrophe in the name, Mr. Copeland often joked, because he was too poor to afford one.

In an industry known for its high mortality rate, the restaurant started turning a profit in three weeks. Because business was so brisk, he added "Famous" to the title, Wohl said. The biscuits came later to the outlets, and to the corporate name, after Mr. Copeland worked with the chefs Warren Leruth and Gary Darling to devise a recipe.

The Popeyes craze was on, fueled by a popular jingle, "Love That Chicken From Popeyes," that Dr. John sang. In 1977, franchising began, and within a decade Popeyes was the third-largest fast-food chicken chain in the country, behind KFC and Church's.

Along the way, Mr. Copeland was married twice—the first time to Mary Alice LeCompte, his childhood sweetheart, and the second time to Patty White. Both marriages ended in divorce, and the first Mrs. Copeland died in 1995.

As he built his business, Mr. Copeland developed his public persona, and he was elevated to the status of a local icon. He was a man who could be counted on to show up in a flashy car wearing flashy, usually black, clothes and looking perpetually tanned and youthful, generally sporting an earring or two.

His 50-foot powerboats roared around Lake Pontchartrain, and when he raced in the United States and abroad, he met such luminaries as the deposed King Constantine of Greece, Princess Caroline of Monaco, Donald Trump, and the actors Chuck Norris, Kurt Russell, and Don Johnson.

Besides winning a shelf full of trophies, Mr. Copeland set up the Off-shore Professional Tour, a charitable fundraiser that became a star-studded event.

Mr. Copeland became what he called a "secret Santa," underwriting gifts for 1,000 needy children that Santa Claus delivered after dark on Christmas Eve. And the man who never finished high school established the Alvin C. Copeland Endowed Chair of Franchising at Louisiana State University.

Mr. Copeland's money also supported the National Food Service Institute and Delgado Community College's apprentice program for aspiring chefs.

Some of his wealth went to set up a Christmas display in his front yard that grew bigger each year—and generated so much traffic that his neighbors sued in 1983 to have it removed. They also groused about his annual party for hundreds of guests featuring a vast menu and a dance floor over the indoor swimming pool.

The outdoor spectacle was staged elsewhere around East Jefferson Parish until 1991, when a scaled-down version returned to Mr. Copeland's home.

Coincidentally, 1991 was the year in which Mr. Copeland's business audacity seemed to catch up with him. In 1988, he made a $296 million bid to buy Church's. The next year, the firm agreed to be bought out for $392 million. But to finance it, Mr. Copeland had to borrow about $450 million from a group of lending institutions.

In November 1990, Al Copeland Enterprises, the umbrella organization for Mr. Copeland's activities, said that it was in default on $391 million in debts and that it would be bankrupt if a lender demanded payment. In September that year, it had failed to make payments totaling $7.5 million. The banks that had lent money for the Church's deal filed an involuntary Chapter 11 petition, putting Copeland Enterprises into bankruptcy.

But while Mr. Copeland relinquished control of his fried-chicken enterprise, he kept control of the spice supply, a move Ricchiuti regarded as brilliant.

"He was dealing with some of the smartest bankers in the world, and he knew what to keep," Ricchiuti said. "It might look like an insignificant component, but he outfoxed some pretty smart people."

The bankruptcy filing came two months after his blockbuster nighttime wedding to Luan Hunter on Valentine's Day in the New Orleans Museum of Art. Fireworks, including the display "Al I'll love you forever Luan" lit up the sky, and the Popeyes helicopter, known as the chicken chopper, hovered low enough to scatter rose petals—and blow up a mini-dust storm.

That marriage, which actually had begun with a Las Vegas ceremony nearly four months before the museum extravaganza, lasted nine years and ended in a bitter custody fight over their son, Alex.

Overshadowing that, though, was the guilty plea of Ronald Bodenheimer, the original judge presiding over the case, to charges that he promised a custody deal favorable to Mr. Copeland in return for a possible seafood contract and other benefits. As a result of a federal inquiry called Operation Wrinkled Robe, Bodenheimer and two of Mr. Copeland's associates went to jail for participating in the conspiracy.

Bodenheimer served slightly more than three years at a low-security prison camp in Alabama. After serving time in a halfway house and home confinement at his Metairie house, he was put on three years' probation.

Mr. Copeland was never charged. Even though that union ended messily, Mr. Copeland headed down the aisle one more time, in December 2000, to marry Jennifer Devall.

The aisle was in St. Louis Cathedral, a fact that set tongues wagging about the propriety of such an event for the repeatedly divorced Mr. Copeland. However, an archdiocesan spokesman pointed out that the ceremony respected canonical rule because only one of Mr. Copeland's weddings— his first—occurred in a church, and his wife from that wedding had died, thereby dissolving what the Catholic Church regards as a lifelong marriage bond.

The wedding had a fairy-tale beginning, with the newlyweds arriving for the reception at Mr. Copeland's house in a horse-drawn pumpkin coach and walking beneath a line of crossed sabers held aloft by people dressed like wooden soldiers.

Despite that sparkling launch, this marriage, too, dissolved into acrimony. Mr. Copeland was arrested on a domestic-violence charge, and, in court papers filed in the divorce, his wife admitted to an extramarital affair. The divorce was granted in 2007.

Mr. Copeland stayed busy. In addition to restaurants, he had invested in three comedy clubs and three hotels. At his death, Wohl said, a menu for a Brazilian-style restaurant was being tested in two Midwestern cities.

That relentless activity was typical of him, Ricchiuti said.

"Once he made it, it was never enough," he said. "Most people get to a certain comfort level, but that didn't appeal to him at all."

— *March 24, 2008*

Revius Ortique Jr.

His life was a succession of firsts

Revius Ortique Jr., a civil rights lawyer who became the first African-American justice elected to the Louisiana Supreme Court, died Sunday in Baton Rouge from complications of a stroke. He was 84.

Justice Ortique had been a lifelong New Orleanian until he and his wife, Miriam Marie Victorianne Ortique, moved to Baton Rouge after Hurricane Katrina ruined their home.

Ortique's life in the legal profession had been a succession of firsts. He was the first black member of the Louisiana State Bar Association's policymaking organization, the House of Delegates, and was not only the first African-American Civil District Court judge but also the first black chief judge of that court. And in his crowning achievement, Justice Ortique was the first African American to win an election to the state Supreme Court.

Elected in 1992, he had to step down in June 1994 when he turned 70, the mandatory judicial retirement age.

But his public career wasn't over. Sixteen days later, Mayor Marc Morial appointed him to the New Orleans Aviation Board. He became its chairman two months later and held that post for eight years.

In addition to his local activities, Justice Ortique was president of the National Bar Association, an organization of African-American lawyers, and five presidents appointed him to commissions and councils, including one panel that investigated the killings at Kent State University and Jackson State College, now Jackson State University, in 1970.

"I am humbled and forever appreciative of your sacrifice, hard work and high standards of integrity," Morial wrote to Justice Ortique when he left the Aviation Board in 2004.

In everything he did, Justice Ortique was "a hard-working man, very disciplined, very focused on the task at hand," said Ronald Burns, a protégé and longtime friend.

Revius Oliver Ortique Jr. was born in New Orleans and served four years as an Army officer during World War II, when he was deployed to the Pacific theater.

A year after returning to New Orleans in 1946, he earned a bachelor's degree at Dillard University. At Indiana University he earned a master's degree in criminology by studying the criminal-justice system in the South.

When Mr. Ortique returned to Louisiana, he earned a law degree in 1956 at Southern University.

Mr. Ortique, who set up a private practice as the civil rights movement was gathering steam, was part of a generation that possessed "a desire to bring about change," said Sybil Morial, a friend for more than a half-century.

In his profession, Mr. Ortique channeled that desire into work on the legal teams in several suits that resulted in equal pay for black employees at companies such as the Celotex Corp. and Kaiser Aluminum.

Although Mr. Ortique was squaring off against big companies while African Americans frequently were regarded as second-class citizens, "he didn't have a problem fighting big cases," said Burns, whose mother was Mr. Ortique's secretary.

"He was on the forefront of a lot of issues relating to civil rights," Burns said. "I think he was well-prepared. He was fearless. Back in those days, when an African-American attorney represented a client, you'd have the deck stacked against you, but he worked pretty hard."

His preparation was meticulous, but his friends said that was no surprise. Burns, who cleaned Mr. Ortique's law office, recalled getting down on his hands and knees to clean grout by scrubbing with a toothbrush because, he said, Mr. Ortique wanted everything just so.

"It taught a good lesson," Burns said. "You do things the right way all the time, and make sure it's done to perfection."

Mr. Ortique's zeal for change wasn't limited to his work. In 1958, he was elected to the first of five terms he served as president of the Urban League of Greater New Orleans. A year later, he was elected president of the National Bar Association, and he served three terms as president of the Community Relations Council, a biracial group formed to promote racial harmony.

As a result of such activities, "he had integrity beyond reproach," Sybil Morial said. "He had a foot in both camps."

Therefore, she said, Mr. Ortique was the ideal choice to be a negotiator for the black community in discussions with white civic leaders on topics such as jobs in major stores and peaceful desegregation of lunch counters, bathrooms and other public facilities in the early 1960s, before access to such places was guaranteed by the landmark Civil Rights Act of 1964.

The talks, which helped end an African-American boycott of major stores, were set up because nobody wanted people in either community to resort to violence, Morial said.

In these sessions, Mr. Ortique's natural low-key, courtly manner was a major asset, she said.

"He never raised his voice," Middleberg said, describing Mr. Ortique's style. "You never heard a foul word out of his mouth. He was always a gentleman. He'd get upset over issues, but he never raised his voice. He never lost control of the situation."

In the mid-1960s, when Mr. Ortique led the National Bar Association, he lobbied President Lyndon B. Johnson to appoint African Americans to the federal bench.

So a White House meeting was set up. Before it started, Johnson announced the appointment of eight African-Americans to judgeships. And during that session, Johnson announced that he was going to nominate Thurgood Marshall, a major civil rights lawyer, to be the first black justice on the U.S. Supreme Court.

In 1993, Justice Ortique represented Louisiana at Marshall's funeral.

Seeking a judgeship of his own, Mr. Ortique ran in 1972 for a seat on the state Supreme Court, but he placed third in a race that Pascal Calogero won. In 1978, the state's highest court appointed him to a seat on the Civil District bench to complete the term of Adrian Duplantier because President Carter had appointed him to a federal district judgeship.

That lasted six months. In 1979, he was elected to fill out the term of Oliver Carriere, who was retiring. He was re-elected, without opposition, in 1984, and he was elected chief judge two years later.

During his tenure on the New Orleans Aviation Board, five additional airlines set up shop at New Orleans International Airport, and an $850 million rebuilding, renovation and expansion program was begun. Justice Ortique also was instrumental in getting the airport named for the jazz immortal Louis Armstrong.

In keeping with his belief in fair play, Justice Ortique held a luncheon for the airport's labor force because, Middleberg said, "there were always luncheons for executives."

But his sense of decorum never wavered. When one man entered wearing a cap, Middleberg said, Justice Ortique asked him to remove it because ladies were present. When he refused, Justice Ortique asked him to leave.

"He was always a gentleman," Middleberg said.

— June 23, 2008

Francis Fitzpatrick

She tracked U-boats in the Gulf of Mexico

Francis Fitzpatrick, a member of a top-secret World War II team in New Orleans that tracked German submarine activity in the Gulf of Mexico, died July 30 in her home at Ware Neck, Va. She was 92.

Mrs. Fitzpatrick, whose husband won a 1951 Pulitzer Prize for his editorials for the *New Orleans States*, was born Francis James Gasquet Westfeldt in August 1915 in Fletcher, N.C., where her parents had a home to escape the New Orleans heat. The family, hoping for a boy, had decided before she was born to name her for a great-uncle.

She attended the Louise S. McGehee School and Newcomb College. In 1936, she and a friend were on a European tour that was supposed to include the Olympics in Berlin. But the heavy military presence there unnerved her, her son Vaughan said, and they left before attending the games. It was at those games that African-American sprinter Jesse Owens won four gold medals, thwarting Adolf Hitler's plan to use the Olympiad as a showcase for German superiority.

She married William Fitzpatrick in 1940. After the United States entered World War II in December 1941, Mrs. Fitzpatrick, who by then had two sons, signed up to take information from people who scanned the Gulf of Mexico looking for German U-boats.

To fulfill this sensitive wartime mission, Mrs. Fitzpatrick reported to the Maison Blanche building, now the Ritz-Carlton New Orleans, where doctors and other professionals had offices above the department store. But unlike the other floors in the Canal Street building, her floor was off-limits to everyone but her group, her son said.

Because she was sworn to secrecy, Mrs. Fitzpatrick didn't reveal many details about the information she received, Vaughan Fitzpatrick said.

In 1951, William Fitzpatrick became the first New Orleans journalist to win a Pulitzer Prize. A year later, he and his family moved to New York after the *Wall Street Journal* hired him as an associate editor. In 1960, he was named editor of the *Norfolk-Portsmouth (Va.) Ledger-Star*.

Mrs. Fitzpatrick lived in Virginia, but in 2006 acquired a vacation home in New Orleans to be near her grandchildren. She was a member of the Garden Club of Virginia's Norfolk chapter and became known for her garden of herbs, which she grew for culinary and medicinal purposes.

— *August 5, 2008*

Ruthie the Duck Girl

A bar-hopping eccentric on roller skates

Ruthie the Duck Girl, a French Quarter eccentric who zoomed from bar to bar on roller skates, often wearing a ratty fur coat and long skirt and trailed by a duck or two, died Sept. 6 at Our Lady of the Lake Hospital in Baton Rouge. She was 74.

Ruthie, whose real name was Ruth Grace Moulon, had been suffering from cancer of the mouth and lungs when the residents of her Uptown New Orleans nursing home were evacuated to Baton Rouge as Hurricane Gustav approached in 2008, said Carol Cunningham, a close friend who watched over her for nearly 40 years.

"I've always looked at Ruthie like a little bird with a broken wing," Cunningham said. "She was always so dear to me."

Miss Moulon, a lifelong New Orleanian, became a French Quarter fixture, achieving legendary status in a city that treasures people who live outside the mainstream.

Along the way, she acquired a coterie of people like Cunningham who found places for her to live, paid her bills and made sure she got home at night.

A tiny woman with a constant grin, she frequently sported a bridal gown and veil on her forays because, people said, she considered herself engaged to Gary Moody, whom she met in New Orleans in 1963 when he was a sailor.

Moody showed up at a 2001 birthday party for Miss Moulon at Mid-City Lanes Rock 'N Bowl, a venue that offers live music and bowling, but the two never got to the altar.

According to a *Times-Picayune* interview that year, Miss Moulon had a stock reply whenever anyone asked if there might be a wedding in her future: "I got engaged; that's enough!"

In 1999, Rick Delaup made her the subject of a documentary, "Ruthie the Duck Girl."

Miss Moulon's daily routine consisted of roaming from one watering hole to another, mooching drinks and cigarettes. She could be sweet one minute and unleash a torrent of profanity the next.

Although people deemed Miss Moulon's behavior unconventional even by French Quarter standards, no one ever diagnosed her mental condition because she refused to see a doctor, David Cuthbert wrote in the *Times-Picayune* in 2001.

"She's not out of touch with reality; she's just not interested," the photographer David Richmond told the *Times-Picayune*.

Miss Moulon's mother, who put her daughter's hair in sausage curls to make her look like Shirley Temple, came up with the idea that little Ruthie should be a duck girl, Cunningham said.

"She dressed her in evening dresses and bought her skates, and she skated through the Quarter with these little ducks following," Cunningham said.

Miss Moulon's mother, who grew up in rural Louisiana, initially let the ducks live in the house, although the two women sometimes fought over them, according to eccentricneworleans.com. On that website, Myrl D'Arcy, an artist, described a visit to the house:

"The duck's living in the bathtub, and the mother wanted to take a bath. Ruthie didn't want the mother to take the duck out of the bathtub because it would upset the duck."

In the documentary, the artist George Dureau recalled a conversation with Miss Moulon after the death of another French Quarter character, Eloise Lopez Arollo Samakintos, who always carried a cross through the Vieux Carré.

"There ain't a whole lot of us left, George," she said.

— September 13, 2008

John "Wimpy" Miller Jr.

His trumpet heralded the end of Mardi Gras

John "Wimpy" Miller Jr., a trumpet-playing lawyer who donned tights and a tunic once a year to herald the beginning of the end of Mardi Gras, died Sunday of Alzheimer's disease at his Metairie home. He was 89.

For 52 years, Mr. Miller was one of a pair of trumpeters whose flourishes signaled the arrival of Rex, king of Carnival, and his queen at Comus' court on Mardi Gras night. Once the two courts meet, toast each other and their subjects, and take a last regal turn around the floor, the Carnival season is over—until the next year.

Mr. Miller, whose trumpet also heralded the arrival of Rex and his consort at their own ball earlier that night, never lost his fascination with the pageantry.

"It's just beautiful when the courts come together with the pomp and ceremony and all the ermines and capes," he said in a 1981 interview. "But by the time the courts meet, I'm usually in the back, changing into my civvies."

He was drafted for the role by René Louapre, a bandleader who for years was a fixture at old-line Carnival balls.

"I played on the floor during the tableau at the 1947 ball," Mr. Miller said, "and I guess I just became part of it."

He stopped after the 1998 festivities because he couldn't play well enough anymore to meet his own standards, said his daughter, Jonnie LaHatte.

Mr. Miller, a lifelong New Orleanian who grew up in the Upper 9th Ward, started his relationship with the trumpet by accident.

When he and some friends were playing marbles, a man asked whether anyone wanted music lessons. "I brought him to my dad, and I said, 'I want to play that thing with the three valves on it,'" Mr. Miller said. "So he went to a hock shop on South Rampart Street and bought one for $10."

He played well enough to win scholarships to St. Aloysius High School and Louisiana State University, where he played in the marching band known as the Golden Band from Tigerland.

While Mr. Miller was in high school, his friends started calling him Wimpy because, like the character in Popeye cartoons, he was fond of hamburgers, his daughter said.

Tulane University's law school offered no music scholarships, but Mr. Miller earned money in gigs with bands led by Irving Fazola, Pete Fountain, Johnny DeDroit, and Al Hirt, who had been a second-grade classmate.

During World War II, Mr. Miller and his band, Wimpy Miller and his Dixieland Group, entertained troops throughout France. Mr. Miller, who was in the Army, performed with Tommy Dorsey's and Frank Sinatra's orchestras when they entertained the troops, said his son, Larry Miller.

He also was awarded a Purple Heart.

After the war, Mr. Miller had a civil law practice and was in-house counsel for insurance companies. He also was a law clerk at First Parish Court in Metairie until he was 82, LaHatte said.

— *October 21, 2009*

Luba Glade

She loved art and was passionate about it

Luba Glade, an outspoken woman who used her passion for art to become a powerful force in New Orleans' art community as a gallery owner, critic, and collector, died Thursday at Poydras Home of lymphoma. She was 87.

A lifelong New Orleanian who graduated from Newcomb College, Ms. Glade ran the Glade Gallery in the 1960s, wrote art criticism for the *States-Item* in the 1970s and was a catalyst in the establishment of the Contemporary Arts Center.

The idea for that building was born in the summer of 1976 at Robert Tannen and Jim Lalande's exhibit of avant-garde art in an un-air-conditioned warehouse in the 9th Ward.

"This is great," Ms. Glade wrote of that event. "We should have something like this on a permanent basis."

Ms. Glade was in a group that approached Sydney Besthoff about donating a building that had been a warehouse for Katz & Besthoff, his local drugstore chain. The center opened there that fall with exhibits that included Fats Domino's pink Cadillac.

"Her biggest pride was her involvement in the CAC," her son Louis Glade said. "She didn't have gobs of money, but when somebody needed a push, she wrote the article saying we really needed a CAC."

A fixture at art openings, frequently wearing outsize jewelry she had bought on trips to exotic destinations, Ms. Glade could be counted on to make a splash, whether it was through a Vice Squad raid in 1967 that shut down an exhibit at her French Quarter gallery, or in a column when she told the principal backer of the blockbuster "Treasures of Tutankhamun" exhibit to stop taking himself so seriously.

She got into trouble with the law over two pieces by Shirley Reznikoff, a Baton Rouge artist, that resembled a "peep show," said Lt. Frederick Soule, the Vice Squad's commander. The police seized the art and returned it, and the show closed before a decision could be reached on whether the pieces were obscene.

Throughout her life, Ms. Glade had a knack for sizing up art and determining what was—or would become—important, Louis Glade said. "When the Whitney Museum came down to do a Southern art show, they came to Mom's gallery to see what she was showing."

Ms. Glade also was a mentor to young artists, including Arthur Roger and Josh Pailet, who run their own New Orleans galleries. Along the way, Ms. Glade collected art, buying what her son called "minor pieces by major artists."

"She bought small pieces that reminded her of big pieces," he said. She brought her art with her when she moved from her house into an apartment, where art covered every space.

"Furniture was not the problem," she said in a 1990 interview, "but I wanted to bring my art pieces."

She kept going to openings. "If I'm alone, I know I'll always see lots of acquaintances—and lots of interesting strangers," she said in a 1998 interview. "They're just as diverse as the art."

When she showed up, "everyone would come rushing to the door because she was walking in," Louis Glade said. "The love she got when she went to art galleries was overwhelming."

— *November 28, 2009*

Connie Marie Thomas

She rebuilt Katrina-battered buildings and souls

The Rev. Connie Marie Thomas, a minister who used her zeal to help repair buildings and souls that Hurricane Katrina had battered, died Nov. 24 of pneumonia at Touro Infirmary. She was 51.

"She had what I would call a pastor's heart," said the Rev. Ramonalynn Bethley, district superintendent for the New Orleans area in the United Methodist Church's Louisiana Conference.

"To me, it is a faith that is lived out in actions toward others—in listening to others, in caring for others and in serving their needs," she said. "Christ can come in a warm meal or a cold glass of water."

Pastor Thomas, a native New Orleanian who had led two churches in the city when Katrina struck in August 2005, helped establish Luke's House, a free clinic at Mount Zion United Methodist Church.

She was no stranger to storm-related losses: Katrina's winds peeled off the roof of her Uptown home.

In another church-related duty, Pastor Thomas was in charge of about 30,000 volunteers who converged on New Orleans after the storm.

That job, which she held for two years, included finding housing for these people, feeding them, and deploying them.

She possessed organizational skills and patience, Bethley said, "and a love for this city and an appreciation for every volunteer that came this way who would tell our story and keep it going beyond Louisiana when they went back home."

Her experience as an executive assistant to Mayor Marc Morial was a big help, said the Rev. Lester Shaw, pastor of Payne Memorial AME Church. "She got things done," he said.

Shaw was her mentor. During a service at Shaw's church, when he delivered the invitation to Christian discipleship, Pastor Thomas later told friends that the Holy Spirit "arrested her" and made her run toward the pulpit.

"It was spontaneous," Shaw said Tuesday. "She confessed that she had been called to the ministry. From there, she began her ministerial studies."

Pastor Thomas, who was a young adult when this happened, had grown up being active in church. She had sung in the youth choir, taught Sunday school, and led Fasting Hearts, a program that encompassed aerobics classes, health lessons and weight-loss guidance.

After graduating from New Orleans Baptist Theological Seminary, Pastor Thomas was ordained as an itinerant elder and assigned to St. Stephen AME Church in Kenner and Mount Zion AME Church in Bridge City.

She moved into the Methodist Church and was assigned to Napoleon Avenue United Methodist Church, where she helped establish the Zion Christian Academy for at-risk youth and the Starburst Leadership Team, which provided a safe environment for young people.

In her ministry, "she wasn't afraid to be open to new and different types of things," said the Rev. Martha Orphe, a friend who is director of the United Methodist Church's Office of Multicultural Ministries.

"She respected tradition," Orphe said, "but if it meant a new way of reaching people and being relevant, she was open to it. Whatever it took to get it done, she would do it."

This spirit of adventure extended to her personal life. When Pastor Thomas and Orphe were on a trip together, Pastor Thomas decided to try parasailing.

"She knew the danger of it," Orphe said, "but she wanted to try it."

— *December 2, 2009*

William Terral

His plasma nourished his garden

D r. William Terral, a pediatrician who was so passionate about garden-ing that he used his own plasma to help his flowers grow, died Dec. 2 at his Covington home. He was 84.

Although Dr. Terral was devoted to his patients in a practice spanning 60 years and four generations, family members said he was happiest when working in his garden. He was especially devoted to his hibiscuses, said Lylen "Mitty" Terral, his former wife.

At one point, Dr. Terral was undergoing a treatment for a thyroid prob-lem in which his plasma was separated from the rest of his blood. Rather than discard the plasma, Dr. Terral took the bags of the dark, viscous sub-stance to his garden and hung them, one by one, from IV poles, with tubes running into the soil.

A visitor asked Mitty Terral whether she was giving the plants a blood transfusion. "I said, 'I'm not, but Dr. Terral is,'" Mitty Terral said. "I really believe that it made the blooms larger."

A native of Farmerville, La., Dr. Terral grew up picking cotton. He was determined that his children know about agriculture, even though they grew up in Uptown New Orleans alongside St. Charles Avenue, said David "Brett" Terral, one of his sons.

Because a swimming pool and patio took up most of the backyard, Dr. Terral set up a garden on the roof of the garage, setting out the flowers and vegetables in whiskey barrels that had been sawed in half. "It was interesting to see passers-by flummoxed by corn growing on top of the garage, along with string beans and tomatoes," Mitty Terral said.

Dr. Terral, who could hold forth at length on a broad range of topics, earned undergraduate and medical degrees at Louisiana State University.

He joined the Army Medical Corps and served two years in Fontainebleau, outside Paris, shortly after the end of World War II.

Because the nearest hospital to Dr. Terral's hometown was 35 miles away, he established a 12-bed hospital, which has since closed.

But by the time he returned from France, he had married a New Orleanian and decided that he didn't want a family practice in a small town, Brett Terral said. So he entered a pediatric residency at Charity Hospital and established a practice in New Orleans. He stayed there until 1991, when he moved across Lake Pontchartrain to Covington to work with another son, Dr. William "Buddy" Terral.

He continued to see patients even after a fall down a flight of stairs in November 2008 left him unable to move his arms and legs.

Ten months after the accident, Dr. Terral returned to work in a wheelchair. He continued to take histories and listen to his little patients' chests with his stethoscope earpieces in his ears as he told a nurse where to place the chest piece.

"It was such a blessing that he was able to practice as long as he did," Mitty Terral said.

— *December 17, 2009*

Stocker Fontelieu

He was a ubiquitous man of the theater

Stocker Fontelieu, a commanding force in local theater for nearly 60 years, died Monday of cancer at Covenant Home in New Orleans. He was 86.

The executive director of Le Petit Théâtre du Vieux Carré from 1961 to 1985, Mr. Fontelieu was best known as a director who worked for many local theatrical organizations, including Gallery Circle Theatre, Bayou Dinner Theater, and Rivertown Repertory Theater.

By the time he retired in 2006, Mr. Fontelieu had directed 340 plays.

"He could draw out of a person with not much experience exactly what he wanted to get," said Janet Shea, an actress who worked frequently with Mr. Fontelieu and later directed him in *Amadeus*.

"He was always very well-organized and knew exactly what he wanted to accomplish," she said, "and he knew exactly how to take steps to do that."

In an interview with Rebecca Hale for her history of Le Petit, Mr. Fontelieu said the most memorable productions he directed were *The Elephant Man*, *A Man for All Seasons*, *West Side Story*, and *Who's Afraid of Virginia Woolf?*

Because he was blessed with stage presence, a powerful, resonant voice, and a knack for the grand gesture, Mr. Fontelieu performed in front of the footlights, too, appearing in 148 plays. He also was in 14 made-for-television movies and 22 feature films, including *Angel Heart* and *Pretty Baby*.

"He was theatrical, but, then, he was theater," said Frank Gagnard, a retired *Times-Picayune* critic.

Some of those who worked with Mr. Fontelieu went on to national show-business careers. Among them were Bryan Batt of *Mad Men*, who performed in *Grease* and *The Robber Bridegroom* in New Orleans, and Ed

Nelson of *Peyton Place*, who played Stanley Kowalski in a local production of *A Streetcar Named Desire*.

Mr. Fontelieu also was in demand for voice-overs. He was Dr. Walrus, one of Mr. Bingle's sidekicks, in a local Yuletide television series for children, and he lent his distinctive voice to commercials as well.

Stepping before the cameras in commercials, Mr. Fontelieu took on roles that included the inventor Thomas A. Edison for a lighting store—"Edison would have bought it here" was his line—and the furniture merchant Morris Kirschman, driving a horse-drawn buggy brimming with merchandise through the streets of early-20th-century New Orleans.

"Everybody knew Stocker's voice, even if they didn't know Stocker," Gagnard said.

Mr. Fontelieu, who never used Charles, his first name, was born in New Orleans and graduated from New Orleans Academy, which has since closed. He enrolled in Tulane as an architecture major, but he left in 1942, shortly after the United States entered World War II, to enlist in the Army.

Mr. Fontelieu wound up in the infantry in the Pacific theater, where he was in the first wave of the invasions of Leyte and Okinawa. During the Okinawa landing in 1945, Mr. Fontelieu suffered shrapnel wounds in his back and legs. He was awarded a Bronze Star and a Purple Heart.

While recovering in a Hawaii hospital, Mr. Fontelieu saw a USO production of Noel Coward's comedy *Blithe Spirit*. It was the first play he had ever seen.

"All I know is that it was hilarious," he told critic David Cuthbert in a 2003 interview for the *Times-Picayune*.

"I loved it," he said. "I was piqued by the overall production as much as the entertainment of it."

When he returned to Tulane, Mr. Fontelieu said in the interview, he saw a poster bearing two words that changed his life: "Theater Department." He checked it out—and changed his major.

Monroe Lippman, the department's director, suggested that Mr. Fontelieu consider working at Le Petit, with which Tulane was affiliated.

The result: His first role, in 1947, as Frank Bonaparte in *Golden Boy*.

Although acting was what most people entered the theater department to do, Lippman "steered me toward directing," Mr. Fontelieu said in the interview.

After he graduated in 1949, the Little Theatre of Monroe, La., hired Mr. Fontelieu to be its general director. He stayed there four years, directing 21 plays, before returning to Tulane to earn a master of fine arts degree in 1955.

During that time, he had been acting at Le Petit. But after finishing his degree, he was hired by Gallery Circle Theatre, on Madison Street in the French Quarter, to be its executive director. He held that position until he went to Le Petit in 1961.

After leaving Le Petit in 1985, Mr. Fontelieu worked at Bayou Dinner Theater from 1986 until 1993.

He was a freelance director and actor for the rest of his career, a period in which he took on such meaty roles as James Tyrone in *Long Day's Journey Into Night* and Matthew Harrison Brady in *Inherit the Wind*.

And then there was the production of Eugene O'Neill's *The Iceman Cometh*, which was staged in January 2000 in the Contemporary Arts Center's unheated garage. Mr. Fontelieu, then 76, played Capt. Cecil Lewis, a role that required him to be in his undershirt for most of the four-hour play.

"At intermission of the first performance, all of the audience got up as one and left," he said in the 2003 interview. "Who could blame them? But, then, they all came back. They'd gone to their cars to get blankets, overcoats, pillows, whatever they could get to help them stay warm. Now that's what I call a theater accomplishment!"

It was, he said, testimony to the lingering power of theater.

Among Mr. Fontelieu's honors were lifetime-achievement awards from the Arts Council of New Orleans, the Southwest Theater Association, and the Big Easy Entertainment Awards.

"Good theater is always needed," he told Cuthbert. "Experiencing live theater is life-enhancing. Like all the arts, it broadens our lives. Theater, like history, is a great teacher. And with all the problems inherent in it, I still look forward to going there."

— *December 15, 2009*

Fred Feran

A runner who boycotted the Nazi Olympics

Fred Feran, a Czech runner who boycotted the 1936 Olympics in Berlin because of the anti-Semitism rampant in Nazi Germany, died Thursday at St. Joseph's Rehabilitation Center in LaCrosse, Wis. He was 92.

In 1947, Mr. Feran and his wife, Jean, settled in New Orleans, where his relatives lived. He carried the Olympic torch through the French Quarter in 2002 en route to its destination, Salt Lake City, for that year's Winter Olympics.

The Ferans moved to LaCrosse, where their daughter, Maureen Freedland, lives, after Hurricane Katrina destroyed their New Orleans home in August 2005.

Mr. Feran was born Fred Feuermann in Zakopcie, Slovakia (later Czechoslovakia), but his family had to move a year later after their house was burned down in a pogrom, an organized massacre of Jews.

As he grew up, Mr. Feuermann started running, and he amassed dozens of medals. He was so fast—and so popular—that he became accustomed to hearing people chant, "Feuermann! Feuermann! Feuermann!" when he ran.

In 1936, the Czech government chose him to compete in the 1,500-meter race in the Summer Olympics, which Adolf Hitler envisioned as a way to showcase the Nazi myth of Aryan superiority.

But two days before the team was to leave for Berlin, Mr. Feuermann and a teammate decided to join a multinational boycott of the games that was led by Jewish athletes. Among the boycotters was Herman Neugass, a champion Tulane University sprinter known as "The Green Wave Express."

It was a tough decision, Mr. Feran said in a 2002 interview, but not as difficult as those he would face as a Jew trying to survive in Europe.

"You can't have everything," he said in that interview.

"The Olympics are not important when your life is at stake," his wife said.

Mr. Feuermann would lose four siblings and dozens of other relatives in the Holocaust.

Those losses haunted him for decades. "He never cried on anyone's shoulder," Rabbi Edward Cohn of Temple Sinai said, "but he never forgot the severe losses of his siblings, and he would often rehearse them, even in his sleep."

In 1939, as World War II loomed, he decided that his best chance for survival would be in Palestine, which the British controlled. Three days before German troops occupied Czechoslovakia, he dropped out of engineering school, and he and his brother Erwin joined about 700 other Jews on the *Agios Nicholas*, a Greek ship.

They were at sea for four months waiting for permission to land. After they debarked, Mr. Feuermann became Mr. Feran because he had been urged to anglicize his surname.

He worked in the oil industry and joined the Czechoslovakian Overseas Army in Jerusalem.

Mr. Feran was demobilized in Brazil, where he met his wife, who also was a Czechoslovakian.

They moved to New Orleans, where his mother's relatives, the Pulitzers, lived. Leah Pulitzer Antin, a co-owner of Antin's Jewelry, sponsored their entry into the United States.

Mr. Feran sold jewelry by day and repaired clocks at night. As word of his expertise as a clock repairman spread, he acquired clients throughout the United States.

— March 2, 2010

Walter G. Cowan

An editor who was meticulous, brave and kind

Walter G. Cowan, a gentle, meticulous journalist who capped a 43-year career by editing the States-Item, New Orleans' afternoon newspaper, for a decade, died over the weekend. He was 98.

He started at the *New Orleans Item* as a reporter in 1936. After leaving town for four years to work in public relations, Mr. Cowan returned to New Orleans to work on the *New Orleans States*, first as a reporter, then as city editor. After the two papers merged in 1958, he became managing editor of the *States-Item* in 1964 and, in 1969, editor. He retired in 1979.

Throughout Mr. Cowan's career, co-workers respected the thorough professionalism that made him scrutinize everything, from the spelling of a name to the credibility of a source, to ensure that a story was solid.

"My great love of Walter was based on his always wanting to help the reporter do a better job," said Rosemary James, a former *States-Item* reporter. "He was one of the best at that. He would take your story and explain why he thought it was weak and give you his suggestions for strengthening the content of the story and the style."

"When I think of Walter, I think of the calm at the eye of the hurricane," said Charles A. Ferguson, his successor.

Born in Bond, Miss., to parents who died when he was a teenager, Mr. Cowan earned money as an adolescent by delivering the (Gulfport-Biloxi) *Daily Herald.*

The 100 customers on his six-mile route paid Mr. Cowan 15 cents a week, and he got to keep half of it—$7.50 a week.

By the time he threw the paper each morning, he had already read most of it while he was rolling it up. The paper route and his interest in reading led him to begin submitting sports stories to the *Daily Herald* and to the *Times-Picayune*, he wrote in a privately published family history.

"To my surprise, the newspapers printed the stories as I sent them," Mr. Cowan wrote. "My friends and teachers were impressed, and I even began entering the *Times-Picayune*'s Biggest News of the Week essay contest."

One of his rivals was Hale Boggs, the future congressman, who was submitting winning entries from his home in nearby Long Beach, Miss.

With a $10-per-week job for a publicist to pay his expenses, Mr. Cowan entered Perkinston Junior College (now the Perkinston campus of Mississippi Gulf Coast Community College). After finishing the two-year curriculum there, Mr. Cowan stayed out of school for a year to earn money so he could enter the University of Missouri.

With $125 in his wallet, Mr. Cowan enrolled. He earned his meals by waiting tables, and he stoked a furnace in return for a room.

While working on the copy desk of the *Columbia Missourian*, Mr. Cowan befriended the seven members of The Reveille staff who had enrolled at the University of Missouri after leaving Louisiana State University rather than submit to Huey P. Long's censorship.

One of those contacts paid off. When Mr. Cowan arrived in New Orleans in 1936, looking for work, one of the Reveille Seven, David McGuire, was on the *Item* staff and helped steer his friend to a job as a reporter for $15 a week.

McGuire also introduced Mr. Cowan to Margaret Martinez, whom he would marry in 1940. She died in May 2002.

Mr. Cowan became an assistant city editor and helped coordinate coverage of the Louisiana Scandals, the blanket term used to describe the dealings of Long's cronies that came to light after the U.S. senator's assassination in 1935. As a result, a host of officials wound up serving prison terms, including the governor, LSU's president, and members of the Orleans Levee Board.

This period provided "the most excitement, and greatest results, of any political upheaval in my career," Mr. Cowan wrote. "The New Orleans newspapers, through the coverage of the scandals, brought a lot of national attention to the state."

In 1941, he moved to Mobile, Ala., to become a public-relations and advertising representative for the Gulf, Mobile & Ohio Railroad.

Meanwhile, World War II was raging. Toward the end of that conflict, the *States* asked Mr. Cowan to return to New Orleans as a reporter, but he had a more pressing concern: He had been reclassified 1-A and was told to be ready to report for active duty in three weeks.

But V-E Day intervened. Because of that factor and the fact that he had a wife and child to support, Mr. Cowan's name was dropped to the bottom of the list. He headed back to New Orleans, where he covered the mayoral campaign in which the reform candidate deLesseps S. "Chep" Morrison unseated Robert S. Maestri.

After nine months, Mr. Cowan was named city editor, a job he held 18 years. He was named managing editor in 1964.

The *States-Item* and the *Times-Picayune* shared the same publisher, the same building and the same editorial board. Part of that changed in 1969, when separate editorial departments were established. Mr. Cowan was named editor.

Despite his genteel manner, Mr. Cowan showed he could be tough, as he was when Gov. Edwin W. Edwards complained about the paper's relentless coverage of the cost overruns and delays that beset construction of the Louisiana Superdome in the early 1970s.

Mr. Cowan never flinched. "The best way to change the public image of the Dome is to see that it is operated efficiently," he said. "If we had had that from the start, then there would be no problems.

"I agree that the Superdome should have a better image, but the *States-Item* does not intend to forfeit its right to report fully what goes on at the Dome. We do want to cooperate in making the Dome a success, but we will tell the story as it happens."

The most explosive story of his later years was one that the *States-Item* helped break: Orleans Parish District Attorney Jim Garrison's free-wheeling investigation of President John F. Kennedy's assassination.

It started late in 1966, three years after the slaying, when police reporter Jack Dempsey wrote in his weekly column that Garrison was preparing to launch the inquiry. No other news organization did anything with the story, Mr. Cowan wrote.

Three months later, Dempsey suggested follow-up work. A search of City Hall records resulted in evidence of extravagant spending, some for trips out of the country. David Snyder, who had unearthed the City Hall files, and Dempsey gave their information to James, who wound up writing the story and confronting Garrison for a reaction.

"Garrison looked at it, threw it on the floor and claimed his probe would be ruined if we published it," Mr. Cowan wrote. "I gave the signal to publish."

It became a sensational story around the world. Eventually, Clay Shaw, a New Orleans businessman, was indicted and tried on a charge of conspiring to kill the president. A jury acquitted him in less than an hour.

Throughout the story's stormy developments, "I relied on Walter for good common sense," James said. "We had others in the newsroom who were willing to go off half-cocked, but not Walter. Walter kept all of that on an even keel. . . . He never expressed an opinion, which was appropriate for a man in his position."

In 1977, Mr. Cowan delivered the commencement address at his alma mater, exhorting Missouri graduates to exercise fully the media's watchdog role, especially in covering corporations, and to fight in courts for the rights of the press.

In introducing Mr. Cowan, the dean, Roy M. Fisher, said the speaker "reflects the strongest and most estimable qualities of American journalism."

His career, Fisher said, "epitomizes the traditions of strong reporting that digs behind the scenes, yet remains objective and provides the reader a balanced story about which he can make up his own mind."

— April 13, 2010

Catherine Clark Mayer

"She was a life force like no other"

Catherine Clark Mayer, a model, artist, art teacher, and community activist who brought an unmistakable flair to whatever she did, died Wednesday at her home in Mandeville, La. She was 93.

"She was a life force like no other," said the artist Emery Clark, a long-time friend. "She truly was the poster child, the icon for everything she did."

Mrs. Mayer, who loved to wear jungle prints and drove a white convertible until she was 90, was a self-taught artist who never let adversity stop her.

After she fell and fractured her hip when she was in her late 80s, Mrs. Mayer sent her daughter out to buy art supplies so she could teach painting to her fellow patients who were undergoing physical therapy, Clark said.

And after learning she had breast cancer when she was 79, Mrs. Mayer was one of nine faces adorning the cover of *The Many Faces of Breast Cancer*, a locally published collection of inspirational stories.

"I believe in 'Attitude, Attitude, Attitude,'" she said in that booklet, "and a great deal of faith."

A native New Orleanian, Mrs. Mayer graduated from high school in Atlanta, where her family lived briefly during the Depression.

While in Atlanta, she reigned over a spring festival as Queen of the May. Among the members of her court, she said, were the future wives of Groucho Marx, William Randolph Hearst Jr., and Frank Sinatra.

In her 20s, Catherine Clark was a model at Gus Mayer department store on Canal Street. She possessed the type of beauty that could turn heads, including Cary Grant's.

She met the debonair movie legend when he wandered into a dance at a downtown hotel shortly before the United States entered World War II. According to a privately published memoir, Grant asked her to slip out with him to the French Quarter, but she turned him down, saying, "No, thank you. I have a date."

Her date was Martin Mayer, Gus Mayer's nephew, whom she had met while she was modeling at the Canal Street store that bore his uncle's name. They married in 1941; he died in 1978.

Grant wasn't the only superstar she met. While Mrs. Mayer was working as an administrative assistant to the St. Charles Hotel's executive director, Clark Gable dropped in for lunch during a layover between trains en route to officer training school in Miami. She was sent to get him out of the hotel through a back door and back to the train station before his presence touched off pandemonium.

"I don't remember any real conversation with him," she said in her memoir. "All I can remember is [saying], 'You're short!'"

During World War II, Mrs. Mayer was an active volunteer in the war effort, and she continued volunteering for the rest of her life. At the Old Ursuline Convent in the French Quarter, where she was a tour guide, Clark said she helped raise money for its renovation.

Mrs. Mayer's infatuation with painting started in childhood, she said, when she was fascinated by watercolors. Her artistic style blended realism with impressionism, Clark said.

In addition to canvases, Mrs. Mayer painted murals for the Women's and Infants' Services unit at what is now Ochsner Baptist Medical Center. She started teaching in her 70s, and she arranged shows for her pupils at the Christwood Retirement Community and the Young Energetic Senior group at the Pelican Athletic Club.

Art, she said, is "letting your imagination go and doing whatever you feel like."

— *April 16, 2010*

Lambert Joseph "Bobby" Gonzales Jr.

He rescued people from roofs after Hurricane Betsy

Lambert Joseph "Bobby" Gonzales Jr., who was part of a Coast Guard detachment that drove through floodwaters to rescue people from their roofs in the wake of Hurricane Betsy, died Sunday at his Metairie, La., home. He was 90.

As Betsy was barreling toward New Orleans on Sept. 9, 1965, Mr. Gonzales and his colleagues were summoned to the Coast Guard base near the Industrial Canal.

When the 9th Ward and St. Bernard Parish flooded, "everyone who had ever driven a 2 1/2-ton truck was pressed into duty to get people off the roofs," said his daughter, Janice Gonzales Barry. "I remember my father telling me that families were huddled together on top of the roofs. They were crammed into the trucks.

"They drove for 36 hours without sleep, driving back and forth. When the trucks were full, they had to pass up people who were begging to be picked up, but there was no room."

In recognition of that effort, the unit received a letter of commendation from Coast Guard Commandant Edwin J. Roland.

"By your meritorious service, you have upheld the highest traditions of the United States Coast Guard," Roland wrote.

Mr. Gonzales spent 28 years in the Coast Guard, retiring in 1968 as a master chief petty officer.

During World War II, his unit established and maintained telephone communication from New Orleans to the mouth of the Mississippi River and in remote areas of the Gulf Coast, his daughter said. It was, she said, an area that had been regarded as too sparsely populated to justify service.

"When the war came, the military realized they needed phones for security reasons," Barry said. "My father was climbing telephone poles."

After leaving the Coast Guard, Mr. Gonzales went to work at Tulane University, where he performed administrative duties such as directing work crews in the housing department and law school. He retired in 1981.

A native New Orleanian who graduated from St. Aloysius High School, Mr. Gonzales grew up in a family of opera lovers. Before his voice changed in adolescence, Mr. Gonzales was in demand as a soprano, his daughter said.

He ushered for operas when he was in high school, and he was a regular listener to the Metropolitan Opera's Saturday afternoon radio broadcasts, Barry said, even when he was stationed in Ketchikan, Alaska, during World War II.

Mr. Gonzales also was an athlete, competing in swimming, boxing, basketball and wrestling. He was the mascot of the New Orleans Athletic Club's championship baseball team of 1933.

In 1956, Mr. Gonzales won the Class B singles championship in the annual Commercial Athletic Association tennis tournament, prompting this appraisal from Jimmie Powers in the *Times-Picayune*: "Gonzales' game is based on steadiness. He keeps the ball in play, preferring to let his adversaries make the errors."

— July 2, 2010

Raul Bertuccelli

He fabricated fanciful floats for Mardi Gras

Raul Bertuccelli, an exuberant member of an Italian float-making family who put his skills to work building floats and outsize walking heads for nearly 30 years of Carnival parades, died June 24 at West Jefferson Medical Center from complications of a stroke. He was 82.

His papier-mâché creations adorned the flamboyant floats of the Rex, Bacchus, Endymion, and Alla parades. He built the cornucopia for the Boeuf Gras float in the Rex parade, as well as figures for the Wonderwall at the 1984 world's fair in New Orleans and the daily Carnival parades there.

He also made the massive Mr. Bingle figure that hovered during the Christmas shopping season outside Maison Blanche's Canal Street store, a building that now houses the Ritz-Carlton New Orleans.

Mr. Bertuccelli made some of his figures move. For the Rex parade, float designer Henri Schindler said, Mr. Bertuccelli's creations included a giant dragon, a lizard, and a lion, all enormous and animated. Even their eyes moved.

Mr. Bertuccelli had grown up building such mobile figures in Viareggio, his hometown in the Italian region of Tuscany, where his father and uncle made floats for the annual Carnevale celebration.

A jester head made by Mr. Bertuccelli's uncle, Sandro Bertuccelli, has become a regular feature of the Rex procession. Blaine Kern, a dominant figure in New Orleans' Carnival who had a float-building company bearing his name, met Mr. Bertuccelli during the 1960s while Kern was studying European celebrations.

The two became friends, and in 1977 Mr. Bertuccelli came to New Orleans with his family to work for Kern.

"He was the best papier-mâché sculptor I ever met in my life," said Kern, chairman of the board of Blaine Kern Artists. "His characters had their own personalities."

"It was obvious that he enjoyed what he was doing," said Barry Kern, Blaine Kern's son and the president of Blaine Kern Artists. "He had that Italian flair that was so incredible."

Said Schindler: "He was like Tuscany—bright, beautiful, warm."

To make his creations, including the outsize heads that marchers wore in the Krewe of Endymion parade, Mr. Bertuccelli used a multistep process that started with a clay sculpture of the figure, said his son Jonathan Bertuccelli. Then he made a plaster mold. After that set, he pulled it off and filled the inside with several layers of papier-mâché, a soggy mixture of paper, flour and water. Once it dried, the result, the younger Bertuccelli said, was light and strong, with room inside for devices to make the figure move.

In 1983, Mr. Bertuccelli left Kern to form Studio 3, a float-building firm, with his sons Jonathan and Giorgio. Giorgio moved to Los Angeles to pursue a music career; Jonathan represents the third generation of Bertuccellis to continue making floats.

Studio 3 has continued to do work for Kern, Jonathan Bertuccelli said. It also worked for the world's fair, creating walking heads that roamed the grounds and mountains that floated atop barges in the Great Hall, now the Ernest N. Morial Convention Center.

For nearly two decades, Studio 3 also made the floats for Houston's Thanksgiving Day parade.

Making floats wasn't all Mr. Bertuccelli did with his hands. As a youth during World War II in Italy, he started boxing U.S. soldiers for food and money. One soldier he trained with was Ezzard Charles, who later won the heavyweight championship.

Mr. Bertuccelli, who was the first alternate in the welterweight division of Italy's team for the 1948 London Olympics, turned professional, winning 31 fights, losing three, and fighting to a tie in one.

He also built floats for carnival parades in three Colombian cities: Bogotá, Cartagena, and Baranquilla.

"He dreamed big," Carnival chronicler Arthur Hardy said.

When float builders in Viareggio learned of Mr. Bertuccelli's death, they honored him by laying down their tools and leaving their warehouses for two days, Giorgio Bertuccelli said.

Instead of a funeral in New Orleans, a party was held at Blaine Kern's Mardi Gras World, where people can see how Mardi Gras is made.

"His life was Mardi Gras," Jonathan Bertuccelli said, "and he didn't want anything with sadness."

— *July 6, 2010*

Sue Hawes

She fought for Louisiana's ecosystem

Sue Hawes, an environmental advocate for the Army Corps of Engineers who specialized in building coalitions to restore and preserve Louisiana's fragile ecosystem, died Friday at Touro Infirmary of liver failure. She was 74.

Because of her knowledge and tirelessness in communicating her concern about such issues as coastal land loss and restoration, she was "the environmental conscience of the corps," said Mark Davis, director of the Tulane Institute on Water Resources Law and Policy.

"There probably wasn't a single restoration project that she was not involved in or lent her expertise to," said Melanie Goodman, a corps colleague and friend.

After Hurricanes Katrina and Rita struck in 2005, Goodman said Ms. Hawes was "heavily engaged" in the design and rebuilding of New Orleans' levee system, which had failed, resulting in the flooding of 80 percent of the city.

In addition to being the voice of wisdom and experience, Ms. Hawes "worked hard to get people to listen to each other and cooperate," said her daughter, Cynthia Van Dam.

With this talent, Ms. Hawes "earned the highest respect and admiration from a diversity of groups, including federal and state resource agencies, local governments, commercial fishermen, oil and gas representatives, land managers, and other interests throughout Louisiana and the nation," Goodman said.

When these groups got together for sessions that could be contentious or boring, Ms. Hawes was "always a breath of fresh air amidst the bureaucrats and pessimists," said David Richard, a board member of the Coalition to Restore Coastal Louisiana.

Even if he and Ms. Hawes happened to disagree on a particular issue, "she always had a sense of humor," Richard said.

An Idaho native who moved to New Orleans about 40 years ago, Ms. Hawes, a biologist, worked at Louisiana State University in New Orleans and LSU Medical Center before landing an internship at the corps' New Orleans office in 1972. She started working there full-time in November 1973.

From 1978 until 1990, Ms. Hawes was chief of the office's environmental section. In 1990, she was named project manager for the environment for the corps' New Orleans District.

In addition to being involved in many projects, as well as scores of meetings with all the groups she strove to make part of a pro-environment coalition, Ms. Hawes was a mentor to young colleagues, said Tom Podany, chief of the protection restoration office for the New Orleans District.

"She taught a lot of people to have the same appreciation for the environment and factor it in" to their work, he said.

Ms. Hawes kept on working despite being beset by a host of health problems, including ovarian cancer, cancer of the tongue and throat, two mild strokes, and several crushed discs, her daughter said.

"She walked with a walker," Van Dam said, "but one of her friends at the corps called her Speedy. Others compared her to a pit bull."

"The way she would rehabilitate was to get back into her job," Podany said.

— *July 8, 2010*

Jean Danielson

"Dean Jean" was demanding, but was a soft touch

Jean Danielson, a professor and mentor who had a knack for spotting and nurturing academic talent during 39 years at Newcomb College and Tulane University, died Monday at Canon Hospice of complications of thyroid cancer. She was 77.

As an associate professor of political science and, later, director of Tulane's honors program, Dr. Danielson made a point of being accessible to students whenever they sought her out.

"Very few of us are willing to or have the complete commitment to students that Jean had," said Tom Luongo, the honors program's director. "Once she was engaged by a student, she was thoroughly engaged. She listened. She loved to talk to them. She was endlessly patient. . . . There are people who come along occasionally who can play that kind of role, but they are few and far between."

Dr. Danielson set high standards for students and demanded a lot from them.

"Some people thought she was like a drill sergeant, but she was a soft touch," said James Kilroy, a former Tulane provost and dean of its College of Arts and Sciences.

The time Dr. Danielson spent with students, especially those whom she was grooming to compete for prestigious scholarships for postgraduate study, paid off. During her tenure, Luongo said, Tulane students won a Rhodes scholarship, 11 Marshall scholarships, seven Truman scholarships, and 22 Goldwater scholarships.

Dr. Danielson, who acquired the nickname "Dean Jean," kept counseling students even after her retirement in 2004 until ill health forced her to stop. Business cards printed up for her bore a made-up title: adviser at large.

"It quite suited her," Luongo said. "If she were still here, we would love to have her playing that role because none of us could do what Jean could do."

Her students appreciated the attention, said Joan Bennett, a former Tulane biology professor who is an associate vice president of Rutgers, the State University of New Jersey.

"She was always ready for a discussion, an argument or theories, and she always listened," said Nancy Marsiglia, a civic leader who, as a political-science major in the early 1970s, took three courses with Dr. Danielson. "I thought the world of her."

With her bowl haircut, deep voice, resonant laugh and ever-present More Red cigarette, Dr. Danielson cut a distinctive figure on the Uptown campus.

Dr. Danielson, a Chicago native, came to Tulane in 1965 after earning bachelor's and master's degrees at Southern Illinois University and a doctorate at the University of Kansas. She was the first woman to earn a Ph.D. in political science at Kansas, and she was the first female member of Newcomb's political-science faculty.

"I had a big mouth," Dr. Danielson said in a 2004 interview with the *New Wave*, a Tulane publication. "I was never afraid to articulate my ideas, so I was something different."

In 1974, she organized Newcomb's first women's studies colloquium. "It was adventurous and out there," Bennett said. "She came into the first class and said, 'We're going to give the broad picture.' Everybody got it. Then she'd take a puff and tell another line, and she'd have everybody with her."

Dr. Danielson received awards recognizing her teaching prowess, and she was elected to Omicron Delta Kappa, the national leadership society.

"The university provided her a family environment, and the students were her kids," history professor George Bernstein said. "She always treated them like adults. If you show that you respect them and care for them, they'll respond, and there was nobody in the world better at that than Jean."

— *July 9, 2010*

Andrew "Moo Moo" Sciambra

He believed in Jim Garrison's assassination inquiry

Andrew "Moo Moo" Sciambra, who as an Orleans Parish prosecutor worked on the investigation that his boss, Jim Garrison, was conducting into the assassination of President John F. Kennedy, died Tuesday at River Region Hospice of complications of a stroke. He was 75.

Even though that inquiry came to naught, Mr. Sciambra was "a true believer" in what Garrison was doing, said David Snyder, who covered the case for the *States-Item*.

"He was incredibly loyal to Garrison," Snyder said. "He was straightforward and not trying to con anybody."

The only person charged in the case was Clay Shaw, a New Orleans businessman. Mr. Sciambra was the Garrison aide who was sent to Shaw's French Quarter home on March 1, 1967, to tell him he was about to be arrested in the plot to kill Kennedy.

Mr. Sciambra's duties included developing the testimony of witnesses, including Perry Raymond Russo, who claimed he had seen Shaw and Lee Harvey Oswald, the man the Warren Commission identified as the lone gunman, at a gathering where, he said, the assassination was planned.

However, Russo changed his story several times and recanted the story two years after the 1969 trial.

Exactly two years to the day after Shaw's arrest, a Criminal District Court jury acquitted him after deliberating less than an hour.

After Garrison left office in 1973, Mr. Sciambra went into private practice. In 1978, he was appointed a commissioner in the Magistrate Section of Orleans Parish Criminal District Court, a position he held for 20 years.

A lifelong New Orleanian, Mr. Sciambra grew up in the Royal Street building that was later used in the 1958 movie *King Creole* as Elvis Presley's house, said his wife, Evelyn Sciambra.

During his childhood, she said, her husband acquired his nickname from a French tenant who lived in the building. "She called him 'Boo Boo,'" Evelyn Sciambra said, "and it turned out to be 'Moo Moo.'"

When he was 9 years old, Mr. Sciambra started boxing at St. Mary's Gym in the French Quarter. In college, he won three Golden Gloves championships in the light-welterweight division.

In the ring, "he was a dancer," Evelyn Sciambra said. "He wasn't a fighter; he was a boxer."

Mr. Sciambra, who had been a student at Louisiana State University, turned professional, his wife said, because his coach was leaving the school to coach professional boxers.

But, she said, Mr. Sciambra had a form of anemia that put an end to his boxing career after only two bouts. So he returned to LSU to finish his undergraduate degree and then graduated from Loyola University's law school.

During the Garrison investigation, when the district attorney's office was the object of worldwide attention, Snyder said he was impressed by Mr. Sciambra's devotion to his job.

"While most of these guys were looking for a judgeship, that didn't seem to be his deal at all," Snyder said.

— July 29, 2010

Jimmy Brennan

The wine cellar was this restaurateur's kingdom

Jimmy Brennan, an owner of the fabled French Quarter restaurant bearing the family surname who developed an award-winning wine cellar there, died July 18. He was 70.

Mr. Brennan, who had been battling cancer, died of myelodysplastic syndrome, a blood disorder that can be the result of cancer treatment, said Theodore "Ted" Brennan, one of his brothers.

A lifelong New Orleanian, Mr. Brennan attended Louisiana State University before heading to the Ecole Hoteliere de la S.S.H. in Lausanne, Switzerland. From there, Mr. Brennan went to Houston in the late 1960s to run the Brennan's Restaurant there. He returned to New Orleans in 1973 to operate Brennan's on Royal Street with his brothers, Ted Brennan and Owen "Pip" Brennan Jr.

His duty was to develop the restaurant's wine cellar. Although it started as part of the job, that task turned into an all-consuming passion, Ted Brennan said. By the time Hurricane Katrina hit in August 2005, the cellar had 35,000 bottles, and it had won *Wine Spectator* magazine's Grand Award every year since 1983.

"He knew his stuff," said Ellen Brennan, Mr. Brennan's sister-in-law. "That was his life."

Although the storm didn't inflict severe damage on the pink building, the power failure ruined the wine cellar. "After four days, we knew the cellar was gone," said Ted Brennan, adding, "The wine broiled."

Among the casualties was the cellar's most precious bottle, a magnum of 1870 Lafite Rothschild. Bought at a 1976 auction, the bottle probably would be worth between $50,000 and $60,000 today, Ted Brennan said.

Before all the cellar's contents could go bad, Mr. Brennan embarked on what he called "the grand tasting" with Lazone Randolph, the chef, and a handful of people who had stayed in the restaurant to protect it from van-dalism and looting.

"I'd call in from Dallas—they couldn't call out—and one of them would tell me, 'This evening, we're seeing if the Lafite '28 is better than the Lafite '29,'" Ted Brennan said.

When the restaurant reopened, restocking the cellar was a top priority. Mr. Brennan outlined the plan, and it is being followed, his brother said.

The cellar has about 14,000 bottles, he said. "It's coming along quite nice-ly. This was his baby."

There was a private memorial service. "We toasted him with a bottle of Dom Perignon 1990, his favorite Champagne," Ted Brennan said, "and wished him bon voyage."

— August 1, 2010

Wendy Roberts

Queen Elizabeth II honored her service

Wendy Roberts, a displaced New Orleanian who was honored by Queen Elizabeth II for her work as leader of this country's chapter of the Daughters of the British Empire, died Saturday at St. Patrick's Manor in Framingham, Mass. She was 88.

A native of Hightown, England, who moved to New Orleans in 1948, Mrs. Roberts had lived in Massachusetts since Hurricane Katrina ruined her home in the Lakeview neighborhood, said Jane Denis, her daughter.

She yearned to return to New Orleans, but it was impossible, her daughter said.

Among Mrs. Roberts' possessions that were swept away was the bejeweled medal that the queen had given her at Buckingham Palace in 1986 to signify Mrs. Roberts' membership in the Most Excellent Order of the British Empire, Denis said.

The Daughters of the British Empire—a charitable, nonpolitical organization for women of British or Commonwealth birth or ancestry—raises money for assisted-living facilities across the United States, Denis said. Mrs. Roberts was its national president from 1983 to 1986.

She was born Dorothy Wendy Green, but she never used her first name. Mrs. Roberts moved to New Orleans with her husband, Geoffrey Roberts, who worked for Texas Terminal Transport and Terminal Shipping Agency.

He had become smitten with New Orleans when he did an internship in the city with Lykes Brothers Shipping Co. Inc., and was eager to return, Denis said.

Mrs. Roberts became active in the Daughters of the British Empire in the early 1950s. In addition to holding the presidency of the United States chapter of that organization, Mrs. Roberts was Great Britain's honorary vice consul for Louisiana.

"She loved her work and was a real ambassador for the city and the state in promoting trade and goodwill between our two countries," said James Coleman Jr., the honorary British consul for Louisiana.

In Queen Elizabeth's Birthday Honors List in 1986, she made Mrs. Roberts a member of the Most Excellent Order of the British Empire.

Mrs. Roberts, whose husband died in 1980, lived alone near the 17th Street Canal. The weekend before Katrina struck in August 2005, her neighbor, a doctor, insisted that she accompany him to University Hospital, where he was on duty, Denis said.

That suggestion probably saved Mrs. Roberts' life, her daughter said, because her home took on 6 feet of water when the 17th Street Canal Levee broke.

She and the doctor rode out the storm at the hospital, which is now the Interim Louisiana State University Hospital, Denis said.

Four days later, a bus took people who had been in the hospital to New Orleans' Louis Armstrong International Airport, where Mrs. Roberts and doctors from the hospital got a ride to New Iberia, La.

Her son-in-law, Serge Denis, flew south and brought her to Massachusetts.

— *August 17, 2010*

Philip Henry McCrory Jr.

He was a pharmacist and coffee entrepreneur

Philip Henry McCrory Jr., who was not only the director of the state's pharmacy but also an entrepreneur who developed a thriving business selling chilled coffee concentrate, died Wednesday of cancer at his Metairie home. He was 65.

A native New Orleanian, Mr. McCrory earned a bachelor's degree in pharmacy at Northeast Louisiana University, now the University of Louisiana at Monroe.

In 1975, he became the first pharmacist hired as director of pharmacy services in the state Office of Public Health. He held that job until the week before he died, said Leah Michael, the assistant director.

The office provides prescriptions to about 90 public health units and clinics around the state. Before Mr. McCrory was hired to coordinate the process at the state level, "they would just give (prescriptions) out with no rhyme or reason," Michael said.

Mr. McCrory also was the state's coordinator of the federal government's strategic national stockpile of pharmaceutical products, which are designed to be sent out in an emergency when a state committee requests them.

This inventory was tapped in the wake of Hurricane Katrina, Michael said, and Mr. McCrory was responsible for managing the distribution.

On the job and off, Mr. McCrory enjoyed a good cup of coffee, and he made cold-drip concentrate in the family kitchen, said Gregory McCrory, one of his sons.

Because his friends liked the coffee made from the concentrate, Mr. McCrory started thinking about selling it, his son said. After first making it in a back room of his house, Mr. McCrory rented a place from his brother Dennis where he could set up the machinery and bottle the results.

He landed his first account, Dorignac's Food Center, in 1987. The company was originally called Coffee Extractors of New Orleans, but it was reborn in 1989 as New Orleans Coffee Co.

Its product, CoolBrew Coffee, comes in seven flavors. About 6,000 bottles are produced each week, Gregory McCrory said, and they are sold in the New Orleans area, two other Louisiana cities—Baton Rouge and Lafayette—and as far east as Pensacola, Fla.

The CoolBrew Coffee plastic bottle includes a small container at the top into which a coffee drinker squeezes the concentrate.

After Hurricane Katrina, the company added a fleur-de-lis to that part of the bottle. That emblem has become a symbol of the region's determination to rebuild after the devastating storm.

Mr. McCrory, who installed solar panels on the family home, received an award in 2004 from Mayor Marc Morial for "creative reduction of energy and waste while producing a quality product," according to the citation.

In recognition of his work in the Office of Public Health, he received the Charles E. Dunbar Jr. Career Service Award from the Louisiana Civil Service League.

— *August 24, 2010*

Jill Jackson

She politely dispensed Hollywood gossip

Jill Jackson, a pioneering New Orleans sportscaster who moved to Hollywood to do a gossip column that ran for decades in hundreds of newspapers, including the Times-Picayune, died Wednesday at the Beverly Hills Rehabilitation Center. She was 97.

Ms. Jackson, who at her peak was syndicated to 1,700 newspapers, never stopped working, composing her columns on a manual Olivetti typewriter, said Loraine Despres, a cousin.

"She was very proud of this," Despres said. "I talked with her a couple of weeks ago, and she said, 'I've never missed a deadline.'"

Ms. Jackson was a throwback to a time in Hollywood when a gossip columnist like Hedda Hopper—a friend of Ms. Jackson's—was powerful enough to make or break careers.

Among Ms. Jackson's friends were the actors Edward G. Robinson, Joan Blondell, and Joan Fontaine; Michael Curtiz, the director whose pictures included *Casablanca*; and Frances Marion, who in 1931 became the first woman to win a screenwriting Oscar.

Ms. Jackson, who also wrote for *Rider's Digest*, which appeared weekly on New Orleans buses and streetcars, was tame by today's standards.

"She did not want to say ugly things about people in print," Despres said. "It makes her memoir less exciting than it would have been if she had really told the dirt."

She also had bit parts in movies, including some that her friend Ross Hunter produced. Among them were *Madame X*, in which she was a police matron, and *Airport*, in which, Ms. Jackson said in a 1993 interview, she played a passenger whose face was obscured by an oxygen mask and a hefty fellow flier.

Although Ms. Jackson's years in Hollywood provided plenty of opportunities to hobnob with movie stars, she had had a notable career in New Orleans before she headed west in 1960.

Born Alice (pronounced "ah-LEESE") Schwartz, Ms. Jackson graduated from Sophie B. Wright High School and Newcomb College, where she was active in the drama club. She also performed in productions at Le Petit Théâtre du Vieux Carré.

Ms. Jackson, who had written for the *New Orleans Item*, one of the city's two afternoon newspapers, became friends with Peggy and Henry Dupré when both worked for WWL-AM. She fell in love with radio when Peggy Dupré asked Ms. Jackson to be on her show, according to a 2008 interview in *New Orleans Magazine*.

Because Ms. Jackson had played golf and tennis, Henry Dupré asked her to cover a women's golf tournament. On the strength of that assignment, WSMB-AM offered her a five-minute sportscast each weekday, and she took it. It was sponsored by Jax beer, a factor that gave birth to the name she adopted and used for the rest of her life.

Ms. Jackson, who moved to WWL-AM, was a lonely pioneer for women on the sports beat. She had to sit outside in the rain for football games because women weren't allowed in the press box. Because Tulane University barred women from football practice, Ms. Jackson spied on the team from a nearby oak tree.

Despite the sexism, she insisted that she loved that time in her life, Despres said, adding that Ms. Jackson once said, "I would have paid them" to do what she did.

Ms. Jackson was eventually elected to the Associated Press' Sportscasters' Club, and she became a member of *Esquire* magazine's sports poll. However, according to the New Orleans Magazine interview, her membership card was made out to "Mr. Jill Jackson."

She got a job as host of a weekly broadcast from Brennan's Restaurant, where she interviewed celebrity diners. In her honor, the restaurant created a salad bearing her name.

One of her more memorable celebrity interviews, Despres said, involved climbing onto the shoulders of Karl Wallenda, a member of the legendary circus family, and talking to him as he stepped onto the tightrope. There was no net. They didn't go farther than a few inches because she was terrified of heights.

"Sometimes, I wish I'd had guts enough to cross that wire," Ms. Jackson wrote in her memoir. "Today, I might be famous. On the other hand, I might be dead."

Ms. Jackson was president of the Hollywood Women's Press Club in the 1970s. The organization gave her a Life Achievement Award in 2004.

— September 10, 2010

Bill Monroe

A TV pioneer and Meet the Press *host*

Bill Monroe, a pioneer in New Orleans television who became NBC's Washington bureau chief and moderator of *Meet the Press*, died Thursday in a Potomac, Md., nursing home. He was 90.

A native New Orleanian who graduated from Tulane University with a Phi Beta Kappa key, Mr. Monroe was WDSU-TV's first news director when he joined the NBC affiliate in 1954.

Although Mr. Monroe was new to television, he was no stranger to broadcasting. In 1946, after serving in Italy for three years with the Army Air Corps during World War II, Mr. Monroe joined WNOE-AM as the New Orleans station's news director.

In 1950, the *New Orleans Item*, one of the city's two afternoon papers, hired him as an editorial writer. Mr. Monroe had had print experience as a New Orleans reporter for the United Press wire service before he went to war.

The WDSU news staff amounted to "three or four people who just read the news," he said in a 1998 interview. "Early television reporters were converted from newspaper reporters."

Mr. Monroe hired a fleet of seasoned journalists, including the reporters Alec Gifford, Ed Planer, and Bill Slatter, and the photographers Mike Lala and Jim Tolhurst.

The station had already made a name for itself in 1951, when it covered U.S. Sen. Estes Kefauver's organized-crime hearings in New Orleans. Five years later, after Earl K. Long was re-elected governor, Mr. Monroe sent Gifford and Lala to Baton Rouge to show what he felt would be an interesting legislative session.

This was long before open-meetings laws, but nobody said anything, Mr. Monroe said in the interview, because everyone seemed to believe that someone had given them permission.

"We were there a week and a half before we were challenged," he said. Long tried to have them removed, but the New Orleans delegation resisted because its members had become stars.

That experiment "put people in touch with the Legislature in a way they hadn't seen before," Mr. Monroe said in the interview. "The Legislature came alive. We got more letters for that than any other thing we did."

During that period, the station started airing editorials that Mr. Monroe wrote and delivered. The station stirred up controversy when it called for calm during the civil-rights period, when New Orleans' public schools were facing desegregation. There were about 50 editorials related to the civil rights movement.

For the editorials, WDSU won a Peabody Award and a national award from the Radio and Television News Directors Association.

In 1961, NBC hired Mr. Monroe to be its Washington bureau chief. He later became the Washington editor of *Today*, and he conducted interviews with an array of officials, including Vice President Spiro Agnew, Attorney General John Mitchell, New York Gov. Nelson Rockefeller, Ralph Nader, and U.S. Sen. Edward Kennedy.

For those interviews, Mr. Monroe won a Peabody Award in 1972. Three days later, he succeeded Lawrence Spivak as moderator of *Meet the Press*, a job he held until 1984.

Because of the position Mr. Monroe held and because he and his wife, Elizabeth Monroe, loved to socialize, they were on the party circuit and gave frequent dinner parties, said Lee Monroe, one of his four daughters. On such occasions, she said, she met dignitaries such as U.S. Supreme Court Justices William O. Douglas and Hugo Black.

Although Mr. Monroe, who possessed a deep voice, could be deadly serious on the air, "he was something of a bon vivant, with a good sense of humor," his daughter said. "He was a jazz aficionado. There was always music."

Mr. Monroe left NBC in 1984 to become editor of the *Washington Journalism Review* (now the *American Journalism Review*). He then became the ombudsman for *Stars and Stripes*, the military newspaper, a job that required trips to Japan every other month.

Mr. Monroe was a former president of the Radio-TV Correspondents Association and a former member of Tulane's Board of Administrators.

— *February 18, 2011*

Jessie Poesch

She was a scholar of Southern decorative arts

Jessie Poesch, a scholar blessed with unflagging curiosity who spent a half-century studying such decorative creations as paintings, pottery and prints, died April 23 at Touro Infirmary of complications from surgery. She was 88.

Dr. Poesch was an art professor at Tulane University's Newcomb College. Her books and articles on topics such as armoires, New Orleans gravestones, Louisiana architecture, and Newcomb pottery fill four single-spaced pages of her résumé.

"She pioneered the field of Southern decorative arts," said William Ferris, a longtime friend and a former chairman of the National Endowment for the Humanities. "She was the dean of the field."

Despite her formidable knowledge, Dr. Poesch was "the nicest person you could want to meet," said Lawrence Powell, a friend and colleague who is director of the New Orleans Gulf South Center at Tulane.

"Brilliance and personal warmth don't always go together," he said, "but she combined them to a rare degree."

Dr. Poesch joined the Tulane faculty in 1963. She officially retired in 1992, and an endowed art professorship was established that year in her honor.

Despite what was supposed to be a change in her status, Dr. Poesch kept an office on campus and she continued to work.

"She had other things to say and other things to research," said Sally Main, a close friend, who collaborated with Dr. Poesch on a 2003 book on Newcomb pottery. "She never stopped being intellectually curious, and she never ran out of things that she wanted to write about."

Shortly before her death, Dr. Poesch finished a book on the Great Dismal Swamp, a 750-square-mile expanse that straddles Virginia and North Carolina and is as big as Rhode Island.

This area, which had been a hideout for runaway slaves, is not only a reminder of the wilderness that once dominated North America but also a magnet for photographers and painters, said Ferris, the senior associate director of the Center for the Study of the American South at the University of North Carolina at Chapel Hill.

Although Dr. Poesch was acclaimed for her work—she was a Fulbright scholar who received grants from the National Endowment for the Humanities—she happened on her career by accident, Main said.

A native of Postville, Iowa, Dr. Poesch graduated from Antioch College in 1944 with a degree in psychology but wasn't sure what she wanted to do. She worked with the American Friends Service Committee reuniting families in Europe after World War II, Main said, and she worked briefly at the State Department.

When Dr. Poesch heard a friend say he was going to take an art-history class, that appealed to her, Main said, so she signed up.

She did an internship at the Winterthur Program in American Material Culture, which is part of the University of Delaware, and earned a master's degree. She also earned master's and doctoral degrees in art history at the University of Pennsylvania.

— *April 30, 2011*

Kathleen "Kathy" Vick

She called the roll at Democratic conventions

Kathleen "Kathy" Vick, the New Orleans political operative who was best known for calling the roll of the states as Democrats picked their presidential and vice-presidential candidates at three national conventions, died Monday of Alzheimer's disease at Poydras Home in New Orleans. She was 72.

An outgoing blonde who was barely 5 feet tall, Ms. Vick seemed to make friends—and political contacts—wherever she went.

"She was a woman with a million friends," former Gov. Kathleen Blanco said. "If you met Kathy, you loved her instantly."

By the time Ms. Vick was elected the Democratic Party's secretary in 1989, she had been a member of the Democratic National Committee for 15 years—long enough to develop a national profile.

Three years later, when she conducted her first roll call at the 1992 convention that nominated Bill Clinton and Al Gore, the suspense of that event had vanished because the party's nominees had been chosen via state primaries since the 1970s.

Nevertheless, political junkies keep their eyes glued to the roll call on television, if only to hear delegation leaders deliver florid descriptions of their states and territories—"Guam, where America's day begins," for example—as they cast their votes.

Even though Ms. Vick's unpaid job as party secretary put her in the global spotlight every four years, she said that wasn't where her interest lay.

"Real life is out in the states and counties, in elections, in state and local politics," she said in a 1989 interview.

Ms. Vick, who grew up in a Republican household in New Orleans' Garden District, graduated from the Louise S. McGehee School and Wellesley College.

She worked for the Associated Press in New York City for two years before returning to New Orleans to work as a volunteer in deLesseps S. "Chep" Morrison's unsuccessful gubernatorial campaign in 1960.

With that campaign, she said in a 1984 interview, Ms. Vick knew she had found what she wanted to do. "It was like a duck falling into water," she said.

Ms. Vick moved to Washington, D.C., to work for U.S. Sen. Eugene McCarthy when the Minnesota Democrat sought the party's vice-presidential nomination in 1964. In 1968, she worked in U.S. Sen. Robert Kennedy's presidential campaign.

She was executive assistant to Michael O'Keefe when he was the Louisiana Senate president.

Ms. Vick also started getting involved in the inner workings of the Democratic Party. She was elected to the Democratic State Central Committee and was its first vice chairwoman.

On the national level, Ms. Vick was president of the Democrats' organization of state party leaders, and she was the first person who wasn't an elected official to lead the party's Rules Committee, which settles squabbles over such matters as seating at the national convention.

"I never thought I'd be a rules junkie. I always thought those people were weird," Ms. Vick said in a 1987 interview, "and now I'm one of them."

Ms. Vick also had a knack for spotting talent, said Raymond "Coach" Blanco, the former governor's husband.

She "recognized something in Kathleen that other people didn't see," he said. "It was kinda way out that she saw in this young mother with six kids who had a future in politics. Kathy had that instinct."

Starting with the Legislature in 1983, Blanco went on to be a member of the Public Service Commission, lieutenant governor, and, in 2003, governor.

Ms. Vick, who also ran a public-relations business out of her Garden District home, was named a YWCA role model in 1990. In 1996, she was inducted into the Hall of Fame of the Louisiana Center for Women and Government.

— *May 14, 2011*

Henry George Schmidt

"What interested him was having a good life"

Henry George Schmidt, a bon vivant with a roguish eye who was a fixture on dance floors around New Orleans well into his 10th decade, died Tuesday at Chateau de Notre Dame. He was 100.

Mr. Schmidt held a series of jobs. In his youth, he sold clothes to Huey Long, including a pair of pajamas that became notorious.

Friends and family members said Mr. Schmidt never was defined by the way he earned a living. To those who knew him, Mr. Schmidt was a free spirit who devoted his life to enjoying the city, often accompanied by his younger son, Jimmy.

He could be counted on to show up, nattily dressed, at restaurants and dances, and at concerts by the New Leviathan Oriental Fox-Trot Orchestra, which his older son, George, helped found.

"He enjoyed life more than anyone I know," said Julia Woodward Burka, a longtime friend. "What interested him was having a good life."

And wherever he went, everyone seemed to know him, Burka said.

Mr. Schmidt was a native New Orleanian who seldom ventured far from the Crescent City, even when he was drafted in World War II. After his family saw him off on the troop train, not knowing where he was going, Mr. Schmidt wound up being deployed to Biloxi, Miss., only 90 miles away, his son George said.

Mr. Schmidt grew up in a musical family. His mother sang in the chorus at the French Opera House, where he played backstage as a youngster; his sister was a vocalist with several bands; and an uncle played piano in a Storyville brothel and, later, accompanied silent movies on the organ in local theaters.

After Mr. Schmidt graduated from Jesuit High School, he worked at Stevens Men's Wear. One day in the early 1930s, U.S. Sen. Huey P. Long happened to walk into the store with his entourage, and, George Schmidt said, his father took it upon himself to tell the Kingfish how to sharpen up his image to make a better impression in Washington.

For instance, he advised Long to wear double-breasted suits, and he told him to get a better set of neckties and a hat with a narrower, more fashionable brim than the one Long had been sporting.

And then one day, Mr. Schmidt sold his most notable client a pair of green silk pajamas with a paisley pattern and a cinch belt. The cost: $12.50, the equivalent of about $175 today.

That outfit became infamous because Long wore the pajamas to receive the captain of a visiting German ship when he paid a courtesy call on Long in his Roosevelt Hotel suite.

International tut-tutting ensued, George Schmidt said, and anti-Long forces even re-enacted the scene for a newsreel to show off what they felt was Long's boorishness.

Years later, George Schmidt said he found the pajamas on display in a bedroom in the Old Governor's Mansion, which has been converted into a museum in Baton Rouge.

Throughout his life, Mr. Schmidt never left his house without being splendidly turned out from top to toe, Burka said, and that included a hat— a Panama in summer, a fedora in winter.

But, she said, Mr. Schmidt advised that there's more to wearing a hat than simply plopping it atop one's head. "He told my husband, 'You've got to wear a hat with a jaunty air,'" she said.

Among the women whom the spiffily dressed bachelor dated were Dorothy Lamour, who went on to star with Bing Crosby and Bob Hope in a series of "Road" movies, and Helen Kane, the model for the cartoon character Betty Boop.

From his youth well into his old age, Mr. Schmidt gravitated toward dances. Peggy Scott Laborde, a WYES-TV producer who interviewed Mr. Schmidt and his son George for her documentaries, remembered dancing with Mr. Schmidt at the Jazz and Heritage Festival to the music of the New Leviathan.

"He was a great dancer," she said in an email, "and this was when he was in his late 80s!!"

After Mr. Schmidt worked briefly as a Goodyear salesman, he and his wife, Jo, ran the Lauralee Guest House on St. Charles Avenue.

Mr. Schmidt later was a clerk and checker for the New Orleans Steamship Association; it was the post from which he retired.

In retirement, George Schmidt said, his father roamed the city, striking up conversations with strangers and tossing off stories about vanished landmarks and the people who had inhabited them.

"When you talked to Dad, it was like an oral-history interview," the younger Schmidt said. "Dad had a historical memory."

— *June 17, 2011*

John "Johnny" Mosca

He presided over a culinary landmark

John Mosca, whose white-frame Avondale restaurant bearing his surname is a Mecca for gourmands craving such garlic-infused specialties as barbecue shrimp, baked oysters, and marinated crab salad, died Wednesday of cancer at his Harahan home. He was 86.

Even though he was Mosca's owner, Mr. Mosca (pronounced "Mow-sca") was no figurehead.

"His whole life was consumed with the restaurant, from the time he was a young man until he died," said Harahan Mayor Vinny Mosca, a nephew.

For years, Mr. Mosca, who was known to everyone as Johnny, arose at 5 a.m. to shop for what the restaurant might need that day; drop off his daughter, Lisa, at school; and do more shopping. He made sausages, his daughter said, and he used to make all the pasta and set it out on the tables to dry.

"He was always moving," she said. "It was his nature just to keep going."

At night, Mr. Mosca was at the bar, greeting customers, mixing drinks, and chatting with friends.

"When you walked in, you always expected to see him," said the writer Calvin Trillin, who profiled the restaurant last year in the *New Yorker*. "He was friendly, but not effusive. He had a dry wit, and a kind of twinkly poker face."

When Mr. Mosca sat, it was at a small table at the end of the bar, near the passageway to the kitchen.

"He was a quiet person who had a gigantic love of his customers," Vinny Mosca said. "Oftentimes, it was hard to decipher that because he was serious at the restaurant to make sure things were working properly. Every once in a while, you'd see him smile."

"He enjoyed being at the restaurant," Lisa Mosca said. "I think that's what kept him active and healthy for so long."

A native of Chicago Heights, Ill., Mr. Mosca went to high school there and worked in a restaurant, also named Mosca's, that his parents, Provino and Lisa Mosca, operated.

He served in the Army in World War II. After he was wounded in Italy, Mr. Mosca was sent to the British forces. Because of his restaurant experience, he was put to work as a waiter to high-ranking officers.

Mr. Mosca's natural reticence probably helped him get that job, Vinny Mosca said. "They knew he wouldn't discuss their business with anyone, and they respected that."

Among the people he served were Gen. Dwight Eisenhower, British Prime Minister Winston Churchill, and Josip Broz Tito, leader of the Yugoslav partisans, when they met at the Villa Rivalta in Naples in 1944.

After Mr. Mosca was discharged, he moved to New Orleans to be with his parents, who had headed south because their daughter, Mary, had married Vincent Marconi, a New Orleanian.

They originally hoped to open a restaurant on the east bank of the Mississippi River, Lisa Mosca said, but that deal fell through.

They found a white building on a lonely stretch of U.S. 90 that used to be Willswood Tavern. Since they needed the income, "they were desperate," Lisa Mosca said, "and they took it. I guess it worked out."

The bill of fare was similar to what they had offered in Illinois, but the family adapted it to take advantage of oysters, crabs, and shrimp, said Mary Jo Mosca, Mr. Mosca's wife. Portions were—and remain—huge, and no one grumbled about the location, slightly more than five miles west of the Huey P. Long Bridge.

"It always had the feel of a neighborhood restaurant, except there was no neighborhood," James Edmunds of New Iberia said in Trillin's *New Yorker* article.

Finding it in the dark could be a challenge to people making the drive from New Orleans, Trillin said. "You had to keep your eye to the left or you'd wind up in Morgan City."

When Hurricane Katrina roared through, the front part of the restaurant was relatively unscathed, Lisa Mosca said, but the back roof, which was old, caved in, forcing the family to build a new kitchen.

The building got new white siding, too, that was the same color as the material it replaced. That was important, Mary Jo Mosca said in a 2006 interview. "Customers don't want to see change. When we stained the floor, they had a fit."

The menu has remained virtually the same during the past 65 years. The only change, Lisa Mosca said, "is now they offer half-orders."

— July 15, 2011

Richard "Buzzy" Gaiennie

A recovering alcoholic who led thousands to sobriety

Richard "Buzzy" Gaiennie, a recovering alcoholic who built Bridge House into a respected center that has treated about 23,000 substance abusers since 1984, died Saturday of multiple organ failure at Ochsner Baptist Medical Center. He was 72.

"The city has lost one of its great champions in the fight against the disease of alcoholism and other addictions," said Laura Claverie, who had worked with Mr. Gaiennie when she was president of the board of the Council on Alcohol and Drug Abuse.

"Buzzy gave everybody a deep awareness of the disease of alcoholism and its tremendous impact on a family and a community," she said. "Most of all, he gave us a sense of compassion. I don't think there was ever anything judgmental about him. He just reached out and wanted to help."

Mr. Gaiennie (pronounced "GAHN-yay") was already in recovery when he came to Bridge House in 1984. "He decided that was what he wanted to devote his life to," his daughter Michelle Gaiennie said, even though it meant selling a Buick dealership that had been in his family for three generations.

When Mr. Gaiennie was hired, he was Bridge House's only staff member. Now 75 people are on the payroll, and Bridge House, a residential treatment facility for men, has merged with Grace House, which offers similar services for women, said Michelle Gaiennie, Grace House's executive director.

Bridge House has moved into a new $9.5 million headquarters. On any given day, Bridge House and Grace House are serving about 215 men and women in a variety of programs, said Else Pedersen, Bridge House's executive director.

"None of this would have been here if it hadn't been for his vision," said Kevin Gardere, a veteran of Bridge House's treatment program who is its director of major gifts. "He was my mentor, my spiritual director—a true leader."

Mr. Gaiennie became chief executive officer of Bridge House Corp., which runs both facilities.

Despite that title and the duties that come with it, he tried to spend as much time as possible with people in treatment, Pedersen said. "He loved to be around people who were looking to improve themselves.... That was his life."

A native of Lafayette, La., Mr. Gaiennie moved to New Orleans with his family during his childhood.

He received his nickname—the only name by which most people knew him—from a grandmother, Michelle Gaiennie said. Mr. Gaiennie longed to be called Richard, but when people heard his family call him Buzzy, "he couldn't get away from it," she said.

He graduated from Loyola University. While in the automobile business, he was president of the Louisiana Automobile Dealers Association and a member of the state Motor Vehicle Commission. Mr. Gaiennie became a licensed addictions counselor.

When Jim Mora was the New Orleans Saints' coach, Mr. Gaiennie was the team's substance-abuse counselor.

A deeply religious man who started every day by praying, he also was a deacon in the Catholic Church. Earlier this year, Mr. Gaiennie announced that he had planned to retire in December.

He felt he had come full circle, Pedersen said, because he appeared in television spots urging people to donate their cars to Bridge House. "I left being a car salesman," she said he told her, "and now I'm right back at it."

— August 16, 2011

Lala Dunbar

A physician who "kept going and going and going"

Dr. Lala Dunbar, who relied on determination and a lifelong love of science to earn a midlife medical degree and become a director of Charity Hospital's emergency department, died Aug. 26 of cancer at her New Orleans home. She was 77.

Dr. Dunbar, who also held a doctorate in biochemistry, worked 12-hour shifts in the emergency department at the Interim Louisiana State University Public Hospital until June, even though she had been battling colon cancer for more than two years, said Deborah Sibley, her research coordinator for 17 years.

"She was an Energizer bunny who kept going and going and going," Sibley said.

Born Lalawanda Mathers in Birmingham, Ala.—she dropped the last two syllables of her first name when she got married—Dr. Dunbar grew up when science was an overwhelmingly male profession.

She earned a bachelor's degree in chemistry at George Washington University, where she was a cheerleader. A picture of her in midair, doing a cheer, ran on the front page of The Washington Post, Sibley said, where it caught the eye of James Dunbar, a Naval Academy cadet who had been on the rowing team that won a gold medal at the 1952 Olympics. They married in 1955.

When her husband was sent to Vietnam, she went to graduate school in biochemistry at GWU. She received no encouragement, she said in a memoir, until she scored a 98 on the first test—34 points above the class average.

She applied twice to medical school and was turned down both times, her son Thad Dunbar said. The reason she was given, Dunbar said, was that, at 40, she was too old.

When a first-year student dropped out around Christmas, she asked for another chance and was told she would be admitted if she could pass an anatomy exam a month later.

Determined to get in, she spent what would have been Christmas vacation studying and dissecting cadavers, her son said. It paid off: She passed, with a grade above the class average.

She graduated and completed a residency in internal medicine at Washington Medical Center. After her husband retired from the Air Force in 1981, they moved to Waynesboro, Miss., where she worked in the local hospital's emergency room.

The Dunbars were divorced in 1983.

During a visit to New Orleans, Dr. Dunbar learned that Charity Hospital wanted someone with her experience. She joined the staff in 1985, taught at LSU School of Medicine and became director of the emergency department's medical side, which handles cases such as heart and asthma attacks and diabetes complications.

She also became a researcher who produced enough articles and book chapters to fill 13 pages of her résumé. For 18 years, her son said, Dr. Dunbar also was active in medical missions to Central America with Trinity Episcopal Church.

For five days after Hurricane Katrina, Dr. Dunbar stayed at the swamped Charity Hospital, said Dr. Keith Van Meter, head of the emergency-medicine section at LSU Health Sciences Center.

During her breaks, she climbed 13 flights of stairs to her office—the hospital had no electricity—to work on her research.

She was unflappable, Van Meter said, even when 10 armed SWAT team members were dropped by helicopter onto the roof of Charity and entered through her window, responding to a report of a sniper atop a nearby building.

"Do you need directions?" Van Meter remembered hearing Dr. Dunbar say calmly. "They were like goslings following behind her."

The report turned out to be false.

Although she stopped working full-time in June, Dr. Dunbar came in to work on her research.

"Her holiday was to come to work," Van Meter said. "She was a marvel."

— *September 4, 2011*

Taffy Maginnis

She knew how to make audiences laugh

Taffy Maginnis, an actress blessed with dead-on comic timing who performed on local stages for more than a half-century, died Monday at Christwood Retirement Community in Covington. She was 84.

Though she never had any formal training, Mrs. Maginnis could reduce audiences to fits of laughter with the way she delivered a line, or just with a look or gesture.

"My sons always said that when Taffy said hello, it knocked you out," said M. I. Scoggin, a longtime friend who performed with her for decades.

Mrs. Maginnis, who also dabbled in puppetry, started acting in the Junior League. Among the plays in which she performed were *The Madwoman of Chaillot, Steel Magnolias, A Christmas Carol*, and *Native Tongues 2*, a program of monologues in which Mrs. Maginnis portrayed an Uptown real-estate agent who gossiped, with gleeful zest, about her profession and its practitioners.

"The essence of a born actor is to be a detective," said Sheila Bosworth Lemann, who wrote that monologue. "An actor uncovers the heart of a character. By uncovering the heart of a character, Taffy could look at a character and go right to the context. That made her a formidable person, on stage and off."

Performing runs in the family. Her sister, Mary Louise Wilson, is a Tony-winning actress, and their brother, Hugh, was a pianist.

Mrs. Maginnis was born in Saranac Lake, N.Y., but she grew up in New Orleans because her father, Dr. Julius Wilson, came to teach at Tulane University School of Medicine. When Ochsner Clinic opened, he was its first medical director.

Mrs. Maginnis was born Helen Octavia Wilson, a name she never used. When she was a child, playmates called her Tavy, Blum said, but her father decided it should be Taffy, and the name stuck.

She graduated from Isidore Newman School. She studied at the Art Institute of Chicago but did not graduate.

For about 30 years, Mrs. Maginnis was the Rex organization's costume coordinator. To take care of last-minute Mardi Gras emergencies, Mrs. Maginnis toted extra gloves and masks, plenty of safety pins, needles, thread— and a staple gun.

In a 1993 interview, she explained gleefully why she liked her job: "It's quite nice being surrounded by so many men."

When Mrs. Maginnis' coffin was rolled down the aisle at her funeral, the mourners gave her a round of applause.

— November 3, 2011

Yvonne "Miss Dixie" Fasnacht

"Everybody who was anybody" went to her bar

Yvonne "Miss Dixie" Fasnacht, the fun-loving, no-nonsense proprietor of two New Orleans bars where gay men and lesbians could socialize comfortably long before anyone thought of coming out of the closet, died Sunday at her home in suburban Metairie. She was 101.

Dixie's Bar of Music, which was in the Central Business District for a decade before Ms. Fasnacht moved it to Bourbon Street in 1949, became a landmark that attracted such luminaries as the ballerina Margot Fonteyn, the actors Helen Hayes and Danny Kaye, newsman Walter Cronkite, and U.S. Rep. F. Edward Hébert.

"Dixie's was the kind of place where Uptown and downtown, straight and gay, celebrities and regular folks rubbed shoulders," a customer said in a 1996 *Times-Picayune* interview that included this observation from another former regular: "Everybody who was anybody ended up at Dixie's."

Despite that lofty reputation, "it was a gay bar," said Frank Gagnard, a retired *Times-Picayune* critic, who was a customer.

"It was more a social center than it was a pickup bar," he said. "It was where gay people went to meet friends. Miss Dixie didn't allow any hanky-panky at all."

"She didn't intend to have a gay bar," said Peter Patout, a former neighbor and longtime friend. "It was a bar, and gays were there. It was known as a gay bar. She didn't advertise it."

Ms. Fasnacht, a devout Catholic who unplugged the jukebox on Good Friday, ran the bar with her sister, Irma, who was stationed at the cash register, a massive, chrome-plated machine that regulars called "the mighty Wurlitzer."

The bar got its name because Ms. Fasnacht, a lifelong New Orleanian, was a musician who played the saxophone and clarinet and pounded the tambourine.

In her youth, she joined a local group called the Harmony Maids. When the Smart Set, an all-female band, came to town and the saxophone player quit, Ms. Fasnacht filled in.

The band later called her to join the musicians in Pittsburgh, where, Ms. Fasnacht said in a 1996 interview, she saw snow for the first time. Because that bowled her over, one of the musicians said, "We're not calling you Yvonne anymore. We're calling you Dixie," Ms. Fasnacht said in the interview. "Anyhoo, I've been Dixie ever since."

That group disbanded and reorganized as the Southland Rhythm Girls, but it fell apart in the late 1930s, so Ms. Fasnacht returned home to New Orleans.

In 1939, she and her sister opened the first Dixie's Bar of Music at 204 St. Charles Ave., across from the St. Charles Hotel. Ms. Fasnacht, who had gone to school with the singing Boswell Sisters, occasionally performed.

During the bar's last years at that site, "we started to get the gay crowd," she said in the interview, "and once you're established, that's it. They're loyal. You can always bet on that."

She repaid that loyalty. In less tolerant times, "when there were raids, she would take the money out of her cash register and bail everybody out," Patout said.

In 1949, the Fasnachts decamped to 701 Bourbon St., where the bar operated until Ms. Fasnacht sold it in 1964.

"I was getting older, and so were the customers," she said in explaining her decision to quit. "Miss Irma and I lived over the bar, and it was hard for her to climb those stairs." Irma Fasnacht died in 1993.

A fixture in both bars was a 35-foot mural of 66 celebrities, with their autographs, that Ms. Fasnacht donated to the Louisiana State Museum.

— November 17, 2011

Arthur Q. Davis

His firm designed the Superdome

Arthur Q. Davis, the modernist architect who was instrumental in redefining New Orleans' skyline, died Wednesday at Ochsner Baptist Medical Center. He was 91.

For 41 years, Mr. Davis and his partner, Nathaniel Curtis, formed the firm that designed such major buildings as the Superdome, the Rivergate Exhibition Center, the New Orleans Public Library's Main Branch, St. Frances Cabrini Catholic Church, and the University of New Orleans Lakefront Arena. The firm won about 50 awards for design excellence. In addition to projects in the United States, the firm designed buildings in Vietnam, Aruba, Scotland, Indonesia, and Germany.

"It was the pivotal firm of the city from the 1950s on," said Tulane University Architecture Dean Kenneth Schwartz. "Their legacy is really extensive, not only in New Orleans but also across the world."

Mr. Davis was a lifelong New Orleanian who, according to a story on the Pirate's Alley Faulkner Society website, took an interest in architecture when he was a boy and happened on a mason laying bricks. The man patiently explained what he was doing, Mr. Davis said, and described how the blueprint, tacked to a piece of plywood, showed what he needed to do to build a chimney.

"I knew I wanted to become an architect from that moment," he said.

Mr. Davis graduated from Tulane University and went to work designing wooden structures that the Navy used to build flying boats. During World War II, Mr. Davis served in the Navy, designing camouflage for the ships of the Pacific fleet, including the U.S.S. *Missouri*, the battleship aboard which Japan surrendered.

He studied at Harvard University, where he earned a master's degree after working under such modernist masters as Walter Gropius and Marcel Breuer.

He interned with Eero Saarinen before forming Curtis and Davis with his fellow Tulane alumnus. Curtis died in 1997.

In 1988, Mr. Davis established his own firm bearing his name. During that period, he designed the New Orleans Arena [now the Smoothie King Center].

In 2009, he wrote a memoir, "It Happened by Design."

Throughout his career, "he always moved forward and never stepped back," said his son, Quint, producer and director of the New Orleans Jazz and Heritage Festival. "He was like some kind of nuclear reactor; he always had the energy to go forward."

— December 2, 2011

Judy Cobb

She designed gowns for Mardi Gras queens

Judy Cobb, who turned out hundreds of meticulously crafted gowns for Carnival royalty for 35 years, died Sunday of cancer at her New Orleans home. She was 72.

Even though so many of her creations had to be all-white and floor-length—factors that might put a crimp in creativity—clients said Ms. Cobb unfailingly managed to inject variety, and a bit of each client's personality, into her work.

"Judy read their personalities," said Alice DePass, her business partner and close friend. "She had a knack of knowing what looks good on what girl. (The dress) doesn't express Judy; it expresses the girl."

For instance, Amélie Brown, who was queen of Carnival in 2009, likes being outdoors. So Ms. Cobb found a lace pattern that looked like branches that would be twining up and down her gown. It featured hundreds of beads applied by hand to every leaf and stem. Brown donated the gown to the Louisiana State Museum.

Each one of Ms. Cobb's gowns could take months to create, from the first sketches to the final fitting, and cost as much as $20,000, DePass said.

Because of Ms. Cobb's experience, she knew not only how to make her creations distinctive but also how to tailor them to the taste of the organizations where they would appear.

"She knew what to do and what to avoid," said King Logan, whose daughter Virginia wore a Cobb creation when she was queen of Atlanteans in 2003. "You might aggravate people if you put more beading or rhinestones into a particular queen's dress if you had the money and wanted to impress people. There are some organizations where the expectation is that the dress will be not over the top, but at the top."

Ms. Cobb, a native New Orleanian, started wielding a needle and thread when she took sewing at Metairie Park Country Day School. Her graduation present was a sewing machine.

DePass, also an enthusiastic seamstress, said Ms. Cobb started sewing for hire by making clothes for her friends. When DePass needed help, she turned to Ms. Cobb, a neighbor, and the two women went into business in 1972.

"Judy had an engineer's mind," DePass said. "Anything I came up with, she could do."

Not all the clients were Carnival royalty. One was a prizefighter who asked Ms. Cobb to design his satin robe and boxing shorts, DePass said in a *New Orleans Magazine* interview.

The business, called Alice Designs, grew through word of mouth, moving into gowns for Carnival because, DePass said, "we knew all the people involved in Mardi Gras."

In the 2010–11 season alone, the shop turned out ball gowns for five queens.

— December 20, 2011

Barbara Wellam Songy

A concerned mother who set up a school cafeteria

Barbara Wellam Songy, a concerned mother who built and stocked a school cafeteria and then ran it for 50 years even though she had no experience in food-service management, died Dec. 27 at her Metairie home. She was 89.

A native of London who had lived in the New Orleans area since 1947, Mrs. Songy was alarmed when she learned in the early 1950s that her son's lunch at Our Lady of Perpetual Help School in Kenner consisted of a luncheon-meat sandwich and a bottle of Dr Pepper, said her daughter, Jeanine Songy Latham.

So Mrs. Songy set to work to see what she could do to ensure that her son and his fellow pupils received healthful lunches.

She learned that the federal government would pay for the kitchen equipment if the school would provide the space, Latham said. Working with the Sisters of Mercy, who taught at the school, she collected $5,000 through fundraisers. The St. Rosalie Society of Perpetual Help matched it so construction could start.

When the cafeteria opened in 1955, Mrs. Songy was asked to manage it on a temporary basis. She wound up staying 50 years, until she retired in the spring of 2005.

"She knew nothing about cooking," Latham said. "Our dad cooked. That's what makes this so ironic."

Even though Mrs. Songy spent most of her life in a field for which she had no formal training, Latham said her mother was blessed with a natural gift for mathematics. During World War II in England, she had been a bookkeeper before going to work in a factory making airplane machinery.

She also taught ice skating. That was how she met Gerard Songy, a member of the 8th Air Force stationed in England. Because he was from Edgard,

La., he had no experience on the ice, Latham said, and Barbara Wellam helped him get back up after he fell.

They married and moved to the New Orleans area in 1947. He worked for Shell Oil Co. as a supervisor at the Norco refinery.

In addition to her cafeteria duties, Mrs. Songy had been an active member of Catholic Daughters of America since 1954. She received the St. Louis Medal for Outstanding Service to the Church and Community.

— January 5, 2012

Dominic "Dom" Grieshaber Sr.

"The marrying judge" loved performing weddings

Dominic "Dom" Grieshaber Sr., who was known as "the marrying judge" because of the thousands of weddings, many in unconventional places, that he conducted during 35 years as a judge in New Orleans' 1st City Court, died Monday at Regency Hospital in Covington, La., of complications of a stroke. He was 87.

Although most couples came to his chambers to be united in wedlock, Judge Grieshaber never hesitated to go where matrimony beckoned. He presided over weddings in the Bultman Funeral Home atrium, at the tomb believed to hold the remains of the voodoo queen Marie Laveau, and, during the 1984 World's Fair, in the aerial gondola as it dangled over the Mississippi River.

"I think he was nervous as hell," said his son Dominic Grieshaber Jr. of that ceremony. "Someone wanted to do one on a Ferris wheel. He said no."

Then there were the leather-clad members of a motorcycle gang called the Galloping Gooses, who were married outside a Downman Road bar, surrounded by their similarly garbed friends while the bride straddled a Harley-Davidson.

Although the judge had expected a tough crowd, "they were very serious about it all," he said in a 1991 interview. "I never heard one curse word the whole time I was milling around . . . and he gave her a rock that would blow your eyes out."

Judge Grieshaber once married a pair of transvestites, each wearing clothes associated with the other sex. And he presided over celebrity weddings, including those of the singer Marvin Gaye and the actor Stacy Keach.

His schedule for Valentine's Day in 1991 showed the diversity of the couples who sought his services. After presiding over the lavish third wedding of the fried-chicken magnate Al Copeland at the New Orleans Museum of

Art, complete with fireworks and petals strewn from a helicopter, he headed to Julia Street to marry the cook and a waitress at the Hummingbird Grill, the legendary eatery patronized by slumming swells, college students, and denizens of skid row.

"People would just call up once word got out that the judge liked doing the strange things," his son said. "There isn't a week that goes by when people don't say, 'Your dad married me,'" said the younger Grieshaber, whose father presided over his wedding.

Judge Grieshaber's explanation was simple: "I love marrying people."

A lifelong New Orleanian until he moved to Covington 12 years ago, Judge Grieshaber lost his father when he was 6. He, his mother and his two sisters moved into the rectory of St. Patrick's Church, where his uncle, Monsignor Raymond Carra, was the pastor. Young Dom wound up singing at Masses, attracting people from all over the city, his son said.

The teenager entered St. Joseph Seminary College in 1936 and stayed for six years. He left to join the Army in 1943, during World War II, and served in Texas for three years. He earned a law degree from Loyola University in 1951 and started a private practice that he maintained until 1964, when he was elected a judge of 1st City Court.

He stepped down from the bench in 1999 when he turned 75, the mandatory judicial retirement age. By then, he was chief judge and, his son said, the judge with the longest tenure in the state.

In addition to presiding at weddings, Judge Grieshaber enjoyed raising wildlife at his family's home on Pitt Street. For a while, he tried breeding rabbits, and he once had a cow named Twinkletoes in the backyard. But when Twinkletoes started nibbling the judge's prize camellias, she was sent back to the farm where Judge Grieshaber had bought her.

Judge Grieshaber was a member of the Camellia Club of New Orleans, New Orleans Spring Fiesta, the Knights of Columbus, and the Greater New Orleans Italian Cultural Society. In 1965, he reigned over the Caliphs of Cairo, a Mardi Gras organization.

— March 29, 2012

Luvenia Breaux

She made sure poor children ate breakfast

Luvenia Breaux, a member of the Women's Army Corps who later started one of the city's first free breakfast programs for impoverished schoolchildren, died March 14 at her New Orleans home of complications of a stroke. She was 94.

Ms. Breaux stopped attending school after the eighth grade, but she wanted to travel. So in 1942, shortly after the United States entered World War II, she joined the Women's Auxiliary Army Corps (later the Women's Army Corps) and headed to Des Moines, Iowa, for basic training.

The armed forces were segregated, but her barracks was not. On her first night there, she said in an interview, some white recruits tried to make a point of isolating her by setting up a dividing line of blankets and other gear. When the commanding officer, a white man, happened to enter, he ordered the recruits who had set up the barricade to leave.

"I think integration began right then," she said in the interview.

From then on, her life in the Army was good, she said. Ms. Breaux was a beautician, office worker, clerk, cook and recruiter. She also got to salute President Franklin D. Roosevelt and share a stage with Louis Armstrong.

Her experiences, bolstered by her training, instilled the self-confidence she carried with her for the rest of her life, said two of her sons.

"She was an aggressive personality, a go-getter," Walter Breaux Jr. said. "She had ideas about things that should be implemented, and she went after them."

For instance, when she was cafeteria manager at McDonogh No. 24 Elementary School in the 1950s, she realized that many of the pupils from poor families were coming to school without a proper breakfast.

Convinced that sound nutrition would help them learn, Ms. Breaux persuaded school-system officials to let her set up a program to give these children free breakfasts, years before the federal government instituted such an initiative, her son Dwight Carter said.

And when she was a PTA member at one of her children's schools, she visited the homes of children who had been truant or were falling behind in their schoolwork, becoming a one-woman liaison, Walter Breaux Jr. said.

Ms. Breaux, who ran unsuccessfully for the Orleans Parish School Board, "was the kind of person who saw a need and was aggressive enough to act on it," he said.

Sometimes, he said, his mother acted on the spur of the moment. For instance, one night, she heard the screams of a woman whom several men were attacking in her yard. Ms. Breaux grabbed her gun and fired it into the air, sending the young men fleeing, he said. "That's how fiery she was."

She was a member of Second Free Mission Baptist Church for 90 years. Friends and family members said she enjoyed attending Sunday School and wearing striking hats to church.

— *March 30, 2012*

Jack Dempsey

Legendary chronicler of cops and criminals

Jack Dempsey, a beefy, boisterous son of the Irish Channel who became a police reporter renowned for an ever-present straw hat and cigar and a dogged determination to get the story first, died Thursday at Live Oak Village in Slidell, La. He was 92.

Mr. Dempsey, who wrote for the *New Orleans States* and, later, the *States-Item*, happened to reign over his realm of cops and criminals during the final decades of the period when an afternoon newspaper was the main source for finding out what had happened during the day.

Until 1958, New Orleans had competing afternoon papers, the *States* and the *New Orleans Item*. They were combined to form the *States-Item*, which merged with the *Times-Picayune* in 1980.

In his heyday, when the *States* and the *Item* relied heavily on street sales, Mr. Dempsey employed what his *States-Item* colleague Angus Lind called "a combination of guile, contacts and natural curiosity" to stay ahead of the competition with the latest development in a sensational crime story.

Once, acting on a tip Mr. Dempsey received that the husband of a murdered woman was going to be charged with killing her, editors at the *States* had an extra edition ready to go, but no word came for three hours.

They were anxious hours, but editors had faith in Mr. Dempsey. When he finally came through with the news at 6 p.m., the presses rolled.

"We sent 12,000 papers downtown, and they were sold out in minutes," Walter Cowan, Mr. Dempsey's boss, told Lind in an interview.

On at least one occasion, Mr. Dempsey relied on sheer brass. In a sensational murder case, the judge heard arguments from both sides over whether the slain woman's child could testify.

When the judge said he would announce his decision at 2 p.m., Mr. Dempsey, who was sitting in the jury box with other reporters, popped up and said: "Make it 1 o'clock, judge! I got a 1 o'clock deadline," Lind wrote.

The judge complied.

Mr. Dempsey, who retired in 1981 after 39 years as a police reporter, "never quit trying to gain an advantage on his competition," Cowan said.

In one case, Mr. Dempsey's scoop was worldwide. In several columns of courthouse news, starting late in 1966, Mr. Dempsey relayed the rumor that District Attorney Jim Garrison was going to launch an investigation of the assassination of John F. Kennedy.

To get his scoops, Mr. Dempsey assiduously cultivated his sources. That meant stopping at Freitag's Bakery every morning to buy hot doughnuts for the police at headquarters, he said in a 1985 interview, followed by a stop at Charity Hospital's emergency room.

"There was an old head nurse there," he said, "and (when) I found out when her birthday was, (I) used to bring her perfume and candy from time to time. So sometimes, she'd let me put on a doctor's smock, and I'd go in and ask the patient what happened. They'd just assume I was a doctor and tell me everything. Got a lot of scoops that way."

Although he aspired to become a boxer like the other Jack Dempsey, whom he met years later, Mr. Dempsey went to Louisiana State University, where he studied journalism. He served in the Navy during World War II and in the Marine Corps during the Korean conflict.

When Mr. Dempsey returned to civilian life, he resumed the role for which he will be remembered.

Mr. Dempsey was a character, and he knew it. At staff parties, he could be counted on to sing "Every Man a King," Huey Long's theme song, in what he called, in the tones of the Irish Channel, "a loud, stentorian verce."

At the end of every dispatch he teletyped from the police headquarters press room, he used the signature "alihot," which stood for "a legend in his own time."

— April 13, 2012

Milton Wise

Loyal customers were devoted to his cafeteria

Milton Wise, who for 39 years ran the beloved cafeteria bearing his name, died Tuesday at his New Orleans home. He was 91.

At Wise Cafeteria, which was on the ground floor of a blond-brick office building, people who filled the tables weren't just customers who happened to drop in. In many cases, they were families who made weekly rituals out of queuing up for such specialties as deviled crabs, red beans and rice, brisket, eggplant casserole, bread pudding and chocolate pie, as well as cafeteria staples like crusty custard in dark green cups, quivering cubes of Jell-O, and carrot-and-raisin salad.

Mr. Wise's father, Herbert Wise, started the cafeteria in 1933 in the Cotton Exchange Building on Carondelet Street. Mr. Wise bought the cafeteria from his father and moved it to 909 S. Jefferson Davis Parkway in 1950. That building has become part of Xavier University.

In the days before the proliferation of New Orleans restaurants and fast-food chains, dining at Wise—or "Wise's," as many New Orleanians put it— was "something special," Jeffery Hobden recalled. He said the lines were so long they reminded him of people waiting to board Disneyland rides.

Regulars had their favorites. Marshall Hevron, for instance, always got the same thing: fried chicken, mashed potatoes, green beans, a biscuit and chocolate cake topped with sprinkles.

The most loyal customer probably was Dennis Waldron, who started eating lunch there every day in 1974, when he was a fledgling assistant Orleans Parish district attorney, then continued the habit when he was elected a judge of Criminal District Court.

As a member of the bench, Waldron said, he officiated at the weddings of the cafeteria's cooks and line servers.

His choice never varied: baked haddock, broccoli, a baked potato, two bran muffins and iced tea.

When a combination of factors, including a bad economy and competition from fast-food restaurants and the Piccadilly Cafeteria chain, drove Mr. Wise to shut his business down on Father's Day in 1989, Waldron was the last person through the serving line. Mr. Wise gave him a tray, some hand-lettered signs and the last 12 bran muffins.

"I placed them in the freezer and ate them with a sense of joy and sorrow in the days that followed," said Waldron, who has since retired from the bench.

But he couldn't bring himself to eat the last one, so he gave it to a courthouse colleague.

"We all considered each other family," Waldron said.

A lifelong New Orleanian who graduated from Alcee Fortier High School and Soulé Business College, Mr. Wise was a first lieutenant in the Army Air Forces in the Pacific Theater during World War II.

Herbert Wise III, a nephew, said his uncle participated in the air escort that brought Japan's representatives to the USS *Missouri* to sign the surrender documents that ended World War II.

— August 23, 2012

Diana Pinckley

She helped rebuild New Orleans after Katrina

Diana Pinckley, a public relations executive and communications strategist who became active on many fronts after Hurricane Katrina as a community volunteer striving to rebuild New Orleans and the Gulf Coast, died Wednesday of cancer at her New Orleans home. She was 60.

In post-Katrina New Orleans, she served on a host of recovery-related committees, most notably Women of the Storm, whose members traveled three times to Washington to lobby for help to restore New Orleans levees and, after the BP oil spill, the ravaged Gulf Coast.

"Diana was a connecter, sharing her talents, love, and insatiable intellect with everyone and every cause she believed in," said Anne Milling, the organization's founder.

"Thank you for your service to our city and state," U.S. Sen. Mary Landrieu, D-La., wrote to Ms. Pinckley the week before she died, adding that she wished Ms. Pinckley "peace and joy (for) knowing you made a big difference."

A native of Jamestown, Tenn., Ms. Pinckley was an honors graduate of Duke University who came to New Orleans in 1973 to be a staff writer in Tulane's University Relations office.

She became its news director and, from 1981 to 1993, its director. In this role, she was the spokeswoman for Tulane's Uptown campus, and she founded *Inside Tulane*, a campus newsletter. The office produced publications and news releases, winning national awards for its work, and it coordinated Tulane's sesquicentennial celebration in 1984.

She left Tulane in 1993 to form Pinckley Inc., which helped develop communications strategies for clients such as the Graduate Management Admissions Council, Ohio University, the University of the Pacific, the business schools at Columbia University and Dartmouth College, and the

University of Louisiana at Monroe. She also was co-author of "New Orleans: River Region Renaissance," a survey of the local economy.

Ms. Pinckley grew up reading mysteries, and she reviewed nearly 350 of them over 23 years for the *Times-Picayune* in her column, "Get a Clue." She also interviewed authors and was, most recently, Tulane Medicine's editor.

Before Katrina, Ms. Pinckley was already involved in civic organizations, serving on the New Orleans Council for Young Children, which established a school-based health clinic in the Lower 9th Ward, and the Committee of 21, which was formed to get more women elected to public office. She also was chairwoman of the board that runs the Crescent City Farmers Market.

"Helping creative people prosper made Pinckley tick," said Richard McCarthy, the market's executive director. "Scan the landscape of good things happening. In all likelihood, there was Pinckley, leading from behind. She never sought the spotlight, though she deserved it. She found far greater pleasure in helping others with talent and good intentions grow."

After Katrina, Ms. Pinckley's volunteer work moved into high gear. She devoted increasing amounts of her time and energy to organizations that were rebuilding New Orleans and the Gulf Coast, most notably Women of the Storm.

Ms. Pinckley kept the organization "informed, engaged and enlightened to the ever-changing currents of political platforms that occurred during the rebuilding efforts post-Katrina and, subsequently, into the coastal-restoration initiatives," Milling said. "No assignment was ever too much or too great. There will be an unfillable void."

Ms. Pinckley also helped bring back the city's public-library system, and she served on the task force that established the Edible Schoolyard, where Samuel Green Charter School students learn to cultivate vegetables and prepare meals as part of the curriculum. She also was vice president of the board of the Foundation for Science and Mathematics Education, which supports the New Orleans Charter Science & Mathematics High School.

Ms. Pinckley raised money for WWNO-FM and was an active volunteer at WWOZ-FM. She frequently went on the air to raise money for the latter station, which was a major passion of hers because of her devotion to New Orleans music. Whenever Ms. Pinckley did a fundraising broadcast, she always exceeded the goal for her time slot.

One such gig occurred shortly after Women of the Storm's third trip to Washington, where Ms. Pinckley was one of a group chosen to go to Vice President Joe Biden's office to meet with his staff. That didn't faze her, but when she was at WWOZ two days later with a renowned local musician, she couldn't contain her enthusiasm, sending out this text in capital letters: "I'M IN THE STUDIO WITH DAVE BARTHOLOMEW!"

In 2006, CityBusiness named her one of its Women of the Year.

She and her husband, *Times-Picayune* reporter John Pope, were avid travelers. They rode the Orient Express from Venice to London on their honeymoon, they explored the Galapagos Islands, and they scaled the Great Wall of China and the ruins of Machu Picchu. Her photographs illustrated his *Times-Picayune* stories of their trips to Scotland, Crete, China, and, most recently, a safari in Botswana.

— *September 28, 2012*

Myrtle Mary Franichevich Mary

She was a mainstay of two Mardi Gras krewes

Myrtle Mary Franichevich Mary, a multitalented Carnival connoisseur renowned for her ability to create costumes, research and stage balls and parades, and run an entire krewe, died Saturday. She was 98.

A lifelong New Orleanian, Mrs. Mary devoted her considerable energy to two krewes: Niobeans, an all-woman organization of which she was a charter member, and Babylon, the all-male club her husband, Dr. Charles Mary, helped found. Both eventually served as captains of their respective organizations.

Mrs. Mary, a seamstress with a flair for stagecraft, designed all the Niobeans' costumes, a year-round task. She converted the third floor of her home into a studio, where she led a team that turned her designs into reality.

Even though Mrs. Mary's husband was Babylon's nominal leader, she exerted a powerful behind-the-scenes role in designing and staging the organization's parade and ball.

Their task, which would begin about 15 months before the ball date, often involved traveling widely in the quest for costumes and props.

Her enthusiasm for all things Mardi Gras continued even when she moved into a retirement home. She was named queen of its 2012 Carnival presentation.

— *January 16, 2013*

[Update: Babylon celebrated its seventy-fifth anniversary in 2014. In recognition of Mrs. Mary's work for the krewe, the 2014 parade was dedicated to her.]

Paul McIlhenny

"The Scion of Spice" led the Tabasco empire

Paul McIlhenny, an ebullient executive who for 14 years led the family-owned company that makes Tabasco sauce and who reigned as Rex in 2006, died Saturday at his New Orleans home, apparently of a heart attack. He was 68.

Mr. McIlhenny, whom the *New York Times* once called "The Scion of Spice," became the company's president in 1998—the sixth family member to hold that title—and chief executive officer two years later. At his death, he still held the latter position and also was chairman of the board of directors, but a cousin, Anthony "Tony" Simmons, was named president last year.

The company, which was founded by Edmund McIlhenny in 1868 on Avery Island, near New Iberia, sells Tabasco sauce in about 165 countries and has 11 websites outside the United States, in North and South America and Europe.

During Mr. McIlhenny's years at the helm of the McIlhenny Co., he worked aggressively to expand the number of items to which the familiar Tabasco logo could be affixed. They include T-shirts, aprons, neckties, teddy bears, and computer screensavers, as well as seven varieties of hot sauce.

In 2009, Queen Elizabeth II granted the company a royal warrant, which entitles it to advertise that it supplies the pepper sauce to the British royal family. In honor of the queen's Diamond Jubilee in 2012, the company turned out a Tabasco-sauce box for its British market emblazoned with drawings of dozens of diamonds.

In the United States, the company provides hot sauce for Air Force One.

In 2010, Mr. McIlhenny was inducted into the James Beard Foundation's Who's Who of Food and Beverage in America. He was an author of a cookbook compiled to mark the McIlhenny Co.'s 125th anniversary.

Mr. McIlhenny entered the family business in 1967, shortly after earning a degree in political science at the University of the South in Tennessee.

Despite his passion for all things Louisiana, Mr. McIlhenny was born in Houston in 1944, along with a twin sister, Sara, because their mother was staying there with her mother while the children's father was in the military during World War II, said his daughter Barbara McIlhenny Fitz-Hugh.

Mr. McIlhenny grew up in New Orleans and spent much of his childhood shuttling between New Orleans and the family's compound on Avery Island. Because of his interest in the wetlands around Avery Island, his passion for hunting and his mother's membership on a committee concerned with coastal-zone management, Mr. McIlhenny became aware years ago of Louisiana's increasingly fragile coastline.

Gov. Mike Foster appointed him to the Governor's Advisory Commission on Coastal Restoration, Protection and Conservation, and he was a vice chairman and board member of the America's Wetland Foundation, whose logo appears on every box of Tabasco sauce sold in the United States.

Although Mr. McIlhenny was serious about coastal restoration and the preservation of Louisiana's wetlands, he generally was a merry man—one friend described him as "Falstaffian"—who strove to inject humor wherever possible.

A few days before he reigned as Rex in 2006, Mr. McIlhenny quipped that if, during the ceremonial toast to the mayor at Gallier Hall, the subject of hot sauce came up, "I'll say that's one form of global warming I'm totally in favor of. We're defending the world against bland food."

He took the throne six months after Hurricane Katrina roared ashore, the city's levees failed and 80 percent of New Orleans was flooded. The Rex den took on about 5 feet of water; watermarks were clearly visible on its floats when the parade rolled.

Because of the storm's impact, some people, including Carnival insiders, had questioned the wisdom of having parades in 2006.

Mr. McIlhenny said in a pre-parade interview that the thought never crossed his mind.

"If there was any time when we needed distraction, digression, diversion from the grind, it's Mardi Gras," he said, "and if there was any time we ever needed it, it's here. We need to let it all hang out and, in the sense of pre-Lenten revelry, make sure we relax and recreate."

— *February 13, 2013*

Frank Polozola

He presided over headline-grabbing trials

Frank Polozola, who presided over headline-grabbing cases during nearly 40 years on the federal bench, including the corruption trial of former Gov. Edwin Edwards and a lawsuit that wound up transforming the state prison system, died Sunday of cancer in Baton Rouge. He was 71.

A lifelong Baton Rouge resident, Judge Polozola was named a federal judge for Louisiana's Middle District in 1980 by President Jimmy Carter. He had been a federal magistrate judge since 1972.

Throughout Judge Polozola's career, he insisted that spectators be silent and lawyers be prepared.

"He worked tremendously hard, and he expected that of everybody else," said his son Gregory. "If he knew your case better than you did, he'd be upset."

In 1984, when cheering broke out over a not-guilty verdict, Judge Polozola ordered that the "thundering herd" be removed.

Judge Polozola was chief judge from 1998 to 2005. In 2007, he assumed senior status, which means a judge can take on a lighter caseload.

The most sensational case to land in his courtroom was the 17-week trial in 2000 of former Gov. Edwin Edwards, who had been accused of extorting nearly $3 million from companies that applied for casino licenses during his last term and even after his retirement in January 1996. Among the six other defendants was Edwards' son Stephen.

Judge Polozola was known as a stickler for decorum, and he showed it in this case. For instance, in an attempt to keep the former governor from firing off his trademark one-liners, Judge Polozola imposed a gag order.

And when two defense attorneys challenged one of Polozola's rulings, he left no doubt about who was in charge. His face turning red with rage,

Polozola threatened to have the lawyers handcuffed, removed from the courtroom and jailed. That didn't happen.

According to a news story, he then said: "I don't care if you hate my guts. Every single lawyer in this case, you're stuck with me."

Edwin Edwards was found guilty on 17 counts of racketeering, mail and wire fraud, conspiracy and money laundering. He served eight years in prison, six months in home detention and three years on probation.

Judge Polozola also presided over the trials of former state Agriculture Commissioner Gil Dozier and Louisiana State University football legend Billy Cannon.

Dozier was found guilty of jury tampering and sentenced to 10 years in prison. Judge Polozola tried to add eight years to that sentence, but an appeals court reversed him.

Cannon, LSU's only Heisman Trophy winner, was convicted of counterfeiting, and Judge Polozola sentenced him to five years behind bars.

Cannon, a dentist, asked that he be allowed to provide free care to poor children instead of going to prison. Even though the judge was an LSU graduate and a passionate sports fan, he rejected that offer, saying, "The court refuses to allow those who have family or fortune or stature in life to commit crimes and receive a slap on the hand."

Cannon was freed after 2 1/2 years.

Judge Polozola earned a law degree at LSU, where he was catcher on the baseball team, lettering twice and playing on the 1961 Southeastern Conference championship team.

Though he wasn't a stellar hitter, "he was so good defensively," said James Field, a teammate, in an interview. "He was a very smart catcher. He would take charge of the infield. Whenever he played, he took charge."

After graduating in 1965, the young lawyer began his career with a clerkship for U.S. District Judge E. Gordon West, who became his mentor.

After a year, he entered private practice with Seale Phelps & Smith, becoming partner in two years.

In 1972, through West's influence, he became a part-time federal magistrate, a position that let him keep his law practice. A year later, he gave up his law practice to become a full-time magistrate. While a magistrate, Judge Polozola handled the preliminary elements in an inmates-rights lawsuit credited with reforming Louisiana's troubled prison system and ending the ugly reign of the Louisiana State Penitentiary at Angola as the nation's bloodiest prison.

He took over the case after becoming a judge, and he wound up settling the 27-year-old litigation in 1998. As part of the settlement, the judge established inmate population limits and issued orders to hire guards and improve medical care. He also oversaw prison construction.

In a 2000 interview, Keith Nordyke, a Baton Rouge lawyer who filed suit on behalf of inmates, said the judge "made Angola clean up its act."

Judge Polozola also set population limits in parish jails. In 1983, Orleans Parish Criminal Sheriff Charles Foti ensured he was in compliance by erecting a tent city near the jail to house the overflow. Video-poker revenue paid for a 482-bed wing that was opened in 2000.

Throughout Judge Polozola's career, "he really believed in the justice system," Gregory Polozola said. "He really believed that he was doing the right thing."

— *February 25, 2013*

Vernon Shorty

His center treated hundreds of addicts

Vernon Shorty, who for more than three decades ran a center in the Desire public-housing complex that treated hundreds of people suffering from a range of addiction-related problems, died Tuesday at Tulane Medical Center of complications from a stroke. He was 69.

Although the Desire Narcotics Rehabilitation Center was set up to treat people struggling to break the grip of substances such as cocaine and heroin as well as alcohol, it was also a place where people knew they could go to get rent money, be tested for HIV and receive counseling, find a way to finish high school, and learn how to manage a budget.

Every day, dozens of people who would never touch drugs or alcohol showed up just to visit on the sofa in the reception room, where two of Dr. Shorty's pet alligators stared out at them from their perch in a glass tank.

"Vernon doesn't see himself as the director of a clinic, but more or less as the mayor of Desire," said Morris Edwards III, the chairman of the center's advisory board in the 1980s, in a 1985 interview.

"He feels responsible for everybody," Edwards said. "He's driven by his almost-unique understanding of what it is to be black and poor."

Dr. Shorty, the clinic's executive director, grew up in Desire, where his neighbors included a prostitute, a thief, and a narcotics addict who supported his habit by selling drugs he didn't use.

"What drove him was helping people," said Edwin Shorty, a nephew. "He gave of himself 'til it hurt."

Before becoming the clinic's director, Dr. Shorty worked for six years at the National Aeronautics and Space Administration's Michoud complex in eastern New Orleans. He started as a janitor and eventually became a clerk in the program that built Saturn boosters for the space program.

By that time, he had moved out of Desire. When he went back to visit, he said in a 1985 interview, he couldn't help noticing changes.

"The guys we had played with were on dope," he said, "and the girls we had dated were on dope. I had a brother that was addicted."

Worse yet, Dr. Shorty said, a friend there who worked at a drug-treatment center told him about the dearth of programs for the people in Desire who needed help.

Dr. Shorty, who had worked in a methadone clinic, met with friends to try to change the situation. The result was the rehab center, which opened on Aug. 4, 1970, across the street from the apartment building where Dr. Shorty grew up.

At first, everyone worked on a volunteer basis. Even after Dr. Shorty was being paid and receiving attention for his work—and becoming an expert at snagging federal grants—he worked a six-day week.

"I guess I'm crazy," he said. "Everybody says, 'I don't know how you can do it.' But do I feel burned out? No way. I'm hyper; I'm ready. When I walk in, I'm ready to go."

Dr. Shorty, who for a time drove twice a week to Baton Rouge to teach a course on drug-abuse education, became the subject of admiring articles, and he was a writer and editor for publications of the National Institute for Drug Abuse. In the mid-1970s, he was the first non-medical doctor to be named co-chairman of a national conference on drug abuse, and he brought the meeting to New Orleans.

"Shorty has the ability to organize people and get things done. It's very admirable," said Dr. Harold Ginzburg, a former assistant to the director of the National Institute for Drug Abuse, in an interview.

In 1972, while he was running the narcotics center, Dr. Shorty earned undergraduate degrees in sociology and history from Southern University at New Orleans. He later received a doctorate from Hamilton University.

Among the honors he received were the Nyswander-Dole Award, which recognizes contributions to methadone treatment; a community service award from the National Association for the Advancement of Colored People; and a presidential citation from the National Association for Equal Opportunity in Higher Education.

In 1988, *Newsweek* magazine named him one of the 51 people whom it identified as "America's Most Unsung Heroes."

— *March 3, 2013*

Charlotte Lang

"She covered every aspect of theater"

Charlotte Lang, a singer, dancer, and actress in local theater, died Thursday of a heart attack at her New Orleans home. She was 50.

Ms. Lang, a lifelong New Orleanian, also designed costumes for New Orleans Opera and several productions in which she performed.

"She covered every aspect of theater," said Kevin Charpentier, a friend and frequent collaborator. "Any time I had a problem, Charlotte knew what to do. She was like a walking encyclopedia."

"She loved the stage, she loved performing, ever since she was a small child," said Martha Lang, her mother, who helped her young daughter stage plays.

When Ms. Lang was a teenager, she learned about costume design from her grandmother. "She loved bold colors in her costumes," retired *Times-Picayune* critic David Cuthbert said. "She was a bold lady, and it was reflected in what she did."

Among the productions for which Ms. Lang performed double duty—on the stage and in the wardrobe room—were the jukebox musical *The Class of '70 Something* and *Chicago*, in which she played the prison matron Mama Morton.

Carl Walker, the director who worked with her on *'70 Something*, called her "an extraordinary collaborator."

"I didn't know where my ideas stopped and Charlotte's started," he said. "We thought so much alike, and I learned so much from her. She could take an idea of mine and make it better."

On stage, Walker said, Ms. Lang was extraordinarily versatile, especially when she was the only understudy for all five characters in the musical *Nunsense*.

280

"She referred to herself as Sister Mary Sybil because she never knew whom she was going to play," Walker said. "She could be a nun in toe shoes at the matinee and Mother Superior that night. That's how quick she was. She could turn around on a dime."

Ms. Lang, who had two aunts who were nuns, attended Xavier University and the University of New Orleans but did not graduate.

Despite a wicked sense of humor and a keen talent for mimicry, "Charlotte was actually regal," said Barbara Motley, owner of the now-closed cabaret Le Chat Noir, where Ms. Lang frequently performed.

"She did characters who came up from the streets," Motley said, citing Ms. Lang's performance as a surly meter maid in *Native Tongues*.

"What amazed me about her was the contrast between the roles she played on stage and the way she was," Motley said.

She also was generous, said Carol Stone Wright, who produced several productions in which Ms. Lang worked. When Wright's daughter appeared in a high-school production of *Leader of the Pack*, a compilation of Ellie Greenwich songs, Ms. Lang did six costumes for her—one for each time she went on stage—and didn't charge for them.

"She had a big heart, and she wanted to help," Wright said. "Every time Laura went on stage, you could hear the audience say, 'Ohhh, another costume.'"

— *March 22, 2013*

Cyril "Big Chief Iron Horse" Green

He led Mardi Gras Indians from his wheelchair

Cyril "Big Chief Iron Horse" Green, the wheelchair-bound leader of the Black Seminoles tribe of Mardi Gras Indians, died March 20 in his sleep at his New Orleans home, hours after participating in the tribes' traditional St. Joseph's Day gathering. He was 46.

Mr. Green, a lifelong resident of New Orleans' 8th Ward, got his name from his wheelchair. He had been in it since a night in November 1990, when gunfire rang out after he had stopped to fix his car. Two bullets hit his neck, and one of them nicked his spinal cord.

A third-generation Mardi Gras Indian, Mr. Green didn't let his disability keep him from sewing his Indian suit, driving his van or getting an associate degree in computer technology at Delgado Community College.

"I'm a wounded Indian, but I'm still in battle," he said in a 1997 interview.

His attitude was hardly surprising, given Mr. Green's Indian heritage, said Cherice Harrison-Nelson, founder and curator of the Mardi Gras Indian Hall of Fame.

"It's in your DNA," she said. "It's a calling; it's not simply putting on a suit. . . . It feeds your spirit and your soul. When all else around you is falling down, this is the kind of thing that gives you hope."

Shortly before he was shot, Mr. Green had become extremely religious, Goodman said, and he felt no animosity toward the unknown shooter who crippled him.

"He did not allow his handicap to bring him down," Goodman said. "He looked at that as God's plan to bring him up, and he was going to do everything to achieve his goals."

That included riding to and from classes at Delgado in his motorized scooter, and setting up a small leather-goods business.

Mr. Green became involved with Mardi Gras Indian activities when he followed a cousin, Kevin Goodman, big chief of the Flaming Arrows, into that tribe.

Mr. Green became second chief of that tribe in 1992, Terrel Goodman said, and he achieved that same rank with the next tribe he joined, the Young Cheyenne. His next move was to form the Black Seminoles and a band with that name that accompanied them when they appeared onstage and in parades at the annual Jazz and Heritage Festival.

"He would dress in his suit and ride up on stage with the whole band and other Indians behind him," Goodman said.

Mr. Green was inducted into the New Orleans Mardi Gras Indian Hall of Fame in 2006, and he received the Crystal Feather, that organization's highest honor.

— March 29, 2013

André Victor Wogan

He worked with coded messages in World War II

André Victor Wogan, who worked with coded messages during World War II, died March 24 at Christwood Retirement Community in Covington, La. He was 91.

A seventh-generation New Orleanian, Mr. Wogan grew up in a French-speaking family. After graduating from St. Aloysius High School, he enrolled at Tulane University, majoring in business. But by that time, the United States had entered World War II, and Tulane awarded degrees early so young men could enlist.

Mr. Wogan joined the Army and became a cryptographer; he was stationed in England and Belgium. In an interview with his grandson Hicks Wogan, Mr. Wogan said he worked with a machine that looked like a typewriter, with different wheels for different codes.

"You'd put (the wheels) into the machine, and you could type into English, and it would convert it into nonsensical symbols," he said, adding that the recipient of the message had the same machine with the same wheels that could translate the message back into English.

When he was in Ghent, Belgium, Mr. Wogan was one of a small group of men who were locked in a room every day with the cryptography machines—and their rifles.

"Theoretically, you could be under attack, and you were supposed to destroy the equipment . . . if they came," he told his grandson. "It never happened."

While in England in 1944, Mr. Wogan and some buddies went into London on a weekend pass. It was a time when a complete blackout had been imposed, and the Germans were lobbing so-called buzz bombs on the city. They got that nickname from people who heard buzzing when a bomb approached a target.

Mr. Wogan said in the interview that he heard that sound frequently. "It was like hearing a little motor passing over you," he said, "and once you'd hear them, if the sound stopped, that meant that they were ready to start dropping. . . . I heard one pass over, and then the sound stopped, and you could hear the explosion off in the distance. It was close enough that . . . we were knocked out of our bunks."

After the war, Mr. Wogan stayed in France to take advantage of courses tailored for American soldiers. He studied at the University of Nancy and, in Paris, at the Sorbonne, taking law courses in French.

At that time, each GI got a carton of extra cigarettes. To get extra money in the City of Light, Mr. Wogan, who didn't smoke, said he and his non-smoking buddies sold their cigarettes on the black market.

When he returned to the United States, Mr. Wogan enrolled at Tulane's law school and graduated in 1949. He became a landman, an oil-company employee who performs duties such as acquiring mineral rights, negotiating leases for exploration and determining, through title research, ownership of land and minerals.

Mr. Wogan worked for Humble Oil & Refining Co., British American Oil Co. and Forest Oil Corp., before joining McMoRan Oil & Gas in 1969. He became senior vice president of the company that became Freeport-McMoRan, and he retired in 1984.

— *March 31, 2013*

James J. Lynch Jr.

He delivered men and materiel to Normandy

James J. Lynch Jr., who as a Merchant Marine Academy cadet made seven shuttle runs under enemy fire the day after D-Day to carry troops and materiel across the English Channel from England to France, died April 10 at his Metairie home of complications of Alzheimer's disease. He was 88.

A native New Orleanian, Mr. Lynch graduated from Jesuit High School, where he was a member of the football and baseball teams that won the 1941 prep and state championships. He entered Tulane University as an engineering student in September 1942, but he left after his first year because he had received a congressional appointment to the U.S. Merchant Marine Academy.

After preliminary training at Pass Christian, Miss., Mr. Lynch boarded the S.S. *George Wythe* in Mobile, Ala., for the customary six months of active duty at sea.

But this was anything but routine, said his son Patrick Lynch, because the ship was carrying troops and equipment as part of the buildup to the massive Allied invasion of Normandy on June 6, 1944.

The day after that historic assault, Mr. Lynch ferried soldiers and supplies on seven runs under enemy fire from Portsmouth, England, to Normandy's Gold Beach. In recognition of his service, he received medals from the U.S. and British governments.

He returned to the Merchant Marine Academy at Kings Point, N.Y., to complete his training—and to play on the varsity football and baseball teams. Nearly a half-century later, Mr. Lynch was elected to the academy's Athletic Hall of Fame.

Upon graduating in June 1945, he received his Third Mate's License, which entitled him to serve on any ocean-going vessel, and commissions from the U.S. Maritime Service and the U.S. Naval Reserve.

After returning to civilian life, he launched his insurance business, James J. Lynch Inc., in 1947 and continued to work until he sold the agency in 2010.

— May 1, 2013

Mercedes Tucker Stamps

She brought music to thousands of youngsters

Mercedes Tucker Stamps, a teacher who for a third of a century brought the gift of music to thousands of New Orleans children, including the musical artists John Boutté, Freddy Lonzo and Earl Turbinton, died Thursday in Iredell Memorial Hospital in Statesville, N.C., of complications of a stroke. She was 87.

Mrs. Stamps had been a lifelong New Orleanian until 2006, when she and her husband, Herbert Walker Stamps, moved to Statesville, his home-town, after Hurricane Katrina destroyed their home.

A self-taught pianist, Mrs. Stamps first played on a piano that belonged to her grandmother, who sang hymns to her. She entered Southern University when she was 16 and graduated with honors three years later.

Her first post-college job was at the now-defunct Gilbert Academy, where she taught elementary harmony, music theory and music apprecia-tion. "Some of the students were older than I was," she said in an interview with the *Statesville Record & Landmark.*

From the outset, she was effective, said the New Orleans music patriarch Ellis Marsalis, who was a student at Gilbert when she was a teacher there.

"We have an expression for some teachers that we call 'old school': deal-ing with fundamentals and not really ever having serious disciplinary prob-lems," he said. "Mrs. Stamps was one of those kinds of people. She was really 'old school.'"

Two years later, she joined the New Orleans public-school system, where she taught until her retirement in 1979. She became the first itinerant music teacher assigned to teach African-American students.

In 1954, when Woodson Junior High School opened, she was its first band director. She stayed there 11 years, until she moved to Clark Senior High School, where she stayed until she retired.

Al Kennedy, a former school-system employee who went on to teach history at the University of New Orleans, wrote about Mrs. Stamps in *Mercedes Tucker Stamps: A Public School Teacher's Contribution to New Orleans Music History*.

In it, he told a story that was emblematic of the days of segregation, when Mrs. Stamps began her career. In those days, when African-American children learned from dog-eared books and sat on second-rate furniture, he wrote that Mrs. Stamps' school was delighted when a gleaming, brand-new grand piano was delivered. One teacher even gave an impromptu concert.

But that didn't last. Someone realized that the piano was intended for a white school, Kennedy wrote. It was taken away and replaced by an upright model that needed tuning.

In a 2004 interview with the *Times-Picayune*, Mrs. Stamps said that her duty as a teacher didn't stop when the school day ended.

"I showed concern about the whole child," she said. "I was concerned about them doing well in all phases of their lives."

— *June 4, 2013*

Joseph Sabatier Jr.

He was on the team that tried to save Huey P. Long

Dr. Joseph Sabatier Jr., perhaps the last surviving member of the medical team that treated Huey P. Long after he was shot, died June 6 at his New Orleans home. He was 98.

On Sept. 8, 1935, Joseph Sabatier was a Tulane University medical student who had been assigned to Our Lady of the Lake Hospital in Baton Rouge. It had been a drowsy Sunday, but the tempo picked up as he and several nurses were leaving a movie theater, he said in a 2007 interview with *New Orleans Magazine*.

They saw vehicles speeding to the hospital where they worked, Dr. Sabatier said. When he got back to his room, there was a message: Report to work at once.

Long, the former governor who still ran the state even though he was a U.S. senator, had been shot repeatedly in the Capitol, the skyscraper he had envisioned as his monument.

By the time the doctor in training reached the hospital, he said, a fully conscious Long was being prepared for surgery. Because of a personnel shortage in the operating room, he was put to work as a scrub nurse, a position he described in the interview as "an assistant to an orderly."

Long lingered for two days. During that period, Dr. Sabatier said, politicians lined up in the hall outside Long's room for one last visit.

The activity didn't stop when Long died on Sept. 10, Dr. Sabatier said, because Baton Rouge was crowded with about 200,000 people who had flocked to the city to be part of the funeral throng. It was hot, and because many of the mourners were elderly, the hospital was kept busy with people seeking medical help.

Dr. Sabatier was born in Iota, La., and grew up nearby in Crowley, where his father, Joseph Sabatier, owned a rice mill.

When he was very young, the doctor-to-be went almost weekly to funerals of people who had died in the influenza pandemic. This piqued his interest in medicine, said his son, William Sabatier, as did the example set by his uncle, Dr. George Sabatier of New Iberia, who charged patients what they felt was fair.

He earned an undergraduate degree at Southwestern Louisiana Institute (now the University of Louisiana at Lafayette) and his medical degree at Tulane.

During World War II, Dr. Sabatier was an Army doctor, starting at Fort Benning, Ga. Overseas, he served in North Africa and Italy, where he was chief of neurosurgery at the 24th General Hospital in Florence. After the war, he and two friends founded the Baton Rouge Clinic.

Dr. Sabatier practiced general surgery there until 1967, when President Lyndon B. Johnson appointed him head of the Louisiana Regional Medical Program, which he led for 10 years.

When that initiative was dissolved, Dr. Sabatier resumed his practice as an emergency-medicine physician and as an administrator at West Jefferson Medical Center in Marrero, across the Mississippi River from downtown New Orleans.

Throughout his career, he made forays into public-policy debates. He was a longtime member of the American Medical Association's Committee on Quackery, and he used that position to oppose attempts to let the state recognize chiropractors as practitioners of medicine. The chiropractors prevailed in 1974.

Dr. Sabatier also was successful in getting fluoroscopes—low-intensity X-ray machines—banned from shoe stores in the 1950s. He opposed the devices because of the potential damage that repeated exposure to these rays could do, his son said, and because they would be operated by shoe-store employees who would have no grasp of what the consequences of using the machines might be.

He retired in 1987.

— June 14, 2013

Dorothy "Miss Dot" Domilise

She was the po-boy queen of Uptown New Orleans

Dorothy "Miss Dot" Domilise, who assembled and served thousands of succulent shrimp, roast beef, hot sausage and oyster po-boys to priests, politicians, and neighborhood regulars at Domilise's Restaurant for more than 70 years, died Friday of congestive heart failure at East Jefferson General Hospital. She was 90.

A native of Franklin, La., who moved to New Orleans shortly before World War II, she married Sam Domilise and started working in the family business in the yellow frame building with the hand-lettered sign at Annunciation and Bellecastle streets in Uptown New Orleans.

Domilise's is a fixture, a proud reminder of what neighborhood restaurants were meant to be. Despite the allure of glitzier eateries, Domilise's has been consistently jammed, especially on Saturdays, with customers clamoring for their fresh sandwiches, embellished with a sauce made from a recipe that Mrs. Domilise kept secret.

Politicians were expected to squeeze in on election days to put in appearances. Pamela Pipes said the restaurant was for years the site for her birthday parties, where she ordered hot sausage and cheese po-boys "with extra extra everything."

Mrs. Domilise and her husband took over the business when his parents died. Sam Domilise died in 1981, "and she just kept going," said retired Criminal District Judge Dennis Waldron, a longtime customer and family friend.

She kept up her routine, working six days a week until a few years ago, when the restaurant started closing on Thursdays. She lived in a small apartment just off the dining area.

"She served every sandwich with lots of love," Waldron said.

— *June 17, 2013*

Bill Johnston

He helped create a fabled music venue

Bill Johnston, a fixture on the New Orleans music scene who was best known as a founder of the down-at-the-heels rock-concert venue The Warehouse, died Tuesday of cancer at St. Theresa's Medical Complex in Kenner, La. He was 69.

Mr. Johnston, a native New Orleanian, had been a manager of musicians, with clients who included the Neville Brothers and Gino Vannelli, and he was the entertainment director at Harrah's New Orleans Casino for four years.

He also did stints as the New Orleans Athletic Club's general manager and as talent buyer for the renovated Joy Theater.

Weeks before his death, he was discussing with colleagues the prospect of reshaping for Broadway a show he had done for Harrah's.

"He was a ball of energy," Vannelli said. "You couldn't contain the man. He was a firecracker."

The institution for which Mr. Johnston was best known was The Warehouse, which he established in 1970 with partners Don Fox and Brian Glynn in a rundown warehouse at 1800 Tchoupitoulas St.

Comfort never was The Warehouse's drawing card. The brick-walled venue near Felicity Street had neither air conditioning nor heating, and concertgoers—about 3,500 could squeeze in—sat where they could. The floor was cushioned with mismatched carpet squares, which could be traded for tickets.

"We hippies didn't care," said Michael Brinkman, a longtime friend who worked backstage. "It was crowded," he said. "It was hot in the summer and cold in the winter. You dressed accordingly. You knew you were going to sweat in the summer and freeze in the winter."

Nevertheless, The Warehouse never failed to attract top-flight talent, starting with Fleetwood Mac and the Grateful Dead on its opening night,

Jan. 30, 1970. After that show, a drug bust at the Grateful Dead's hotel gave rise to the "Busted, down on Bourbon Street" lyrics of the group's song "Truckin."

From then on, until its closing night in September 1982, The Warehouse was host to the likes of Joe Cocker, Bob Marley, Richie Havens, and Leon Russell, as well as groups such as Pink Floyd, The Who, The Band, Cheap Trick, the Allman Brothers, Talking Heads, and Jefferson Starship.

Jim Morrison's last concert with the Doors—on Dec. 12, 1970—was at The Warehouse. "He was so smashed that he fell into the drums," Brinkman said.

In May 1976, The Warehouse was host to the Rolling Thunder Revue. Folk legend Bob Dylan headlined the 3 1/2-hour concert with a list of performers that included Joan Baez, Kinky Friedman, Roger McGuinn, Scarlet Rivera, and Ramblin' Jack Elliott.

"His passions were music and promoting it," said Teresa Riccobono Johnston, Mr. Johnston's wife.

The awareness that this would be his life's work hit him when he was a young adult. After leaving Holy Cross School, he served in the Air Force and moved to Chicago, where he worked at a series of bars as a manager, bartender and bouncer, said Jessy Williamson, a Mandeville filmmaker who has produced a documentary about The Warehouse.

One bar Mr. Johnston managed was Barnaby's, where, Williamson said, he became friendly with members of The Big Thing, the house band, which became Chicago Transit Authority and, later, Chicago.

In 1969, Mr. Johnston accompanied the band to New York City for a gig at Fillmore East, a funky music venue on Manhattan's Lower East Side.

When he saw his friends perform there before loudly cheering fans, "he said, 'Oh, my God, we have to have something like this in New Orleans,'" his wife said.

Mr. Johnston persuaded Fox and Glynn to move to New Orleans with him to create a music venue in a 30,000-square-foot brick building on Tchoupitoulas Street. He left The Warehouse in 1975, Williamson said, to concentrate on promoting and managing musicians.

The Warehouse's last booking—Talking Heads and 3-D Beat—was in September 1982. By then, "the hippies had grown up," Brinkman said. "It was past being a hot venue for young people looking for air conditioning."

In addition, Williamson said, more venues for these musicians were available.

The Warehouse was demolished in April 1989. Williamson's documentary about it, *A Warehouse on Tchoupitoulas Street*, was shown at the 2013 New Orleans Film Festival.

Meanwhile, Mr. Johnston, who was inducted into the Louisiana Music Hall of Fame, moved on to other projects, including *Joint's Jumpin'*, a rhythm-and-blues revue he created for Harrah's. Larry Sieberth was the music director.

From the beginning, Sieberth said, Mr. Johnston wanted to retool the show as *Joint's Jumpin' Jukebox* for Las Vegas or Broadway.

"Bill's last request to me was to keep the show going," Sieberth said. "Bill was an idea man. He had ideas—big ideas—and he had the courage to make them happen."

— August 8, 2013

Barry Henry

A movie palace was this doctor's passion

For most of Dr. Barry Henry's 76 years, the Saenger Theatre was the center of his life.

He helped save the motion-picture palace on Canal Street from demolition, he spent years repairing and playing the theater's Mighty Morton Wonder Organ, and he turned his Napoleon Avenue home into a shrine of Saenger memorabilia.

A portrait of Julian Saenger, president of the theater chain bearing his name, hangs in Dr. Henry's dining room, and a swatch of the Saenger's original carpet is on the floor, with the theater's name emblazoned on a scroll across a heraldic shield. And he had a vast collection of Saenger mementos that included photographs, playbills, stock certificates and an invitation to the Saenger's 1927 dedication.

Ever since the theater had been overwhelmed by Hurricane Katrina and the subsequent flooding, Dr. Henry had followed the progress of the Saenger's $152 million renovation, and he had been looking forward to attending the first performance in the renovated theater, said Michael Fitzgerald, his companion.

But that won't happen.

In a twist that Dr. Henry probably would have dismissed as melodramatic, he died of cancer on Monday—four days before the theater's reopening—at his home.

"It's so coincidental, it's shocking," Fitzgerald said.

Dr. Henry, a native of Vicksburg, Miss., had played the piano since he was 5 and moved on to the organ.

In 1972, when he was a young radiologist, he asked the building engineer if he could play the Saenger's organ.

At that time, it wasn't used much, and he said in an interview last year that he heard noises and swishing water when he sat down to play. So he came back at night with a tool kit to work on the organ from 8 p.m. until 1 a.m.

"It was his love of music that helped save the Saenger," Fitzgerald said.

In 1974, Dr. Henry heard rumors that the Saenger was going to be demolished, so he rallied a group of theater mavens that became known as City Lights to save the Saenger and other downtown picture palaces. In 1977, the Saenger was named to the National Register of Historic Places.

Even though that designation ensured the theater's survival, Dr. Henry maintained his interest in the Saenger, down to the smallest details.

When the theater was being restored in 1979, Fitzgerald said, Dr. Henry saw a swatch of carpet bearing the Saenger name that was bound for the dumpster.

"It had been under a concession stand," Fitzgerald said. "The workers thought it was just trash and were ready to heave it. He knew those people, and they gave it to him."

Dr. Henry took it to his home in New Orleans' Broadmoor neighborhood. In August 2005, Fitzgerald thought to take it out of their house when they evacuated as Hurricane Katrina threatened, thereby saving it from the floodwaters that inundated 80 percent of New Orleans, including their part of the city.

Dr. Henry had been a New Orleanian since the mid-1950s, when he came to Tulane University. He earned undergraduate and medical degrees there and was a member of Nu Sigma Nu medical fraternity. After an internship in San Francisco, Dr. Henry served two years in the Air Force's Strategic Air Command. He was honorably discharged as a captain.

He returned to New Orleans for a radiology residency at Charity Hospital. He was in the radiology departments at Charity and the Veterans Affairs Medical Center, and he had a sub-specialty in neuroradiology. Dr. Henry joined Jefferson Radiology Associates and stayed with that group until 1997. He was a member of several radiology and medical groups, and he taught part-time at Tulane University School of Medicine.

Throughout this period, he kept up his interest in the Saenger, amassing memorabilia, working on the organ and even playing it when Bob Hope and Johnny Carson performed there.

In an interview last year, Dr. Henry said that he was looking forward to being in his beloved theater on its reopening night.

"I'm heartsick that it played this way," Fitzgerald said, "but God has other plans."

— *September 26, 2013*

Liselotte Levy Weil

She fled Hitler's Germany and felt survivor's guilt

Liselotte Levy Weil, who settled in Louisiana after fleeing her native Germany as the Nazis were beginning to persecute Jews, died Friday in her New Orleans home. She was 92.

Liselotte Levy and her brother, Leo, were teenagers when they emigrated to the United States early in 1939, two months after seeing their father, Ferdinand Levy, beaten to death by Nazi thugs during the violence that was part of Kristallnacht, the Night of Broken Glass, in November 1938.

"We are glad to be here, so glad," she said in a 1939 interview with the *Meridian* (Miss.) *Star*.

Their mother, Rosa Levy, and sister, Margot Levy, perished in a Nazi death camp. It isn't clear why they didn't get visas to come to America, said Plater Robinson, who is writing a biography of Mrs. Weil.

She and her brother were "racked by guilt, racked by feelings that her mother and sister were trapped," Robinson said. "Whatever they could do was not enough."

Throughout Mrs. Weil's years in America—first in Eunice, La., and, since 1983, in New Orleans—"she kept a lot bottled up in order not to offend others" by giving vent to her emotions, Robinson said.

Her parents, Ferdinand and Rosa Levy, operated a kosher butcher shop. He had fought for Germany in World War I and survived the battle of Verdun, in which nearly 1 million soldiers on both sides were killed, Robinson said.

But when Adolf Hitler came to power in 1933, Levy hurled his military medals into the Rhine River, Robinson said, and started writing letters to relatives in Kosciusko, Miss., in an attempt to get visas for his children, so they could escape a country that had turned hostile.

He received no reply, Robinson said. But a postmaster in nearby Mc-Cool, Miss., sent Levy's letters to Winnsboro, La., where a cousin of the Levys—Isaac Greenwald—lived, and he started the process that resulted in visas for Liselotte and Leo.

Without his help, "we would never have gotten out of Germany," Mrs. Weil told Robinson. The documents arrived Nov. 8, 1938—the day before the start of Kristallnacht, a series of coordinated attacks throughout Germany and Austria in which nearly 100 Jews were killed, thousands were arrested and herded into concentration camps, and hundreds of synagogues and Jewish-owned schools, businesses, and homes were ransacked.

The Levys' home wasn't spared, Robinson said, and Ferdinand Levy was beaten to death in front of his family when he tried to resist the marauders.

Rosa and Margot Levy were sent to a ghetto in Lublin, Poland, and then to Belzec, an extermination camp in Nazi-occupied Poland, where they are believed to have died in 1942, Robinson said.

Liselotte and Leo Levy landed in New York City in January 1939. In the Meridian home of the family that had met them, a reporter who interviewed the siblings noted that they refused to say anything about what Jews were enduring in their home country lest their statements get back to Germany and make matters even worse for their family and other Jews.

Leo settled in Winnsboro with Isaac Greenwald and died in 1998, Robinson said. Liselotte was adopted by Amelia Greenwald, a cousin who lived in Eunice, La., where she operated a dress shop called La Vogue. Before settling there, Greenwald had been a nurse in a psychiatric hospital in Europe in World War I.

In 1959, Liselotte Levy married Leo Weil, a fellow Jewish refugee from Germany who lived in Eunice. After his death in 1983, Mrs. Weil moved to New Orleans.

— *October 14, 2013*

Elvin Ragnvald "Vald" Heiberg III

He apologized for the Katrina levee failures

Lt. Gen. Elvin Ragnvald "Vald" Heiberg III, who apologized because he felt he hadn't done enough to protect New Orleans from Hurricane Katrina-related flooding when he headed the local Army Corps of Engineers office in the 1970s, died Sept. 27 of cancer, in Arlington, Va. He was 81.

Gen. Heiberg, who led the Corps of Engineers from 1984 to 1988, commanded the corps' New Orleans District office in 1974 and 1975.

During that period, he proposed barriers at the eastern end of Lake Pontchartrain that would be shut when a storm approached. The plan ran into opposition from environmentalists and from local officials, who objected to sharing the cost of the project, which federal law requires.

A federal judge ordered a study of the barriers' impact. The fight raged on, with the corps backing the barriers and local groups opposing them.

In 1985, when Gen. Heiberg was head of the corps, his staff urged him to give up, he said in a 2007 letter to the editor of the *Times-Picayune*.

"I was discouraged and decided to stop fighting," he said in the letter, in which he called that action "the biggest mistake I made during my 35 years as an Army officer.... I gave up too easily."

When Katrina struck on Aug. 29, 2005, New Orleans' inadequate levee system was overwhelmed, and 80 percent of the city was flooded.

Alfred Naomi, a former senior project engineer in the corps' New Orleans office, told the *New York Times* that the barriers sought by Gen. Heiberg would have improved overall safety and reduced the Katrina-related damage.

In his letter to the *Times-Picayune*, Gen. Heiberg cited a report from the American Society of Civil Engineers that, he said, "appears ... to reconfirm the need for those barriers, or something like them."

Eight years after Katrina's devastation, New Orleans has a $14 billion ring of walls, levees and gates.

Regardless of whether Gen. Heiberg's plan would have been successful, he "showed integrity and moral certitude that you don't find a lot in today's society," Naomi told the *New York Times*. "Right or wrong, he took the hit—and took some responsibility."

Gen. Heiberg, who was born in Schofield Barracks in Hawaii, followed his father and grandfather to the U.S. Military Academy, where he graduated fifth in his class in 1953. He also graduated from the Industrial College of the Armed Forces and earned three master's degrees: one in civil engineering at the Massachusetts Institute of Technology and two from George Washington University—one in government, and one in administration.

He taught in West Point's social sciences department and was operations officer of the 3rd Brigade of the 3rd Infantry Division in Germany.

In 1968 and 1969, he commanded the 4th Engineer Battalion in Vietnam, receiving a Silver Star, and was special assistant and executive assistant to the director of the Office of Emergency Preparedness during the Nixon administration.

Gen. Heiberg worked for a year as an aide to Army Secretary Howard "Bo" Callaway before coming to New Orleans. When he left New Orleans, he moved on to head the corps' Ohio River Division and then to serve as senior engineer on the staff of the U.S. Army, Europe.

In Saudi Arabia, Gen. Heiberg supervised a project that the corps led for the country's national guard, and he led the cleanup and rebuilding effort after Mount St. Helens' eruption in 1980.

After being the corps' director of civil works from 1979 to 1982, Gen. Heiberg was named deputy chief and, in 1984, chief of engineers, the youngest person to hold that title since 1838.

He retired in 1988 and worked for several consulting firms, including Heiberg Associates Inc., which he founded, and Dawson & Associates, for which he was a senior adviser.

Robert Dawson, the latter firm's founder, praised Gen. Heiberg's "combination of intellect and leadership." "Our nation has lost a remarkable soldier, scholar, statesman and builder," he said, "and we will miss a great friend."

Gen. Heiberg, who was elected to the National Academy of Engineering in 1995, was buried in Arlington National Cemetery.

— *October 7, 2013*

Ruth Rogan Benerito

She made permanent-press possible

Ruth Rogan Benerito, the chemist who led the New Orleans team that discovered how to make permanent-press fabrics, died Saturday at her Metairie home. She was 97.

Dr. Benerito and her colleagues worked at the U.S. Agriculture Department's Southern Regional Research Center. In the late 1950s, they discovered a way to make fabric that would never need ironing by treating cotton fibers so that all the chainlike cellulose molecules were chemically joined, according to an article on the Chemical Heritage Foundation website.

Hydrogen bonds would make cellulose molecules stick together, but those are easily broken, making the fabric susceptible to wrinkling. The New Orleans researchers found a way to strengthen the bonds between cellulose molecules by inserting short organic molecules between them, like the rungs of a ladder, according to the article.

The resulting product—an enormous, wrinkle-resistant molecule—became a boon to college students and overworked parents everywhere.

"When I was old enough to take care of my own clothes, I was so glad," said Liddy Tripp Hanemann, the daughter of Verne Tripp, one of Dr. Benerito's colleagues. "To this day, I think, 'Oh, great, I don't have to iron it.'"

In recognition of her achievement, Dr. Benerito was inducted into the National Inventors Hall of Fame in 2008.

Dr. Benerito, who held more than 50 patents, was the first woman to receive the Southern Chemist Award, and President Lyndon B. Johnson presented her with the Federal Women's Award. Among the other honors she received were the Garvan Medal, the Agriculture Department's Distinguished Service Award and the Lemelson-MIT Lifetime Achievement Award.

A lifelong New Orleanian who made inroads in what had been regarded as a man's field, Dr. Benerito entered Newcomb College when she was 15. After graduating with a chemistry degree, she earned a master's degree in the subject at Tulane University and a doctorate in physical chemistry at the University of Chicago.

Between earning her master's and doctoral degrees, she taught at Newcomb and at Randolph-Macon Woman's College, now Randolph College, after it started admitting men in 2007.

Dr. Benerito started working at the Agriculture Department's research center in 1953. She also helped develop a fat emulsion that was used to feed long-term hospital patients.

She retired from the center in 1986 and joined the chemistry faculty at the University of New Orleans, teaching there until she was 81.

Although she was lionized for this discovery, Dr. Benerito consistently insisted that she was part of a group that helped develop a process that textile scientists had been studying for more than a century.

"No one person discovered it or was responsible for it," she told the *New York Times*. "But I contributed to new processes of doing it."

— *October 8, 2013*

Betty Guillaud

A gossip columnist extraordinaire who stood out

Betty Guillaud, a *Times-Picayune* columnist who swanned her way through a succession of soirees and swankiendas as she chronicled the fun and foibles of the denizens of the Big Easy, a nickname for New Orleans that she helped popularize, died Saturday at The Sanctuary hospice of complications of Alzheimer's disease. She was 79.

As a member of a profession in which all too many of its practitioners seem interchangeable, Ms. Guillaud stood out, with a powerful, throaty voice that could be heard across a bustling newsroom; a hearty laugh that seemed to bubble up from somewhere around her knees; and a smile that could radiate joy or, on rare occasions, gleeful malice that she could direct at anyone who stood in the way of getting the information she wanted.

Ms. Guillaud (pronounced "Ga-LAUD") dressed to be noticed, choosing vivid colors and, often, a bright scarf or over-the-top hat—or both—as well as brassy, but classy, jewelry.

Her modus operandi was simple. She fired up one of her pencil-thin More cigarettes, slipped off an earring, picked up the telephone, and waited for someone to answer, which was her cue to announce, "Hello, dahling, this is Betty Guillaud," in basso-profundo tones reminiscent of Lauren Bacall, and start asking questions in a style that masked bluntness with Southern charm.

"She was eagle-eyed and eagle-eared," said David Cuthbert, a colleague and friend. "Anything worth getting at any event, she got it. Any person worth getting, she got it."

"I think of Betty Guillaud as the Auntie Mame of journalism," said Chris Bynum, a newspaper colleague and longtime friend. "She liked to stir things up and turn an assignment into an adventure. As a gossip columnist, she made irreverence an art form. She showed me that never second-guessing what might be around the corner is the spice of life."

Born Betty Jean Kilgore in Hawkinsville, Ga., she grew up in Mobile, Ala., where she wrote the "Tween Us Teens" gossip column for the *Mobile Press Register*. She took night classes at the University of Alabama's Mobile campus but did not graduate.

After working briefly for the *Montgomery Advertiser*, she moved to New Orleans when she was 20. In New Orleans, she met and married Andrew Guillaud.

She joined the *States-Item* as a feature writer in 1960, but she left in 1963 after the birth of her second daughter. She returned in the early 1970s. During that hiatus, she wrote for the newspaper on a part-time basis, but she also was Nancy Nation, the spokeswoman in advertisements for National Food Stores, and she was named to the *States-Item*'s best-dressed list.

Shortly after returning to the *States-Item*, she took over the social column. In 1978, she was given the Lagniappe column after Tommy Griffin retired.

"That was a position that just seemed made for Betty," said Patsy Sims, a *States-Item* colleague and longtime friend. "Her personality and flair brought new life and pizazz to the column and made it a feature that even folks not interested in society looked forward to each day.

"Really, it was Betty on the page, and people came to love it—and her."

Her column was in the style of Walter Winchell and Herb Caen: a series of brief items and plenty of bold-faced names. Because of all the names that Ms. Guillaud dropped, and because her column prose matched her flamboyant style, her column became "must" reading.

Even though Ms. Guillaud wrote a feature column—for the *States-Item* and the *Times-Picayune* after the newspapers merged—she frequently broke news. In the late 1970s, she dined with Jordan's King Hussein and Queen Alia when they visited New Orleans, and she wrote about it. She also interviewed Margaret Mead, Albert Schweitzer, and Dr. Jonas Salk.

David Cuthbert recalled the morning when Bettye Anding, Ms. Guillaud's editor, strode toward the newsroom's city desk brandishing that day's front page, which contained a story that Ms. Guillaud had reported in her column two weeks earlier.

"Don't you guys ever read your newspaper?" Anding shouted.

Whenever celebrities came to town, Ms. Guillaud always knew where they were staying, who was with them and what they ordered from room service.

She not only homed in on them but also frequently wound up hanging out with them, even in retirement. A few years ago, her daughter Laure Starring said, the two of them were shopping on Magazine Street when Ms. Guillaud spotted the actress Lindsay Lohan in a boutique. Starring said that when she emerged from a fitting room, her mother and the actress were chatting.

Ms. Guillaud also delighted in hinting strongly at the names of Carnival royalty before the krewes announced them, a practice that got her banned from at least one old-line ball.

In 1988, Ms. Guillaud was assigned to report on the festive parties during the Democratic National Convention in Atlanta and the Republican National Convention in New Orleans—a next-to-impossible task in Atlanta because she and Millie Ball, who shared that duty, had received no invitations.

"We had to become party crashers," Ball said, adding that they were able to do their job at the Democratic conclave only because then-U.S. Rep. Lindy Boggs let them go through her pile of invitations and invited them to attend those events with her.

At the end of 1998, Ms. Guillaud retired, marking the event with a succession of parties, capped by an uproarious lunch at Commander's Palace where colleagues wore sunglasses and boas, and the French Quarter entertainer Chris Owens and her band not only performed but also led guests in a second line through the restaurant's Patio Room. The next year, the Press Club of New Orleans gave Ms. Guillaud a lifetime achievement award.

"She was a good columnist, a good journalist, but also a personality," Cuthbert said. "She brightened the landscape of New Orleans."

— *November 18, 2013*

Josie Marino Ortolano

She ruled New Orleans' snowball market

Josie Marino Ortolano, a powerhouse in the local snowball business who not only devised a stream of fanciful flavors such as wedding cake and blueberry hill but also sold the extracts and equipment for making and serving the hot-weather treats, died Wednesday in Metairie. She was 103.

"She was always creative," said Georgiana Janusa, her niece and god-daughter. "She was always thinking of something else she could do."

Mrs. Ortolano and her husband, George Ortolano, were partners not only in marriage but also in business, starting with a snowball stand at Magazine and Delachaise streets in Uptown New Orleans.

In 1931, the year they were married, a snowball cost 3 cents for a relatively small scoop, Janusa said, and the ice was shaved by hand from blocks that icemen delivered.

The stand was quite a magnet, especially in the days before air conditioning, when people desperate to cool off would invest in snowballs before heading back into their hot homes for the night.

While shaving the ice by hand might have exemplified artisanship and customer care, it wasn't good enough or fast enough for George Ortolano, who, Janusa said, loved to fool around with machinery. So in 1936, he invented the SnoWizard to shave the ice, and he and his wife developed a business to make and sell the machines, along with supplies such as cups, syrups, straws, and spoons.

This was when Mrs. Ortolano came into her own. While her husband was responsible for the machines, Mrs. Ortolano handled the snowball-supply side of the business and developed flavors to be poured over the ice, using not only sweet syrups but also ice cream and evaporated milk to make distinctive cream varieties.

Wedding cake, for instance, combined coconut and almond, and she added chocolate sauce to condensed milk to create chocolate cream, which, Janusa said, was a perennially popular choice.

Perhaps Mrs. Ortolano's most audacious creation was the snowball sundae, which consisted of ice, several scoops of ice cream, crushed pineapples, a maraschino cherry and, of course, evaporated milk.

At its peak, Janusa said, the couple used 250 pounds of ice each day.

Mrs. Ortolano's formal education stopped before she got to high school, but "she was the backbone" of the business, Janusa said.

She did more than sell equipment and keep up with orders. When people came in with machines that needed fixing, she fed them if they happened to arrive around mealtime, Janusa said.

Mrs. Ortolano, who also rode in the all-female Krewe of Venus Carnival parade, retired in the early 1990s, and her husband died in 1997. Their snowball stand has closed.

— *November 27, 2013*

George Rodrigue

He created the Blue Dog and became a superstar

George Rodrigue, a Cajun bricklayer's son whose fanciful painting of a beloved pet became an iconic image that was displayed in advertising campaigns and on the walls of celebrities' homes and the White House, died Saturday of cancer at Methodist Hospital in Houston. He was 69.

Mr. Rodrigue, who was born in New Iberia, drew on his Cajun heritage for his works, starting with a series of portraits and landscapes in which oaks hung with Spanish moss appeared frequently. When one of his early paintings was displayed in Paris in 1975, the newspaper Le Figaro declared Mr. Rodrigue was America's answer to the French post-impressionist Henri Rousseau.

He became internationally celebrated and cherished for his Blue Dog paintings, which were inspired by a deceased pet named Tiffany.

The blue spaniel-terrier mix, with a white nose and yellow eyes, first appeared in 1984. Since then, it has turned up in advertising campaigns for Absolut Vodka, Neiman Marcus, and Xerox Corp.; in posters for the New Orleans Jazz and Heritage Festival; in Harrah's New Orleans casino; and on an apartment wall in the situation comedy "Friends."

Whoopi Goldberg and Tom Brokaw are among the celebrity collectors of Blue Dog art, and Bill Clinton commissioned one for his 1993 presidential inauguration, showing him with Al Gore, who would become his vice president.

When Kathleen Blanco was governor, she displayed Mr. Rodrigue's works at the Governor's Mansion. In a statement on Saturday, Blanco, a longtime friend of the Rodrigues, said: "Louisiana has lost a magnificent artist who loved and chronicled the lives of our people. His legacy is reflected in the inherent beauty and messages of his unique body of work. We will miss him dearly."

Although the Blue Dog paintings may look like nothing more than tributes to a special pooch, they, like Mr. Rodrigue's other works, draw on Cajun traditions and folklore, said William Andrews, director of the Ogden Museum of Southern Art in New Orleans. The Blue Dog is a gentle, friendly version of the loup-garou, the werewolf or ghost dog that hides in sugarcane fields and haunts mischievous children.

"The genius of his work is that it always goes back to his Cajun heritage," Andrews said. "He did a wonderful job of leaving a trail of bread crumbs. All of those crumbs will lead you back to his roots. You'll go into the woods and find amazing things there."

The Blue Dog did more than decorate walls and put an appealing face on advertising campaigns. After Hurricanes Katrina and Rita and the subsequent flooding laid waste to much of south Louisiana, the Blue Dog appeared with an American flag, both partly submerged, to raise money for storm relief.

The canine's eyes, "normally yellow, are red with a broken heart," Mr. Rodrigue wrote in September 2005.

He followed that poster with Blue Dog prints urging help from the Federal Emergency Management Agency and pointing out the need for stronger levees.

Within a year, the Blue Dog Relief drive had raised $700,000, including $100,000 to help the New Orleans Museum of Art reopen.

In 2009, he founded the George Rodrigue Foundation of the Arts, which advocates the importance of the visual arts in education. His son Jacques is the foundation's leader.

Because of such initiatives, Mr. Rodrigue will be remembered for his "generosity of spirit, giving back to the community," said Bradley Sumrall, the curator of the Ogden Museum of Southern Art in New Orleans. "His generosity affected everyone he came in contact with."

Mr. Rodrigue, the subject of 12 books and retrospective exhibitions, started painting in the third grade, when he was bedridden for four months with polio.

In 1962, he entered the University of Southwestern Louisiana as an art major. He did not graduate. However, in 2009, the university—by then the University of Louisiana at Lafayette—awarded him an honorary doctorate.

In 1967, he enrolled at the Art Center College of Design in Los Angeles as a graphic arts major, but he returned to New Iberia in 1967, when his father died, and enlisted in the National Guard.

A year later, Mr. Rodrigue became art director for a Lafayette advertising agency, but he left that job a year later to paint full-time.

He had an exhibit at the Art Center for Southwest Louisiana in Lafayette, and Gov. John McKeithen commissioned a painting as a gift to Jean-Jacques Bertrand, Quebec's prime minister.

In 1970, an exhibit of his landscapes was mounted at the Old State Capitol in Baton Rouge. A year later, he finished The Aioli Dinner, his first painting with people. It is on display at the Ogden Museum; Jacques Rodrigue and Mallory Page Chastant were married in front of it.

During that decade, Mr. Rodrigue's reputation continued to grow. His book, *The Cajuns of George Rodrigue,* was chosen as the official U.S. State Department gift for visiting heads of state during the Carter administration.

In 1986, Mr. Rodrigue was commissioned to paint President Ronald Reagan. Three years later, he painted three Cajun Easter eggs for the annual White House Easter Egg Roll.

After the Blue Dog paintings caught on, Mr. Rodrigue was the subject of a documentary, *Rodrigue: A Man and His Dog* with Whoopi Goldberg.

Mr. Rodrigue, who was honored by the Salon des Artistes in Paris and given the Gold Medal for the Arts in Italy, told the *New York Times* that he was always bemused by people's reactions to pictures of his iconic canine, saying that some people burst into tears.

"The yellow eyes are really the soul of the dog," he said. "He has this piercing stare. People say the dog keeps talking to them with the eyes, always saying something different."

The paintings, he said in the interview, "are really about life, about mankind searching for answers. The dog never changes position. He just stares at you, and you're looking at him, looking for some answers. . . . The dog doesn't know. You can see this longing in his eyes, this longing for love, answers."

The Blue Dog turned up on Jazz Fest posters featuring Louis Armstrong, Pete Fountain, and Al Hirt. It was natural to have an iconic Louisiana artist depicting iconic New Orleans musicians, said Quint Davis, the festival's producer and director.

"He took (the posters) to another level," Davis said. "It was a great marriage."

— *December 15, 2013*

Charles "Pete" Savoye

He predicted the massive Katrina flooding

Charles "Pete" Savoye, an early, outspoken opponent of the Mississippi River-Gulf Outlet who warned that the waterway would lead to massive flooding in St. Bernard Parish, died Sunday at his Covington, La., home. He was 83.

When Hurricane Katrina struck on Aug. 29, 2005, and the levees failed, Mr. Savoye's prediction came true: Water rushed into the shortcut to the Gulf of Mexico and inundated St. Bernard Parish, including the home Mr. Savoye had occupied for 52 years.

He moved across Lake Pontchartrain to Covington, where he lived until his death.

The waterway, commonly known as MR-GO (pronounced "Mr. Go"), was closed in 2009. On March 28, 2009, when that process began, Mr. Savoye was in a group that took a boat ride into the outlet to toss rocks into the water, marking the symbolic start of a process that would lead to bigger rocks being dumped to close the waterway.

Mr. Savoye spoke tirelessly for years to all sorts of organizations, including the Army Corps of Engineers and the St. Bernard Parish Council, about the potential peril that became a reality in August 2005.

Because of the waterway, the chances of flooding increased tenfold, Mr. Savoye said in a letter to the editor of the *Times-Picayune* in 1997: "In 1965, when Hurricane Betsy hit, it was because of the MR-GO that the 9th Ward and parts of St. Bernard flooded.

"Before the MR-GO, we had 8,000 acres of land that was a buffer zone to help protect us from a hurricane surge. Today, we have about 70 billion gallons of water waiting to be pushed into our parishes that we never had before."

When Mr. Savoye made his presentations, he brought along a homemade model to show the potential harm the MR-GO could cause. It is now part of the Katrina exhibit in the Louisiana State Museum on Jackson Square in New Orleans.

Mr. Savoye grew up in the Lower 9th Ward and graduated from Francis T. Nicholls High School. He moved to Chalmette in 1953 and worked as a carpenter at the Kaiser Aluminum and Chemical plant for 29 years. An avid outdoorsman, he was president of the St. Bernard Sportsmen's League for 18 years and a member of the advisory committee for coastal zone management for 16 years.

— *January 1, 2014*

Emile E. Martin III

He defied Plaquemines Parish's political machine

Emile E. Martin III, a lawyer who never shrank from opposing the Perez political machine that ran Plaquemines Parish for decades, died Monday at his Belle Chasse home. He was 92.

"He was always anti-Perez before it was safe to be that way," said Michael Kirby, a retired state appeals judge. "He had this passion to see things done right and to take up for the little guy against the giants."

Nothing daunted him, Kirby said. "He was never afraid to take on anybody or anything. He might be wrong, but he'd go down fighting. . . . He always fought for what was right."

Mr. Martin locked horns with Leander Perez, the family's patriarch, over desegregation because Mr. Martin believed schools should be integrated, said Johnette Martin, his daughter. Perez was an ardent segregationist.

Mr. Martin "said we have to provide an equal education for black children," his daughter said. "That was the ending point of my father's working with Leander Perez."

He lost his job as the parish's inheritance-tax collector, Johnette Martin said, and his law practice suffered because people were afraid their cases would be doomed if Mr. Martin represented them.

But he carried on, frequently representing poor people who paid him in produce because they had no money, Johnette Martin said. "We would see people come to the back porch and leave a box of produce to pay my dad," she said. "Once he was paid with a freezer-ready butchered cow.

"My father was a good man. He cared about people."

Mr. Martin, who was elected to a state district judgeship in 1982, after the Perez family lost its clout, was a native of Port Sulphur whose father served on the Plaquemines Parish Police Jury. He was a baker with the Seabees on a ship in the South Pacific during World War II.

After leaving the service, he earned undergraduate and law degrees at Louisiana State University and set up a law practice in Plaquemines Parish. In addition to practicing law, he worked with civic organizations and was an avid fisherman.

Mr. Martin ran for the Legislature in 1959, but he and the other members of his ticket lost because they were running against the Perez machine.

He kept practicing law until he was elected to the 25th Judicial District bench, where he served one eight-year term.

Among the lawyers who appeared before him was Mark Pivach, a former neighbor.

"He was always fair," Pivach said. "He would always listen and do what he thought was right."

Mr. Martin resumed his law practice after leaving the bench. Throughout his career, he was adamant once he took a position, his daughter said. "He had the heart of a lion."

Although Mr. Martin could be firm, he had a wry sense of humor, Kirby said. "At one point, his staff pitched in and bought him a sweatshirt that said, 'Grumpy.' He said, 'I'm not grumpy; I'm irascible.'"

— February 18, 2014

Fred Bronfin

He helped ward off air attacks in World War II

Fred Bronfin, a New Orleans lawyer who tracked enemy aircraft during World War II and devised plans to intercept them, died Wednesday in New Orleans. He was 95.

A lifelong New Orleanian, Mr. Bronfin earned undergraduate and law degrees at Tulane University, where he was elected to two scholastic honor societies: Phi Beta Kappa, for liberal-arts students, and Order of the Coif, for law students. He also was chosen to join the Tulane Law Review staff.

About a year after the United States entered World War II, Mr. Bronfin enlisted in the Navy, where he was trained to be a fighter director. People holding this relatively new position were taught how to use radar to plot the course of incoming enemy planes and deploy aircraft to ward off an attack. It was, his son Dr. Daniel Bronfin said, an assignment that played to his interest in technological advancements.

Mr. Bronfin served at Midway and at Pearl Harbor, where he was a member of the Pacific Fleet Radar Center. He later was named officer in charge of the school that trained fighter directors.

After the war, the Navy transferred Mr. Bronfin, a lieutenant, to Washington, D.C., and New York City, where he used his skill as a lawyer to help terminate wartime contracts and evaluate work in process. Another Navy lawyer performing this task was Richard Nixon, the younger Bronfin said.

In New Orleans, Mr. Bronfin practiced law for more than 45 years. For about 40 of those years, he was senior partner of Bronfin & Heller. He had a general practice that included estate, corporate and tax work.

He was a member of the New Orleans Estate Planning Council and the New Orleans Bar Association, and he was listed in *Who's Who in America* and *Who's Who in American Law*.

— *July 27, 2014*

Ervin Aden

A D-Day survivor who led his Army unit across France

Ervin Aden, who strode ashore on Utah Beach on D-Day and was the only Army officer in his original troop to survive until the end of World War II, died Monday in his New Orleans home. He was 97.

Mr. Aden, a first lieutenant who received a battlefield promotion to captain, led his unit through 55 days of fighting across France after the Normandy landing.

He was seriously wounded outside the town of Villedieu-les-Poelles after he and four fellow soldiers destroyed a security unit for a German tank, killed an undetermined number of enemy soldiers, and captured 25 of them.

He received a Purple Heart, but he eschewed other recognition because he wanted to put the war behind him, said Darryl Berger, his son-in-law.

In 1984, when his wife, Iona Mae Aden, had his combat boots bronzed, her husband broke down and cried—and started telling stories about the war, she said in a 1994 interview.

Mr. Aden and family members traveled to Normandy for events that commemorated the 40th, 50th and 60th anniversaries of the invasion.

In New Orleans, which he had considered home since his Army days, Mr. Aden wore his khaki captain's uniform and waved the Stars and Stripes when he rode in the parade to mark the opening of the National D-Day Museum (now the National World War II Museum) in June 2000. In a ceremony at the museum last September, the French government conferred upon him the Legion of Honor, that nation's highest decoration.

A native of rural Nebraska, Mr. Aden worked alongside his father on the family farm until a scout for the Cincinnati Reds noticed his talent on the baseball diamond. In 1940, he played second base for the Reds in Mexico and other countries in Latin America.

At the end of that year, he enlisted in the Army to get his one-year commitment behind him. But by the time Mr. Aden's year was running out, the United States had entered World War II, and Mr. Aden's year-long hitch turned into five years of service.

He was sent to Camp Livingston near Alexandria, La. During a brief security mission to New Orleans in January 1942, he met Iona Mae Heuer, whom he married in May 1943, five months before he was shipped overseas as a first lieutenant.

His troop—Troop C—consisted of highly trained soldiers who were part of the 4th Cavalry's reconnaissance squadron. After the men landed on Utah Beach on June 6, 1944, Lt. Aden led them through darkness, on the fringe of enemy territory, to report to Gen. Maxwell Taylor.

From then on, Lt. Aden and his men fought across France as Allied forces struggled to reach—and liberate—Paris. Of the five Troop C officers, Lt. Aden was the only one to live to see victory in Europe in May 1945.

On Aug. 1, 1944, Lt. Alden and his men joined the battle to liberate Villedieu-les-Poelles. When he was checking on another troop, he found a smoldering armored vehicle that had taken fire from a German tank in the nearby woods. In an attempt to rescue the GIs trapped in the vehicle, Lt. Aden led four men—soldiers whose names he did not know—to the outskirts of town and proceeded along a ridgeline to find the German troops who would be protecting the tank.

The Americans found the Germans in a farmhouse, which Lt. Aden and his fellow soldiers hit with a round from a bazooka, followed by automatic small-arms fire. The five Americans captured 25 Germans.

As they were leaving, the men came under fire from the German tank. One round injured Lt. Aden in his right leg, buttocks and lower back, but he retained command, and two of the German prisoners carried him back toward American lines.

By that time, it was dark, raising the risk of death by friendly fire. Lt. Aden called out as his group of soldiers and prisoners reached safety, and a sergeant recognized his voice. At that point, Lt. Aden passed out, Berger said, without ever learning the names of the men who had accompanied him or the fate of the GIs in the armored vehicle.

Recovery took more than a year, during which time he was promoted to captain. Although he didn't lose any limbs, Berger said his father-in-law's movement was impaired for the rest of his life.

— March 25, 2014

Daniel Levy Jr.

This mathematician owned French Quarter nightspots

Daniel Levy Jr., a mathematician who owned and operated a string of French Quarter restaurants and nightspots, died Monday of cancer at his Metairie home. He was 89.

A native of New Orleans' Mid-City neighborhood, Mr. Levy graduated from Jesuit High School and the U.S. Military Academy, and he earned a master's degree in mathematics at Columbia University.

He served in the Army in post-World War II Germany and returned to West Point to teach math. But after three years at the service academy, his family was growing—he eventually fathered 11 children—and military housing and pay didn't keep pace, his son Timothy Levy Sr. said.

So Mr. Levy returned home in 1956 to help his father run his family's businesses: Dan's International Settlement, a Chinese restaurant; Dan's Pier 600, where Pete Fountain and Al Hirt performed together early in their careers; Hirt's namesake club; and the Old Absinthe Bar, which included a comedy club where the satirical revue *Nobody Likes a Smart Ass* played for 17 years.

Mr. Levy, whom then-Mayor Moon Landrieu appointed to the Vieux Carre Commission, was a charter member of the Krewe of Bacchus.

His home in Bucktown, a neighborhood near Lake Pontchartrain that had started as a fishing village, was the site for many gatherings of his sizable family, Timothy Levy said.

In addition to his 11 children, Mr. Levy had 52 grandchildren and 45 great-grandchildren.

"His family made him tick," Timothy Levy said, "and his family kept him ticking this long."

— April 2, 2014

Mickey Easterling

She craved attention—and never failed to get it

Mickey Easterling, a philanthropist and party-giver whose trademark style—an outlandish hat, a loud laugh, a Champagne glass in one hand and a cigarette holder in the other—guaranteed the attention she craved, died Monday at her Lakefront home. She was 83.

"She loved the limelight. She loved the attention," said her daughter, Nanci Myke Easterling. "She was flamboyant. She had flair. She was outrageous."

For a first-night party to celebrate Lena Horne's one-woman show at the Saenger Theatre in 1983, Ms. Easterling opened her house to hundreds of guests, who crossed the threshold beneath "Lena" spelled out, in script, in black neon. White party tents dotted the backyard, and each guest received a gift-wrapped box supper from the Fairmont (now the Roosevelt) Hotel.

"She lived life to the fullest," said William Fagaly, a curator at the New Orleans Museum of Art. "She was her own person."

In a 1998 interview for the *Times-Picayune*, David Cuthbert wrote that the walls of Ms. Easterling's home office were hung with portraits of herself by George Febres, Douglas Bourgeois, Jean-Jacques Giraud, and Douglas Johnson.

Out by the pool, Cuthbert said, was a nude sculpture that, Ms. Easterling said, was "the quintessential me—shoes, hat, cigarette and Champagne glass."

For people who might not have known her, Ms. Easterling gave a hint to her saucy personality by frequently wearing a pin spelling out "#1 Bitch" in sparkling stones.

"Wearing that pin all the time was so my mother," her daughter said. "She was proud of the fact that she was aggressive and in-your-face tough."

People beyond her circle of acquaintances learned how tough she could be shortly after the dawn of the 21st century.

That was when *The Galatoire's Monologues*, a theatrical program consisting of letters about the French Quarter restaurant, included Ms. Easterling's complaint about the venerable establishment's decision to use machine-made ice instead of hand-chipped ice to cool patrons' drinks.

To dramatize her concern, Ms. Easterling once had a block of ice delivered in a tub, complete with ice picks, to her table at the restaurant, said W. Kenneth Holditch, co-author of *Galatoire's: Biography of a Bistro*.

She appeared to go through life with a swagger that more than compensated for her height of only 5 feet.

"Sure, I have a big ego," Ms. Easterling said in a 1993 interview. "I like power. Why not? It's my Napoleon attitude. And by the way, I'm not a tall woman, but I'm taller than Napoleon."

Despite the bluster, "there was a soft spot that not everybody got to see," Nanci Easterling said. "She was the type that could be brought to tears."

Sister Jane Remson, director of the New Orleans chapter of Bread for the World, said Ms. Easterling worked on behalf of New Orleans Artists Against Hunger and Homelessness. "It was in her heart," she said.

Ms. Easterling, whose favorite charities included Children's Hospital, Easter Seals, and St. Jude's Children's Research Hospital in Memphis, contributed to activities at the New Orleans Museum of Art and the Mahalia Jackson Theater of the Performing Arts.

She supported artists such as George Dureau and endowed a chair in theater at Loyola University. She also helped underwrite the restoration of the Saenger Theatre.

But there were other causes, institutions, and individuals that Ms. Easterling joined that people never knew about, Fagaly said.

"She had a heart of gold," he said. "If she knew someone who needed help, she would quietly help. I find that admirable."

She was born Marycathyren Gambino. Her father, Michel Gambino, operated dairy farms on the West Bank, across the Mississippi River from New Orleans, and founded the Westside Creamery.

She graduated from Mount Carmel Academy and did not go to college, her daughter said.

Her marriage to Vern Easterling, an investor who operated a tugboat business, ended in divorce.

Ms. Easterling operated an import-export business and made investments, said her daughter, who said she didn't know anything else about those activities.

"My mother was a very secretive person," she said.

"There was an air of mystery about Mickey," Fagaly said. "She really enjoyed that."

There was nothing mysterious about Ms. Easterling's personality. Starting with her hats. She told Cuthbert she had been wearing them since she was 2 years old, taking a break only in the 1960s, when, she said, bouffant hairstyles made millinery impossible.

In her house, Cuthbert said, Ms. Easterling stockpiled hundreds of hats, stuffed inside hatboxes in closets and even in the bathroom, that bore the names of such renowned fashion houses as Dior, Lily Daché and Mr. John.

"I change the hats twice a year—the first day of spring and the first day of fall," Ms. Easterling said. "That's when I decide which ones are coming out to play, which ones go back on the shelf, and which of the damn things I'll never put on my head again."

There was no telling where she and her hats might go, be it the Bombay Club in the French Quarter or a Mozart festival in Salzburg, Austria.

Before her health made travel impossible, Ms. Easterling spent part of each year in Tangier, Morocco. On one of those trips, she said, King Hassan II, the country's ruler, thanked her for turning in a diamond necklace she had found on the floor of his palace.

That attention Ms. Easterling craved in life continued with her memorial service. Billed as a celebration of her life, it was held at the Saenger Theatre, and it featured Ms. Easterling's body sitting, on stage, on a wrought-iron bench in a garden setting, with a Champagne glass in one hand and a cigarette holder in the other.

— *April 20, 2014*

Ted Sternberg

He was the local lord of Lot-O Burgers

Ted Sternberg, who lent his name to a chain of Frostop stands that dispensed root beer in frosted mugs—no ice—and enormous sandwiches called Lot-O Burgers, died April 18 in Woldenberg Village. He was 85.

At the peak of his career, he owned 15 Ted's Frostop outlets in Louisiana and Arkansas. Each was identifiable by an elevated outsize neon-ringed mug of root beer.

Mr. Sternberg's burgers were so colossal that he served them on loaves intended for po-boy sandwiches, he said in an interview on the Travel Channel's *Burger Land* program.

In that interview, Mr. Sternberg said he got the idea of buying a Frostop franchise when he came back from the Korean conflict—he had been a Japan-based fighter pilot—and wanted to own his own business.

Through his job at a real estate company, he met a man who was developing the Frostop franchise, his wife said. "Frostop was doing well," he said in the interview, "and I bought a franchise."

"One thing led to another and then another," Susan Sternberg said.

Despite competition from industry giants such as McDonald's, Burger King, and Wendy's, Mr. Sternberg kept his franchises going for 50 years, working out of an office at the Uptown New Orleans Frostop near Tulane University.

Mr. Sternberg, whose given name was Samuel Theodore Sternberg, retired after Hurricane Katrina.

— *May 12, 2014*

Courtney Giarrusso

She persevered despite her handicap

Courtney Giarrusso, who overcame towering odds to earn a master's degree, died Tuesday at Touro Infirmary of complications from pneumonia. She was 33.

Born with the spinal-cord defect spina bifida, Ms. Giarrusso was paralyzed from the shoulders down and incapable of even the smallest movement. For instance, operating the mouse on her computer—something she did when she didn't want to use voice commands—was a struggle.

Yet she persevered, with an optimistic spirit that amazed her friends and the teachers at Our Lady of Holy Cross College, where Ms. Giarrusso earned a master's degree in mental-health counseling in 2012.

"She had the most wonderful spirit," said her mother, Civil District Judge Robin Giarrusso. "She never felt sorry for herself."

"I don't know how I would have the upbeat attitude," said Joan Fischer, director of the college's Thomas E. Chambers Counseling and Training Center. "I don't know how I would keep going, but she does."

She was also smart. Ms. Giarrusso was one of the top students in the college's postgraduate counseling program, and she finished the comprehensive examination in half the time allowed, said Carolyn White, the program's director.

At Ms. Giarrusso's side throughout those years was her mother, who juggled her schedule to meet her daughter's needs so she could drive her to class, take notes, type her papers, and help her on tests.

"If you don't like to sleep, it's relatively easy," Robin Giarrusso said in an interview. "You don't think about it. You just do it."

Ms. Giarrusso moved around in a sleek black high-tech wheelchair. At home, she was propped up on pillows in her bed, which had an air mattress that redistributed pressure to reduce the risk of bedsores.

In an interview two years ago, Ms. Giarrusso said she had always wanted to be in a profession that helped people. Counseling was ideal, she said, because it would let her talk to people all day long.

Ms. Giarrusso, a graduate of Edna Karr Magnet School, lived with her parents in the Lakewood South neighborhood until Hurricane Katrina struck in August 2005. The family had to flee when the nearby 17th Street Canal wall was breached and their community was flooded. They headed first to the Fairmont (now Roosevelt) Hotel and then to Baton Rouge before settling in Algiers, across the Mississippi River from downtown New Orleans.

According to Crescent City Jewish News, Ms. Giarrusso suffered a broken arm in a fall and had to be hospitalized for two weeks in Baton Rouge during that post-Katrina period for treatment of dehydration and bedsores.

Nevertheless, she continued her studies online and went to classes at night, graduating from the University of New Orleans in 2007.

— *May 28, 2014*

Rowena Spencer

A pediatric surgeon devoted to her young patients

Dr. Rowena Spencer, a pioneering pediatric surgeon who worked tirelessly to get the best possible treatment for the patients she called her babies, died Tuesday at Mount Vernon Nursing and Rehabilitation Center in Alexandria, Va. She was 91.

A Shreveport native who had moved to New Orleans in 1949, Dr. Spencer left the city just ahead of Hurricane Katrina in August 2005, said Brig. Gen. Lewis Spencer Roach, a nephew.

Throughout her surgical career, which lasted until her retirement in 1984, Dr. Spencer set a series of precedents. She was the first woman surgeon in Louisiana, the first pediatric surgeon of either sex in the state, and the first female surgical intern at Johns Hopkins Medical Institutions in Baltimore. She taught at the Louisiana State University School of Medicine, where she was the first woman in the department of surgery to hold a full-time faculty appointment.

Dr. Spencer developed an interest in conjoined twins, who are joined early in pregnancy before structures such as the neural tube have developed to the extent where skin closes over them.

She separated four sets of conjoined twins and wrote a medical textbook on the subject after retiring in 1984 from her surgical practice.

"She was driven by a genuine desire to help children," said Dr. Charles Hill, who was Dr. Spencer's partner in her New Orleans practice. "She had an unwavering strive for perfection, not only in that but in everything she did."

"She was dedicated to her babies to the nth degree," Roach said. "She would fight for them like a tigress."

Her guiding philosophy was simple. "Babies are people. They need more than bottles and a diaper," Dr. Spencer said in an interview with Charles A.

Fishkin, a friend and former patient of Dr. Spencer's whose father had been one of her colleagues.

She was devoted to them. When her young patients were going to get X-rays, Dr. Spencer brought them into the room, Fishkin said. She carried them into the operating room and, after surgery, into the recovery room as she talked or sang to them.

Dr. Spencer once went eight years without taking a vacation, Fishkin said, and she often slept at the hospital so she could monitor her young patients after surgery.

"If it's my baby and I am responsible for it, I am going to be there," she told Fishkin. "You can't just turn around and walk off."

This commitment was lifelong. "I have loved babies since the day I was born," Dr. Spencer told Fishkin. "My purpose wasn't to be a pioneer. I just wanted to hold those babies."

This was evident during her childhood in Catahoula Parish, where her father, Dr. Lewis Cass Spencer, was an orthopedic surgeon and, later, a public-health official.

When she was growing up near the banks of the Little River, "she was a babysitter of anyone she could lay hands on," Roach said. "When there was a major flood when she was in high school, she took care of a baby that was malnourished in a shelter and took it home."

The two were reunited 60 years later, Roach said.

Dr. Spencer graduated from LSU and earned a medical degree at Johns Hopkins, where she was one of four women in her graduating class. She underwent further training in surgery and pediatrics at the Karolinska Institute in Sweden and at Children's Hospital of Philadelphia, where she worked with Dr. C. Everett Koop, who helped develop pediatric surgery as a medical subspecialty. Koop went on to become surgeon general during the Reagan administration.

In New Orleans, Dr. Spencer trained at Tulane University and Charity Hospital. She raised eyebrows in the 1950s, when segregation was still the rule, because she insisted that all her patients at Charity be treated in the same ward, regardless of their race, Fishkin said. But she stood firm.

"Babies are babies," she told Fishkin. "If they need help, they need help."

Once Dr. Spencer decided on a course of treatment, she never second-guessed herself, Hill said. "There was no hesitation at all."

Because of her passion for her calling and her determination to do the right thing for her little patients, she frequently ran afoul of the predominantly male medical establishment, Roach said, because she never hesitated to speak out. As a result, he said, she told him, "I suffered the tortures of the damned."

Although Dr. Spencer was devoted to children, she never had any of her own. "She didn't have the opportunity," Roach said.

She was profiled in *Louisiana Women: Their Lives and Times,* which was published in 2009.

— *May 15, 2014*

Alden "Doc" Laborde

He founded three firms to serve the offshore-oil industry

Alden "Doc" Laborde, a Louisiana entrepreneur who founded three publicly traded companies to serve the offshore-oil industry, died Friday at his New Orleans home. He was 98.

In a career that extended into his tenth decade, Mr. Laborde organized Ocean Drilling and Exploration Co., better known as ODECO, in 1953 to build the world's first offshore mobile drilling barge.

A year later, he established Tidewater Marine to build offshore service vessels. And in 1985, he was a co-founder of Gulf Island Fabrication Co. to build offshore oil-drilling platforms.

Despite his string of successes, Mr. Laborde was modest about his achievements, including election to the National Business Hall of Fame.

There was, he said in a 2003 interview with *Louisiana Life* magazine, no grand design to his career. At the outset, Mr. Laborde said, "we were doing this all by the seat of our pants."

A native of Vinton, La., who grew up in Marksville, La., Mr. Laborde graduated from the U.S. Naval Academy in 1938. His son John "Jack" Laborde said his father remained a passionate alumnus, with a vanity license plate that read "BEAT ARMY."

Mr. Laborde served in World War II as the commander of three combat vessels in the Atlantic and Pacific theaters.

Back in civilian life, Mr. Laborde decided to work in the oil industry, starting as a roustabout on a drilling rig. He proved to be a quick study who could devise methods to solve problems and make work more efficient.

When he worked for Kerr-McGee Corp., he was a drilling engineer who became a mud engineer, the crew member responsible for ensuring that the specially treated mixture performs functions such as lubricating and cooling the drill bit, carrying the drill cuttings to the surface, and forming a filter on the bore-hole wall to prevent the invasion of drilling fluids.

While he held this position, Mr. Laborde acquired his nickname, Doc, because mud engineers always were called mud doctors, Jack Laborde said.

When Mr. Laborde started at Kerr-McGee, a platform was built for each new rig. He regarded this process as inefficient and costly, his son said, especially in light of the boom Mr. Laborde foresaw in the wake of President Dwight D. Eisenhower's following through on a campaign promise to lift the moratorium on offshore drilling.

Mr. Laborde believed that a mobile, submersible offshore drilling rig was feasible, but Kerr-McGee officials did not, so he left the company to find investors for his invention and the new company, ODECO, that would manufacture it.

After being turned down by several companies, Mr. Laborde found an investor: Murphy Corp. (later Murphy Oil Corp.) Charles Murphy Jr., the company's leader, loaned him $500,000 and helped him round up other investors.

The first rig was named "Mr. Charlie" in honor of Murphy's father, Murphy Oil's founder. Shell Oil Co., ODECO's first customer, used it to drill an exploratory well 30 feet deep near the mouth of the Mississippi River.

The rig lived up to expectations, and it was kept in service for 20 years before being taken to The Rig Museum in Morgan City, La. Demand for portable rigs grew, and ODECO became a world leader in producing them. It has become part of Diamond Offshore Drilling Inc.

Mr. Laborde and his family moved from Morgan City to New Orleans in the 1950s because the drilling-rig company relocated to the Industrial Canal, just outside the city, his daughter Susan Couvillon said.

Offshore oil rigs need supplies. But Mr. Laborde noticed that the retooled Navy ships, shrimp boats and similar vessels used to carry pipes, food and other equipment to the rigs weren't equipped for such work, so he designed a boat to fill this need—a vessel with the pilot house up front and supplies in the rear.

Gathering 10 friends to underwrite the production of these boats, Mr. Laborde formed Tidewater Marine (now Tidewater Inc.) in 1954. Like ODECO, it was a big success.

Thirty-one years later, when Mr. Laborde was 70, he and a partner, Huey Wilson, founded Gulf Island Fabrication Inc., which became a leader in making drilling and production platforms.

But that wasn't his finale. Thirteen years later, he designed the MinDoc, a stable, floating drilling platform designed to work in deep, turbulent waters.

And he was the principal owner of All Aboard Development Corp., an oil and gas exploration and production company.

Throughout Mr. Laborde's career, he wanted to be on the drilling rigs as much as possible. His son remembered this statement from his father at a crowded meeting: "We don't have too few chairs. We have too many people. You need to be on the drilling rigs, where your customers are."

At the core of his life was his strong Catholic faith, said Anne Milling, a longtime friend. "He lived his religion; it wasn't something he just gave lip service to," she said.

As a member of the St. Vincent de Paul Society, he delivered food boxes weekly to poor people until he was too weak to do so, and he never trumpeted it, Milling said. "It was just his own thing, his way of reaching out to others who are less fortunate."

He was a close friend of Archbishop Philip Hannan, so much so that he asked to use the casket that Hannan ordered but that his family decided not to use when Hannan died in 2011, said Linda Newton, a former funeral director at Lake Lawn Metairie Funeral Home.

Besides being a friend, Mr. Laborde was a trusted business adviser to Hannan, Milling said. "He didn't make a major decision involving business dealings without Doc Laborde."

Mr. Laborde was one of the first people Hannan called with the news that Pope John Paul II would be coming to New Orleans in September 1987, Milling said. Mr. Laborde was on the host committee for the visit.

He received honorary doctorates from Loyola and Xavier universities and Catholic University of America, and he was awarded the Presidents Medal by St. Mary's Dominican College and the Integritas Vitae Award by Loyola.

Pope John Paul II named him a knight commander of the Knights of St. Gregory the Great, and Tulane University declared him an honorary alumnus and inducted him into its Engineering Hall of Fame.

— June 6, 2014

THE FUNERALS

Warren McDaniels

Celebrating a life with salutes and music

They prayed over Warren McDaniels amid the majesty of Gallier Hall on Friday morning, and his fellow firefighters gave a solemn final salute to their former chief at the department's French Quarter headquarters.

But between these moments of somber pomp to honor McDaniels, who died Sunday, they danced. Lord, how they danced.

The movement started slowly, as the Treme Brass Band played a slow, keening rendition of "Amazing Grace" while McDaniels' glossy mahogany coffin was hoisted aboard a fire truck, a swag of black cloth draped along each side. A stiff breeze blew the towering purple, green and gold head-dresses of the three Mardi Gras Indian chiefs who were at the head of a procession that included about two dozen of McDaniels' fellow members of the Zulu Social Aid and Pleasure Club in their golden blazers.

Then, with barely enough time to draw breath, the musicians tore into "In the Sweet By and By," and the strutting started. At the epicenter of the musical movement was Jennifer Jones, the band's grand marshal, whose spats-covered shoes tapped, hopped and glided from St. Charles Avenue onto Poydras Street, keeping time with a black umbrella bearing treble clefs and fleurs-de-lis in golden sequins.

She was in the spotlight, and she knew it, beaming a 1,000-watt smile as she moved her parasol so dramatically that the dove atop it bobbled.

"I'm a dancer," Jones said. "I work on instinct."

High-pitched notes from Kenneth Terry's trumpet bounced off the high-rise office buildings, and workers and tourists couldn't resist joining in. Everyone seemed to be brandishing at least two cameras.

"I wanted to be part of it," said Gretchen Carroll, taking a break from her job as a manager at Pan American Life. "It was too good not to come out."

As she clapped time, Carroll greeted most of the Zulus. They are her friends because Carroll is a member of the Walking Warriors, an affiliated marching club.

"I love to second-line," she said.

While this was a familiar ritual to her, it was absolutely foreign to Robert Dempster, a musician from Detroit. Within a block, though, he was bopping along.

"I love it," he said, shouting to be heard over the exuberant notes of "I'll Fly Away."

"I wanted to hear the soul of New Orleans, and I'm getting it," Dempster said. "I'm getting goose bumps just from walking. I'm a lucky guy."

The music and dancing were so exuberant that this part of the cortege pulled nearly a block ahead of the slow-moving fire truck bearing McDaniels' coffin, followed by family members and mourners who included Mayor Ray Nagin; his wife, Seletha; and City Councilwomen Jacquelyn Brechtel Clarkson and Cynthia Willard-Lewis.

Even though there were, basically, two parades, Sandra Rhodes Duncan, the funeral planner who staged the event, wasn't upset as she walked between the two groups.

"They're supposed to be happy," she said, gesturing toward the musical marchers. "He's going home."

The farewell to McDaniels, New Orleans' first African-American fire chief, began in a vast peach-colored room in Gallier Hall, where about 350 mourners gathered to honor the son of the Lower 9th Ward who had led the Fire Department for nine years.

Dozens more spilled out into the corridor. They crowded into the room where McDaniels had lain in state, a rose in his lapel, since midday Thursday, his coffin flanked by firefighters standing at attention, bearing gleaming axes.

Although McDaniels had been a high school dropout, he returned to school to earn a GED. He joined the Fire Department in 1969 and ascended through the ranks in a 33-year career.

McDaniels retired at the end of 2002; he was 63 when he died.

"Chief McDaniels often said, 'I did pretty well for a poor boy from the Lower 9,'" Assistant Superintendent Edwin Holmes Sr. said, prompting chuckles.

But McDaniels' rise wasn't easy, said his successor, Charles Parent.

Early in his career, Parent said, McDaniels told him about a meal at a station house. When the young McDaniels had finished, a white captain picked up his plate and silverware and tossed them into a wastebasket.

But, Parent told the mourners, McDaniels took it in stride. "I was a hungry young man," McDaniels told him, "and I figured he'd run out of plates before I got full."

Speaker after speaker praised McDaniels for opening the Fire Department to women and minorities and for instituting the first-responder program, in which firefighters learn how to deliver basic medical care because they're usually the first to arrive on the scene.

"He was really focused on what was best," Nagin said. "He loved the community, and he wanted to make it better."

At the end of the service, as a trumpeter played "Just a Closer Walk With Thee," the casket was borne out toward St. Charles Avenue.

The pallbearers were flanked by double rows of white-gloved, saluting police officers and firefighters who were from not only New Orleans but also departments around the state, as well as the state fire marshal's office.

With a whistle blast from Delrone Perkins, Zulu's grand marshal, the mile-and-a-half walk began.

Shortly after the procession turned into the French Quarter, it passed beneath an American flag suspended between two fire-truck ladders, a traditional mark of respect.

At the parade's destination—departmental headquarters in the 300 block of Decatur Street—shiny fire engines were front and center, behind row upon row of firefighters in their dress uniforms.

Kenneth Terry played "Taps," and a gleaming silver bell was rung nine times in "last alarm," another mark of respect.

Then, as everyone in uniform saluted, the casket was lowered from the fire engine and placed inside a white Lincoln Continental hearse for the ride to Biloxi National Cemetery in Mississippi.

It was time to be solemn again: The Treme Brass Band played "Just a Closer Walk With Thee," and the Zulus and Jones swayed as they advanced in slow, exaggerated steps.

But that was brief. The band soon launched into "Big-Legged Woman," and the dancing resumed.

And Perkins, Zulu's grand marshal, let himself smile.

"It was a beautiful day," he said. "This was the best one we've had in a long time. Chief Warren was a great man, and we saw him out in style."

— March 1, 2008

Al Copeland

The fried-chicken king gets a flashy farewell

Surrounded by friends, family and the trappings of his extravagant lifestyle, fried-chicken magnate Al Copeland was laid to rest Monday after a Mass in which the man everyone knew for his outlandishness was described by a priest as a humble, penitent man who spent his last weeks trying to "get right with the Lord."

"Most people knew Al Copeland as someone who lived in the fast lane," Monsignor Christopher Nalty said during a Mass at Holy Name of Jesus Church. "They didn't realize that he knew that the Catholic Church was the road to heaven."

Copeland, who built the Popeyes fried-chicken franchise into the third-biggest such franchise in the country, died on Easter in Munich, Germany, of complications from cancer treatment.

Although Copeland may have eschewed much of his characteristic bravado in his final months, mourners saw plenty of reminders of his over-the-top style when they reached the family mausoleum in Metairie Cemetery. Nine cars, eight motorcycles, a sport-utility vehicle and a dune buggy were parked nearby in a semicircle. A motorcycle was at the gate, as was Copeland's outsize speedboat, with tongues of flame painted on each side.

"Al did everything in life big," said television anchor Eric Paulsen, a friend. "He's going out big."

Copeland's body was borne in a horse-drawn hearse with oval windows that let everyone see the gleaming bronze casket. Leading the way was the New Orleans Spice Jazz Band, which played a doleful medley of "My Way" and "St. James Infirmary" as grand marshal Jennifer Jones took long, slow steps in her spats-covered shoes, her gloved hand over her heart.

The path leading to the mausoleum's door had been strewn with white rose petals, and tiny beads resembling Christmas lights—reminders of

Copeland's over-the-top yuletide displays at his suburban home—had been threaded through some of the white flowers that banked the stand where the coffin rested.

The mausoleum door was open, revealing a stained-glass window depicting an oil lamp throwing off beams of light.

Copeland, who had suffered from cancer of the salivary gland, died at 64. One of the speakers at the cemetery was his brother, Gilbert, who was 10 years his senior.

"Thank you, brother, for setting the example of how to live and how to die," he said. "I can say, with confidence, that nothing will ever be the same."

Although Copeland may have set a fast pace with his business ventures, his love of speedboats and fast cars, and his four marriages and four divorces, the mood at the Uptown church and the mausoleum was determinedly low-key, with no big emotional displays.

The Mass began after a three-hour visitation, during which about 2,000 people drifted past the closed coffin, funeral director Frank Stewart said.

The casket was ringed by 23 nosegay arrangements of white flowers—tulips, roses, hydrangeas, and gardenias—with nine big ones for Copeland's children and 14 smaller ones for his grandchildren.

Outside, 14 stretch limousines, all but two of them white, filled the horseshoe on Loyola University's campus; Copeland's white Rolls-Royce and Bentley were parked on St. Charles Avenue.

By the time the Mass started, nearly all of the pews in the Gothic church, which can hold 760 worshippers, were filled. Among those present were three of Copeland's ex-wives; his first wife died in 1995.

Although there were allusions to Copeland's fast-track life—his neighbor Jay Polite said living next door to Copeland was "like living next door to Elvis"—the dominant impression was of a desperately ill man, confined to a wheelchair, who stopped off at the Vatican six weeks ago en route to Germany because, Nalty said, he wanted to get his spiritual affairs in order, starting with an audience with Pope Benedict XVI.

"Leave it to Al to go right to the top," Nalty said. But because the pope was on retreat, "Al got stuck with me," said Nalty, a New Orleans native who is a member of the Roman Curia, the small bureaucracy that runs the Catholic Church.

Perhaps it was for the best, Nalty said. "Al didn't speak Italian and German, and the pope didn't speak no yat."

What followed, Nalty said, was a series of sessions with "a Catholic man who knew he needed God's mercy."

Their time together included a trip to Lourdes, the French village where otherwise inexplicable cures have been attributed to a spring dug by St. Bernadette, who said she had seen the Virgin Mary.

The experience, which included bathing in the water, resulted in healing that wasn't physical, but spiritual, Nalty said.

"Al asked for God's mercy," he said. "I know Al received God's mercy. . . . I have the sure and certain hope that I will see Al again, and it will be right with Jesus."

At the cemetery, where about 300 friends and relatives brandished small black-and-white-checked finish-line flags, Nalty said, "May the Lord now welcome him to the table of God's children in heaven."

Because 11 was Copeland's lucky number, 11 white doves were released, followed by 111 gold and white balloons.

At New Orleans funerals, jazz bands always end with something upbeat. This time, the selection was the commercial jingle "Love That Chicken From Popeyes."

— April 1, 2008

Revius Ortique Jr.

Mourners recall a trailblazer and perfectionist

Revius Ortique Jr., the first African American elected to Civil District Court and the state Supreme Court, was remembered Friday as a stickler for getting things exactly right.

He was, friends said at his funeral, a stern perfectionist who corrected lawyers' grammar, told men to take off their hats when ladies were present, and felt so strongly about the appearance of his lawn that he got down on his knees to edge it with scissors.

This instinct, former New Orleans Mayor Marc Morial said in a rousing eulogy, was so strong that not even death could force Ortique, who died Sunday, to change his ways.

"We say to St. Peter: 'Open your pearly gates. Let the angels, saints and prophets stand at attention because there will be order in Section H. . . . The justice is on the way,'" said Morial, president of the National Urban League, to applause from mourners at Franklin Avenue Baptist Church.

"At a time when baggy pants and split infinitives are too common among the young people, I hope we'll lift up this man's life as a role model," said Morial, who appointed Ortique to the New Orleans Aviation Board in 1994 after his retirement from the state's highest tribunal.

Speaker after speaker marveled at the titles Ortique amassed during his 84 years: Lawyer. Civil rights activist. Negotiator. National Bar Association president. Member of five presidential commissions. Chairman of more boards than anyone could remember. Judge. Chief judge. And, finally, state Supreme Court justice.

Because of Ortique's achievements and the example he set, just being around him was empowering, restaurateur Leah Chase said. "He always made me feel big," she said. "He made me feel I could soar to the greatest heights."

Ortique could be tough, Chase said, as he was when he was trying civil rights cases or negotiating with representatives of New Orleans' white power-er structure in the early 1960s to give black New Orleanians access to lunch counters and jobs in quality stores.

"Only God could break Justice Ortique," Chase said. "He wouldn't bend for anybody."

Her restaurant, Dooky Chase's, was important in the life of Ortique and his family as the only white-tablecloth establishment where African Americans could dine before civil rights legislation was passed in the 1960s.

During that period, the restaurant became the de facto headquarters for civil rights activists, including Ortique.

As Ortique's family grew, Dooky Chase's became the place for major family celebrations, said Dr. Alden "Chip" McDonald III, one of Ortique's three grandchildren, because Ortique wanted them to remember the place where history was made and the importance of what was developed there.

This, McDonald said, was what his grandfather always told him about the importance of that tradition: "It was getting through the tough times that made the good times possible."

The 90-minute memorial attracted a host of political figures, past and present. Mayor Ray Nagin sat alone in a front pew; U.S. Rep. William Jefferson, former Mayor Sidney Barthelemy, Lt. Gov. Mitch Landrieu and Orleans Parish Criminal Sheriff Marlin Gusman were there, as was Sybil Morial, Marc Morial's mother and the widow of former Mayor Dutch Morial. State judges in black robes, including Chief Justice Pascal Calogero, marched down two aisles as the service started.

At the front of the sanctuary, Ortique's body, clad in a judicial robe, lay in a cherry-wood casket. When the service started, the coffin was closed and covered with a spray of anthuriums.

Although most speakers discussed Ortique's professional accomplishments, Bishop Roger Morin reminded worshippers of the joy Ortique took in his family: his wife of 60 years, Miriam Marie Victorianne Ortique; their daughter, Rhesa McDonald; and their three grandchildren.

In a sharp contrast to all the titles that speakers had been using, Chip McDonald employed one that was humble and endearing: Pops.

"Pops, we love you," he said. "Rest well. You did good. In each of us, there's a piece of you. For that, this world is a better place."

He closed with his grandfather's standard toast: "Hear, hear," intoned three times. Gesturing, McDonald urged the mourners to join in. The chant grew stronger each time.

The toast was repeated at Ortique's grave, after white-gloved pallbearers guided the casket into the Ortique-McDonald tomb at St. Louis Cemetery No. 3.

Along the way to the graveyard, a man in a tattered T-shirt and jeans did something the perpetually proper Ortique would have approved of as the cortege passed: He took off his baseball cap and put it over his heart.

— *June 28, 2008*

Lindy Boggs

Saying goodbye to Maw-Maw

E ven in death, Lindy Boggs could attract a crowd.

Drawn by love for the woman her grandchildren called Maw-Maw, the hundreds who converged on St. Louis Cathedral on Thursday—a mixture of longtime friends from New Orleans and Washington, Capitol Hill colleagues, and French Quarter denizens—heard soaring choir performances, a surprise solo from Mayor Mitch Landrieu, and a procession of speakers who extolled Boggs as a wife, mother, congresswoman and ambassador.

"We are gathered today to thank God for the life of the Honorable Lindy Boggs," Archbishop Gregory Aymond said. "May she now share with him eternal glory."

"She was more than good. She was great," said U.S. Rep. John Lewis, D-Ga. "Grace was in her DNA, grace was in her steps, and heaven was in her eyes. She never gave in. She never gave out. She kept the faith. She kept her eyes on the prize."

Lewis, House Democratic Leader Nancy Pelosi, D-Calif., and former U.S. Sen. John Breaux, D-La., described Boggs as a colleague who was determined to win, especially on issues involving the betterment of Louisiana and the rights of women and minorities, while wrapping her determination in genuine gentility and graciousness.

Boggs, who died Saturday at the age of 97, "could wrap you around her little finger and make you love every minute of it," Breaux said.

Because of Boggs' strength and tenacity, Landrieu said he rejected any attempt to describe her as a steel magnolia.

"I would prefer to remember her as a live oak," he said, "whose roots are as deep as the nation itself, who is as sturdy as anything God has ever created, who has branches all of us can rest on when we get tired, who produces shade to protect us and who produces thousands and thousands of acorns."

Landrieu, who later sang "Ave Maria" during the celebration of the Eucharist, drew laughter and tears when he imagined what Boggs' arrival at heaven must have been like, starting with this request of God: "Hello, darlin', may I come in?"

After being assured of everlasting life as a reward for her service on Earth, "She found the one thing that none of us could find in the mountains of Alaska," Landrieu said. "She found Hale," her husband, who was the House majority leader when his airplane vanished there in 1972.

"They gently grabbed hands," Landrieu said, "and they walked off into the eternal sunset to receive their just reward."

His audience included veterans of Boggs' nine successful House campaigns, some of whom wore their "We Love Lindy" buttons. Some, including Landrieu's sister, U.S. Sen. Mary Landrieu, D-La., wore purple, one of Boggs' favorite colors.

In the continuous stream of mourners were the French Quarter entertainer Chris Owens; Luci Johnson Turpin and Lynda Bird Robb, longtime Boggs friends who are the daughters of Lyndon and Lady Bird Johnson; seven residents of Lindy's Place, a New Orleans home for homeless women; and Zach Tamburrino, the maître d' at Maison Bourbon Jazz Club, who often escorted Boggs back to the door of her Bourbon Street home.

"She always trusted me to get her home," he said. "If someone was dropping her off, she'd always say, 'He'll take care of me.'"

Former Gov. Kathleen Blanco attended, as did the restaurateurs Leah and Dooky Chase, New Orleans City Councilwomen Jackie Clarkson and Susan Guidry, and Sybil Morial, the widow of one New Orleans mayor and the mother of another, who said she regarded Boggs as a role model.

"We had her a long time," she said, "but we still didn't want to let her go."

That was a theme that Aymond, the principal celebrant of the 75-minute Mass, discussed in his homily.

While acknowledging the grief that the mourners felt, "her over 60 years of public service remain as an inspiration," Aymond said. "As we bid our farewell to Lindy, our gratitude for all she has done for our city, our state and our country (leads us to) say, 'Well done, good and faithful servant, and we hope to see you again in the Lord's kingdom.'"

The Mass was wrapped in the panoply of the church, complete with men and women wearing black capes of five religious organizations, thundering organ music to accompany singers from the choirs of the cathedral and St.

Peter Claver Church, and a host of priests and deacons who helped administer the elements of the Eucharist.

Those elements were brought to the altar by 11 of Boggs' descendants. Other grandchildren and great-grandchildren read Scripture and intercessions during the prayers.

Two granddaughters, Elizabeth Boggs Davidsen and Rebecca Boggs Roberts, discussed their grandmother's legacy.

"This is not the end of an era," Roberts said. "Each of us and our children is made in her model. We know there's a little bit of Maw-Maw in each of us."

Although the Mass was thoroughly Catholic, the New Orleans part of it took over at the end of the service, when Boggs' casket was rolled up the aisle while the singer Leah Chase sang a soulful version of "Just a Closer Walk With Thee."

The mood was revved up by "The Battle Hymn of the Republic," complete with drum rolls at the start of each verse, as the coffin proceeded through the doors and into blindingly bright sunshine and 90-degree heat.

At that point, the Treme Brass Band played a dirge while purple-fringed lavender parasols, decorated with purple flowers, were distributed. Then the musicians, following jazz-funeral protocol, tore into "I'll Fly Away" as the cortege sped away, bound for St. Mary's Cemetery in New Roads, La., Mrs. Boggs' childhood home.

Though the song created an upbeat mood, the restaurateur Ti Adelaide Martin said she couldn't help feeling sad as the music faded.

"It's just the finality of it," she said. "We thought she was going to be around forever."

— *August 1, 2013*

ACKNOWLEDGMENTS

This book is the brainchild of my wife, Diana Pinckley. After several years of seeing the diverse types of people who had died on my watch, she suggested that their obituaries should be collected in a book that would not only remind people of these remarkable folks but also give an idea of the wonderfully quirky place that New Orleans is.

Diana died in September 2012. I wish that she were able to see her idea become a reality.

Susan Larson, a close, longtime friend of Diana's and mine, has taken on the task of helping me pull this anthology together. The title was her inspiration, and she has helped me with the difficult task of deciding whom to include.

I am grateful for her counsel, and for the help and support of other good friends, including Brett Anderson and Nathalie Jordi, Emily Clark and Ron Biava, Brooke and Karen Duncan, Linda Ellerbee, Sue Grafton, Walt and Jodie Handelsman, Kenny Harrison, Karen Kersting, Anne and King Milling, Chris Schultz, Ellen Sweets, Gwen Thompkins, and Fran and George Villere.

Because these obituaries first appeared in the newspaper, they are the property of NOLA.com|The Times-Picayune. I am grateful to my editor, Jim Amoss, for helping to negotiate the path that led to permission from the parent company, Advance Publications, to publish the obituaries in this book.

At the University Press of Mississippi, I have been lucky to work with Leila Salisbury, Anne Stascavage, Craig Gill, Steve Yates, John Langston, Valerie Jones, and Deborah Upton, a superbly patient and painstaking copy editor. Their enthusiasm for this project has been wonderfully encouraging.

The obituaries would not have been possible without the help of local funeral directors, including Sandra Rhodes Duncan, Billy Henry, Ceatrice Johnson, Linda Newton, Patrick Schoen, and Stephen Sontheimer. Over the years that I have been writing obituaries, I have built good working relationships with these men and women, and they have developed sound news judgment about which clients would make good obituary subjects.

I must pay special thanks to the families and friends of the subjects of these obituaries for being patient with my questions at a stressful time and for providing valuable insights.

Occasionally, I have received notes from these people thanking me for what I had written and telling me how much it meant for them to see accounts of their friends' and relatives' lives in print. I have been surprised and touched by these letters, and I am humbly grateful for them.

Printed in the United States
by Baker & Taylor Publisher Services